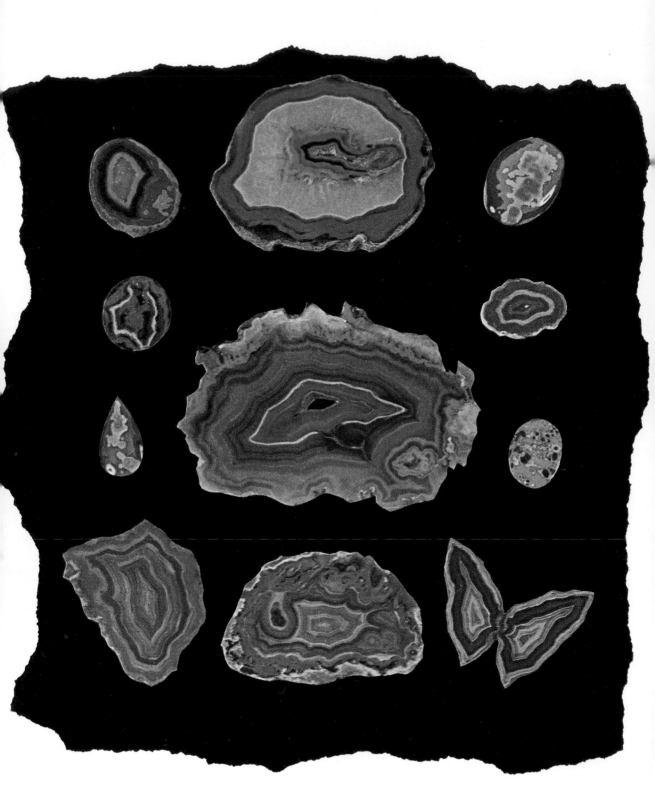

THE BOOK OF AGATES

And Other Quartz Gems

THE  BOOK

And Other Quartz Gems

OF  AGATES

By Lelande Quick

CHILTON BOOK COMPANY
Philadelphia   New York   London

Copyright © 1963 by Chilton Book Company

First Edition

Second Printing, June 1970

All Rights Reserved

Published in Philadelphia by Chilton Book Company,
and simultaneously in Ontario, Canada,
by Thomas Nelson & Sons Ltd.

ISBN   0-8019-0964-3

Library of Congress Catalog Card Number 63-8919

Designed by William E. Lickfield

Manufactured in the United States of America by
Quinn & Boden Company, Inc., Rahway, N. J.

Dedicated to

THE LOS ANGELES LAPIDARY SOCIETY
where I served and where I learned

Preface

THIS IS not a scientific textbook. It tells all about agates but it does not tell, except in a general way, exactly how agates are made because the details would be boring to many and really useful to none. They are available in many other books. They are details on which no one agrees at this time, for the details are only conjectures.

The author believes that this is a needed book on the quartz gem minerals. Needed by whom?—Needed by the more than three million followers of the rock hobby in America, particularly by the half million or so who are cutting and polishing rocks and learning the details of America's fastest growing craft hobby—gem cutting. Since more than 90 per cent of all the gems they will cut into cabochons or faceted stones are in the quartz family, a book is needed that gives complete details of that group.

The book is designed to acquaint the collector with places all over North America where he can gather his own gem rocks; to show him what he can do with them after he finds them; to acquaint him with the interesting history of agates and define their types; to tell about other quartz varieties such as the opal, jasper, and petrified wood; and to give him the most complete information that has ever been gathered on the gem materials forming the quartz group.

The information contained in this book has mostly come out of the personal experience of the author in helping to organize a great many of the gem and mineral societies of the United States; his experience in lecturing to many universities, museums, and service clubs from coast to coast; his rock travels in the field; but particularly his experience as the founder of the *Lapidary Journal* and its editor and publisher for thirteen years.

The greatest part of the work has to do with collecting-spots in every state and all over North America, and it is hoped that the book will be enjoyed by the armchair traveler and found of great benefit by the actual gem hunter or rockhound. The gathering of the profuse illustration material has been almost as great a task as writing the book itself and this is also a great contribution to the available information on the rockhound's favorite gem—the agate.

LELANDE QUICK

La Jolla (San Diego), California

Acknowledgments

AFTER A book is written it is difficult to set down credits for help received, and one always fears that the name of an important adviser may be left out. However, in the case of this book, the author received no personal help of any kind, except in the great problem of securing adequate illustrations.

The information contained herein about the field locations has come out of the author's long and valuable experience as editor and publisher of the *Lapidary Journal* for thirteen years and as a monthly contributor of lapidary information in a page in *Desert Magazine* for a period of more than fifteen years. It has also come out of a large personal experience in field collecting in several states, particularly in California.

To refresh my memory and to check on some facts, frequent reference has been made to old issues of the *Lapidary Journal*, but the magazine has never been directly quoted. The author is indebted, too, to references taken from the great work on gemstones, *Gemstones of North America*, by John Sinkankas. Several of the "trail" books mentioned in Chapter 12 were also consulted. Many other sources in an extensive library on the subject were consulted, but none of them made any important contribution to this work, which is based predominantly on personal experience and knowledge, with the exception of frequent reference to the *Dictionary of Gems and Gemology* by Robert M. Shipley.

In the matter of the wide variety of pictures, however, several sources deserve appreciation and credit. Paul E. Desautels, Associate Curator, Division of Mineralogy and Petrology of the Smithsonian Institution, was most generous and cooperative with pictures. Archie B. Meiklejohn, of the Los Angeles Lapidary Society, was very helpful in searching out old pictures of the Society's field trips and shows. Leo Berner, of the same Society, supplied many photographs of petrified wood from many localities. Several other club members supplied photographs. The mining bureaus of several states were helpful in information and in supplying photographs and maps.

The final manuscript was efficiently typed by Wilda Boyer of La Jolla, California.

LELANDE QUICK

La Jolla (San Diego), California

Contents

THE BOOK OF AGATES
And Other Quartz Gems

Chapter 1

What Are Agates?

THE COLLECTING instinct is nowhere as highly developed as among the American people, who will collect anything from matchbook covers to fancy-colored diamonds. These activities are called hobbies, which the dictionary defines as "occupations of interest to which one gives his spare time."

In this realm of hobbies the fastest growing during the past several years has been the hobby of collecting and cutting rocks. It was estimated by the United States Bureau of Mines in 1959 that approximately three million persons in the United States followed rock collecting as a hobby. Many of these people have merely a passive interest in rocks, picking up a rock here and there and toting it home for their garden or as a memento of a pleasant visit or excursion. The great percentage of these rock hunters, however, become amateur lapidaries or gem cutters and process their finds into gemstones of great beauty or articles of usefulness. About 40,000 rock hunters have formed more than 900 clubs or societies in North America, where they regularly meet to study rocks, exchange information, and conduct field excursions to hunt specimens. Formed into regional federations, they hold yearly displays of their lapidary and jewelry work, exhibitions that always contain thousands of beautiful items. A visitor to any one of these shows can hardly fail to notice that easily 90 per cent of all the gems displayed belong to the quartz family, in which the agate predominates.

It is for these agate fanciers that this book is written; to bring to them the most comprehensive information on agate that has ever been gathered between the covers of one book. This information comes from the experience of countless amateur gem cutters known to the author throughout his years as editor and publisher of the *Lapidary Journal*, a magazine for gem cutters and silversmiths. It is a compilation of much of the information that has appeared in print in other books on minerals and gems, and in magazine articles about the quartz family minerals and about agates in particular.

George Kunz, probably America's greatest gemologist, began one of his books on gems by saying that the love of precious stones is deeply implanted in the human heart. He was referring, of course, to all gemstones and not to the few that are generally regarded as the precious stones — the diamond, ruby, emerald, sapphire, and sometimes the pearl, which is not a gemstone at all but an animal rather than a mineral substance.

All other gemstones are popularly regarded as semiprecious and in too many minds that word is a synonym for semiworthless. Ask a number of people the question, "What is a precious stone?" You will receive many answers, guided by a person's temperament or profession or business. The tendency to use the two words precious and semiprecious is rapidly diminishing, and in the jewelry trade itself the custom is to refer to the diamond, hardest but not the rarest of gemstones, and then class all other gemstones as "colored stones." In this class of colored stones the most prolific are the agates, the most interesting group of gems in the world. While one hundred sapphires out of one hundred may all look exactly alike, one finds that one hundred agates result in one hundred varieties of design or color or both. No two agates are ever alike and it is this diversity that makes agate lovers. No other gem offers so much in color and interesting markings.

Thinking on the subject of precious stones has changed a great deal through the years. For instance, Edward W. Streeter, in his authoritative work *Precious Stones and Gems*, published in 1877, separated gems into two classes—"jewels, or gems proper, perfectly pure" and "half pure precious stones, colored or tinted." It would be difficult indeed to classify gems in that manner today. However, Streeter had many ideas that do not conform to today's thinking. For instance, he said that "agate, strictly speaking, does not belong to mineralogy." His thought was that agate was not a mineral because it was a collective substance, a conglomeration of silicates or quartz minerals.

The thing that makes the so-called precious stones precious is their relative rarity and hardness, the emerald being the rarest of the group. The diamond is not rare but the market is well controlled. Hardness makes for durability and it is this particular quality that people like to buy so that their gems will withstand the ravages of time.

For a measuring rod the gemologist and mineralogist use the Mohs (to rhyme with hose) scale of hardness. This scale grades all minerals (and nearly all gems are minerals) into a hardness scale of ten points. Diamond is the hardest substance known and is rated at ten, while talc is the softest mineral and is rated at one. The quartz family of minerals, which includes agate, is rated at seven, a degree having great durability and a hardness great enough to permit the finished gem to take a high polish and retain it.

In this book our aim is to discuss the agate particularly and to give some attention to other chalcedony and quartz gems also. The agate is the favorite gemstone of the nearly three million gem hunters and gem cutters of America. The popular term for these gem hunters is rockhound. While the word is not found in any dictionary, it is only a matter of a short while before it will be, for it is widely accepted and has been used in many books and hundreds of magazine articles in the nation's foremost publications.

It is the popular impression among rockhounds that chalcedony is a form of agate, usually a term used specifically for gray agate. However the reverse is true, for agate is a form of chalcedony. It is not known how this word (pronounced kal-*sed*-oh-knee) originated. It was once popularly supposed that the word derived from Chalcedon in Asia Minor, but this is no longer accepted.

Agate belongs to the quartz family of minerals. There are many varieties of quartz of an extremely fine-grained type among the tectosilicates known as chalcedony. Many of these are used as gem materials. Among them, in addition to the agate varieties, are jasper, petrified wood, chrysoprase, tigereye, and common and precious opal.

In the general opinion of most collectors, chalcedony is usually concretionary and the color is uniform. When patterns are involved, such as moss or bands, the material is regarded as agate. In this book, however, we shall make it a practice to call all forms of chalcedony agate, which is the term in popular use.

At this point at the beginning of the book it is perhaps wise to correct a popu-

Three specimens of quartz crystal Chinese snuff bottles with rutile needle-like inclusions. In the smaller bottle the inclusions look like seaweed at the bottom of the ocean. Illustrations courtesy of Charles E. Tuttle Company, Rutland, Vermont, from *Chinese Snuff Bottles* by Lilla S. Perry.

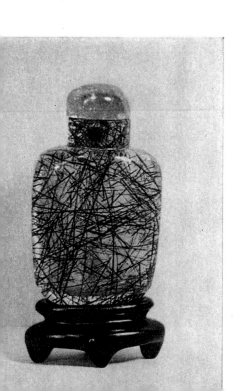

Moss agate Chinese carved snuff bottle
with moss- or fern-like inclusions.

Another example of a Chinese carved
agate snuff bottle. It is a brecciated
jasper, or conglomeration of cemented
pebbles in chalcedony, and is called
pudding stone in the gem trade. Illustrations courtesy of Charles E. Tuttle
Company, Rutland, Vermont, from
Chinese Snuff Bottles by Lilla S. Perry.

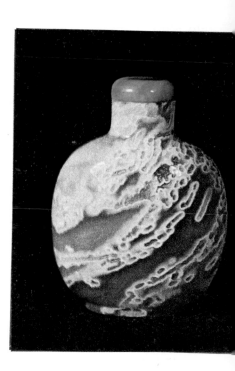

Chinese snuff bottle with streamers
milky quartz in chalcedony. Cutti
through the ends of the streamers giv
them the appearance of macaroni. T
material is known in the gem trade
macaroni agate.

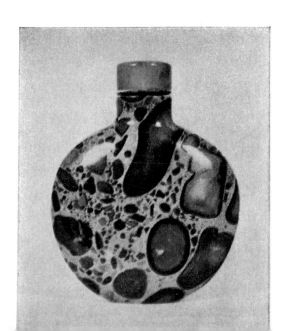

lar impression that agates were formed by volcanic action and under great heat. Volcanic action created cavities and gas pockets in the volcanic ashes that later were filled by cold silica, into which filtered various minerals as coloring agents. The cavities then became solidified, producing the agates that we dig today.

Agates are widely distributed, for quartz minerals are found in nearly every corner of the world. More than 200 varieties of quartz have been detailed in the literature, and most of these varieties have been chalcedony and cuttable for gems. It seems relatively safe to say that there is more interest in agates than in any other of the two hundred or so quartz varieties, or indeed in any other gem mineral species.

In the United States and Canada there is wide interest among rockhounds in the field of agates and this is because, in many sections of North America, there are localities where agates abound. In the 1930's, when interest in agates was coming to the fore and the early agate societies were forming in Oregon, there were localities where agate-filled thundereggs were so abundant that it took about ten years for the hunters to carry away the agates that were located on the surface of the ground. It is not so easy now as it was at that time to find agates on the surface, but after a little hard labor and digging at the known locations, rockhounds are still uncovering more than enough agates for their needs. Some of the old locations are bulldozed from time to time and great quantities of new thundereggs are uncovered.

However, in the desert regions of the west, inaccessible to bulldozers, it is still necessary to dig, as the surface material has long since been carried away. New locations are being discovered every year, however, and it is a thrill indeed to find such an area and realize that you are the first one to pick up some agates or petrified wood where they have lain undisturbed for perhaps a million years.

Chapter 2

Agates in History

HISTORIANS have been unable to place a definite date on man's first interest in agates, but from agate trinkets found in ancient graves the gathering of agates must date back to the Stone Age itself. It is generally agreed that pretty stones were man's first permanent possessions, after he had invented the spear, followed by the bow and arrow.

In selecting stones like flint, a type of quartz, which he could fashion into spear- and arrow-heads, it was inevitable that he found stones that appealed to him by their beauty—and thus were born the first instincts of art. When man first began to settle into villages and communities, after abandoning the nomadic life, he started to fashion other things out of stone. See the ancient axhead of agate in the accompanying photograph. This is a Sumerian agate axhead believed to date back about five thousand years.

As early as 3500 B.C. we find that the Egyptians had a well organized industry for mining rock crystal north of Assuan and amethyst near Gebel Abu Diyeiba, and they collected the agates from the same desert areas. Three thousand years later agates became an article of trade among the Arabians. These agates are believed to have come from India, where much good agate material could be obtained and where it is obtained to this day.

The earliest inhabitants of Mesopotamia were the Sumerians and they are believed to be the first people in history to recognize the value of precious stones as ornaments. As far as is known, they understood and practiced the lapidary art and made cylinder seals, signet rings, beads, and many other ornamental objects. In excavations made at Kish by Marshall Field for the Field Museum of Natural History in Chicago, great quantities of agate beads were found. These beads were worn by both sexes. The beads were also made of carnelian (red agate) and lapis lazuli (blue stone), but the agate beads predominated. The source of the agate has never been determined.

The first mention of agate in literature on the subject was made in a treatise *On Stones* by Theophrastus (372–287 B.C.). He referred to it as a beautiful stone sold at a high price, deriving its name from the river Achates in Sicily where it was believed to have been found for the first time. Pliny the Elder repeats this in his Natural History, written about A.D. 77. He detailed all the knowledge of agates up to that time, and since his account is so interesting we repeat it here.

He wrote: "The achates was in older times highly valued but now it is cheap. It was first found in Sicily near the river also called Achates. Later it was found in many places. It occurs in large masses and in various colors, hence its numerous names: iaspisachates [agate-jasper], cerachates [chalcedony], smaragdachates

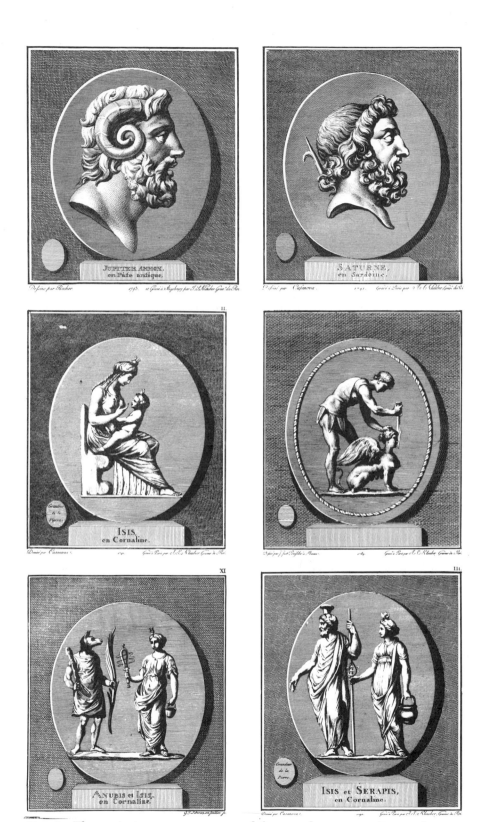

JUPITER AMMON,
en Pâte antique.

SATURNE,
en Sardoine.

ISIS,
en Cornaline.

ANUBIS et ISIS,
en Cornaline.

ISIS et SERAPIS,
en Cornaline.

FIG. 1. The ancient cameos were carved from sardonyx, carnelian, and agate by J. S. Klauber, famous engraver to the king of France, between 1789 and 1793. (*Engravings courtesy of Walter Kohn.*)

[green agate], haemachates [red agate or agate with red jasper veins or spots], leucachates [chalcedony], and dendrachates [moss agate]. As to the variety called autachates, as it is burned it gives off a smell like that of myrrh. This is a reddish variety resembling coral, hence it is called coralloachates: and the same is spotted with gold as is the sapphiros. This variety occurs frequently in Candia where it is called the holy or sacred agate, for according to the common people it is a cure for the sting of poisonous spiders and of scorpions. This property I could well believe the Sicilian agate has, for as soon as scorpions breathe the air of the Roman province of Sicily, no matter how venomous they may be, they immediately die. The Indian agate has the same properties and many other wonderful ones besides; for on them you will find represented rivers, woods, and farm horses; and one can see in them coaches, small chariots, and horse litters and in addition the fittings and trappings of horses. Physicians make agate mortars with which they reduce their drugs to fine powder. [They still make agate mortars and pestles to this day for pharmacies and laboratories.] It is believed that to look on the agate rests the eyes. If held in the mouth agate quenches and allays the thirst. [Even today in many desert areas inhabitants hold pebbles in the mouth to allay thirst.] Phrygian agate has no green in it. That from near Thebes in Egypt has no red or white veins. It also protects against scorpions. The Cyprian agate has the same virtue. Some insist that the supreme beauty and value of the agate is for it to be clear and transparent like glass. Those found in Thrace and near the mountain Oeta, upon Mount Parnassus, on the isle of Lesbos and in Messene, have the image of flowers, such as grow in the highways and the paths in the fields. Similar ones come from the Island of Rhodes. But the magicians know of other sorts: those that resemble a lion's skin are reputed to be

more potent against scorpions. In Persia they believe the perfume of agates turns away tempests and other unusual storms, and it also subdues violent river floods. To determine which stones are proper for this purpose the magicians throw them into a caldron of boiling water. If they cool the same, it is certain that they are suited for the above named purpose. But to be efficacious they must be worn tied by the hair of a lion's mane. Those agates, however, which display the pattern of a hyena's hide, the magicians cannot abide, as they cause dissension in the home. They also hold that provided a wrestler wear an agate, all of a color, he becomes invincible. As a test of this they put it and the different colors used by painters into a pot of seething oil. After it has boiled therein for two hours it will, provided it is genuine, impart to the oil and paints the color of vermillion. So much for the agates."

After reading Pliny's account of the other known gems of the time it becomes quite apparent that his discussion of the agate treats it almost with contempt. At the time of Pliny's death in A.D. 79 (he died in the same eruption of Vesuvius that destroyed the cities of Herculaneum and Pompeii) it was a mark of the highest prestige to own a cup made of agate. Just as a man is marked today by his possession of a Cadillac or Lincoln, so was the ancient Roman marked by the possession of an agate bowl or cup to "cool" his wine. It was the popular belief at the time that crystal was ice turned to stone, and thus a crystal or agate bowl was supposed to cool wine.

It will be noted that in his discussion of the agate Pliny seldom mentions the cups. He was inclined to treat with disdain and contempt the lavish display of jewels worn by women at the time. Never in the history of the world were jewels more revered or respected. It was said that people were inclined to mourn more over a broken agate cup than the body of a leading citizen. This was a time when the Emperor Caligula's wife, Lollia Paulina, wore $1,700,000 worth of jewelry made of emeralds and pearls to a wedding party.

Elsewhere in his History, Pliny speaks of men who "search amid the regions of the clouds for vessels [crystal] with which to cool our draughts and to excavate rocks, towering to the very heavens, in order that we may have the satisfaction of drinking from ice." He censured the employment of drinking cups set with other precious stones.

Many Romans had special keepers for their cabinets of crystal and agate cups and some even had individual names for each cup. One prominent Roman woman, not particularly rich, bought a crystal drinking cup for the equivalent of $5,913. It was reported at the time that, when Nero received bad news of a revolt and a lost battle, he exercised his wrath by smashing two agate bowls against the wall. He felt that he could punish his enemies no more than by destroying two objects that were so revered.

The largest crystal vessel ever reported was one which the Empress Livia Augusta dedicated in the capitol. It was said to weigh fifty pounds. Another vessel was reported that held twenty-four quarts. When Alexandria was conquered, Augustus chose as his reward from the spoils a single crystal cup.

No one was more extravagant with agate cups than Nero. He is reported to have paid a price equivalent to $39,675 for one cup. He confiscated the cups and bowls of many of his courtiers when they died. One of his consuls possessed so many cups that, when he died, Nero had to display them in his private theatre. This same consul once pledged the health of a lady of his fancy and then bit out the piece of the rim that her lips had touched. Although marred by the act, the cup was considered of greater value than any other in Rome. This is probably a myth since no one ever had teeth strong enough to bite a piece out of an agate cup. It is possible, however, that he could have broken the cup at the rim if it was very thin. When dying, the Consul Titus Petronius asked to see a large cup for which he had paid $12,000. He then broke it into a thousand pieces to keep Nero from getting it.

Much of the time, Pliny refers to the cups and bowls as being made of myrrha, which is a vague term, just as we would say today that a substance was a "hard stone." The Chinese likewise caused similar confusion by calling all hard stones jade. The term myrrha not only included agate and chalcedony but onyx and fluorspar and perhaps other materials.

As earlier stated, the first mention of agate in the literature was by Theophrastus about 300 B.C. However, one must not overlook the fact that, while agate is not mentioned by that name in the Bible, varieties of agate, such as carnelian, and other quartz gems are mentioned in many places. The first mention of agate in the Bible occurs very early, in the second chapter of Genesis, the first book of the Bible. Here mention is made of the onyx form of agate. Most notable of these mentions is the instruction for making Aaron's breastplate about 1250 B.C. A full account of the breastplate was contained in an article by A. Paul Davis in the *Lapidary Journal* for June, 1960.

The account of how the breastplate was to be made for Aaron, Moses' brother, is given in the 28th and 39th chapters of Exodus. The original breastplate was probably destroyed in 586 B.C. when the Temple and all its furnishings were carried away by the Babylonians. The Temple was rebuilt about 519 B.C. and apparently a second breastplate was made at that time, according to the Babylonian Talmud. This breastplate must have existed down to the time, in 54 B.C., when Crassus and the Roman army plundered the Temple and carried away all of its jewels. There is no record of another breastplate being made when Herod the Great ordered the Temple rebuilt in 20 B.C. A replica of the breastplate was made by Davis, who gives his account of it in the *Lapidary Journal* article.

The breastplate consisted of four rows of three precious stones each, on which were inscribed the names of the tribes of the twelve sons of Israel in the order of their birth. The only precious stones known at the time were those of Egypt, the Near East and those found along trade routes to the Near East. Of the twelve stones used, six of them were of the quartz family. Reuben's stone was red jasper, Simeon's was citrine or yellow quartz. Naphtali's was rock crystal or clear quartz. Issachar's or Dan's was amethyst or purple quartz, Zebulun's was yellow jasper and Benjamin's was chrysoprase or green chalcedony.

Many authorities disagree on the kinds of stones. Possibly the best piece of research ever done on the subect was for an article in the *Lapidary Journal* for August, 1960, by E. L. Gilmore, who possesses a thorough knowledge of gems and whose research was most complete. While Davis used a red jasper in his replica, Gilmore claims that the stone was sard or sardonyx, a reddish-brown agate type of chalcedony, named for the city of Sardes, one of its early sources. The Bible mentions the word sardius and Gilmore is no doubt correct when he says that sard was a stone so well known by the ancients that the translation of sard should be accepted as correct.

Gilmore is in disagreement with Davis on the second stone, or citrine (sometimes called topaz quartz). The stone was green and not yellow and was probably a peridot. Benjamin's stone, the chrysoprase, is given as agate in the Standard Revised 1958 edition of the Bible. It seems clear from the making of the breastplate that, about 1500 B.C., the peoples of the Holy Land and Egypt were familiar with all types of agate

and other quartz-family gems, that they were available from local sources and that they were the favorite precious stones of the day, probably because of their availability.

We are unaware of any talismanic claims made for agates at this time, but in ancient times the literature indicates a wide belief in the efficacy of wearing agates because of their wonderful virtues. In King's *Natural History of Precious Stones*, published in 1865, he reports that the author of "Lithica" wrote these lines about the agate:

> Adorned with this, thou woman's heart shall gain,
> And by persuasion thy desire obtain;
> And if of men thou aught demand,
> shalt come
> With all thy wish fulfilled rejoicing home.

In ancient times, according to Kunz, it was believed that anyone who wore an agate would be guarded from all dangers and would be enabled to vanquish all terrestrial obstacles. The wearer was supposed to be endowed with a bold heart. The preferred agates were black with white veins and pure white.

Kunz also reports that wearing of agates was supposed to induce sleep and pleasant dreams. Cardano wrote in 1585 that he had tested agates to see what their effect would be on his personal life and that he found the wearing of agates to make him "temperate, continent and cautious; therefore they are all useful for acquiring riches."

Perhaps the most curious and suggested use for agate occurred in 1709 when a Brazilian priest contrived an idea for an air ship. The ceiling of the airship was to be made of coral agate set in a network of iron. The sun's rays were supposed to heat the agate roof and generate magnetic power. In recent years agate amulets, particularly beads, made in Idar-Oberstein, Germany, have been exported to the Sudan and other places with great financial success. The agates are very popular with many

African tribes and are even used as currency in some sections.

Regardless of the merits of the definitions of precious and semiprecious stones in an earlier chapter, it appears to have been the opinion of earliest man that certain stones were not dead; they were "genuine" and possessed a "soul" of their own. This sensitivity to the supposed strange powers emitted from such stones marked them as precious. As far back as human history can be traced, precious stones have been important in leading to the fulfillment of human desires.

To the more than 40,000 inhabitants of the city of Idar-Oberstein in Western Germany, however, the word precious stone has a different meaning—it means life. For here we have 25,000 people who are all artisans at the trade of gem cutting, in every phase of it, and who have family roots in practically every country in the world where precious stones are found, and from where they are exported to the busy hands in the old home in Germany. There are 450 agate cutting mills alone. These skilled artisans can cut the tiniest diamond or diamonds as large as a peanut, are able to carve delicate figurines in agate and other materials and can carve the finest cameos from agate or shell. They can accomplish any feat of the lapidary craft. Furthermore, these people have been supplying the world with gems for more than 2,000 years and many of the items, particularly the agate bowls earlier described, were brought from Idar to Greece and Rome before the days of Christ.

Two thousand years ago Caesar had conquered France and was marching North. The Roman armies soon captured Augusta Trevirorum, the present-day city of Treves. Along the valley of the Moselle River passed the Roman legions on their way east to Moguntiacum, now Mayence. They crossed the mountain range and penetrated a valley running parallel to the Moselle Valley to join

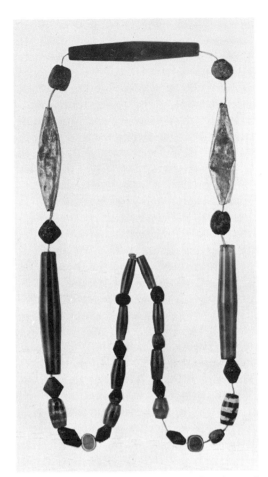

Fig. 2. Necklace of agate, lapis lazuli, and gold. About 3000 B.C. From excavations at Kish by Field Museum, Oxford University. (*Photo courtesy of Chicago Natural History Museum.*)

the Rhine. There they came upon a small and unimpressive group of buildings beside a swiftly flowing mountain stream between precipitous walls of rock. The settlement was known as Hidera, present day Idar. The people were peasants and hunters but in the winter, when they could not farm or hunt, they occupied themselves with processing the surrounding country's rocks into things of great beauty. The surrounding hills were filled with great quantities of agate, topaz, and amethyst, the favorite stones of the day. One can imagine with what delight the Roman soldiers came upon a whole district filled with these precious items and

9

met a people who knew how to do the lapidary work involved—just like the Roman silversmiths and gem cutters at home.

In a short while the Roman gem dealers realized the great potential of Idar and they took gigantic grindstones from the nearby Palatinate and used the rushing waters of the Idar River to run them. In A.D. 314, Treves was raised to a bishopric and nearby Idar grew in importance. After the fall of Rome, Idar also declined but the artisans continued to make their ornaments and gems, although they had to again depend upon agriculture and hunting for a living. At no time, however, did the grindstones of Idar become silent, and they ran steadily for two thousand years until, of late years, the old grindstones were replaced by electrically-driven motorized lapidary machinery. In the museum at Idar, however, some grindstones are operated in the old way, with men lying on their stomachs while working, just to show visitors the old methods.

Intense activity did not return to Idar, however, until the twelfth century when the new German rulers took over the ancient craft and restored it to prosperity. The Counts of Oberstein, who owned the agate quarries on the Weisselberg and the chief deposits on the Galgenberg in Idar, encouraged the inhabitants to refine the raw materials and offer them in international trade. The town prospered for a long time and the gem cutters organized themselves into a guild, prohibiting anyone from leaving the valley and taking his trade elsewhere. But in time the local deposits were exhausted and it was necessary to send men into the outside world to look for sources of supply. Thus, in time, every family in Idar had members in other countries looking for and sending them supplies of gem cutting materials. When vast quantities of agates were discovered in Uruguay, and other materials in Brazil, the town started to

flourish as it never had before, interrupted only by World War II. Today the city of Idar-Oberstein is flourishing but, unfortunately, this is principally because it is now also a center for manufacture of synthetic gems. The reader is urged to visit this charming city when on a European trip, visit the unusual museum, and see all phases of the lapidary art. Visitors report that the food, beer, and wine are other highlights.

Besides the work of Germans in agate, there is no other section of the world where skilled artisians and lapidaries are carving figurines and objects of art from chalcedony and agate, except in China, where the materials are not emphasized because jade is the favorite gem material. The Chinese workmanship, however, exceeds in artistic value that of the Germans. Under Communist rule, trade in agate treasures and other gem figurines has been discontinued. There is a flourishing quartz crystal cutting trade in Japan.

The greatest interest in agate at this time is found in the United States and Canada, where several hundred thousand amateur gem cutters have home workshops in which they fashion gemstones, principally agates. The agate is favored in these home lapidary shops because it is easily cut and polished and takes a high polish that is durable, the material being hard enough to withstand abuse if worn in jewelry. Agate is the prime favorite because of its great variety in color and interesting patterns. Agate is the only form of chalcedony that has a steady market in the gem trade, and only agate designated as moss agate commands the Federal tax on precious stones. Readers are warned to pay no tax on agates other than moss agates. If the agates are set in jewelry, of course the tax must be paid on the jewelry piece.

Another reason agate is popular is that it is so readily available to rock hunters, or rockhounds as they are called today. As mentioned previously, there are about three million of these rockhounds in the United States alone, most of them searching all over North America for agates. Of these, about 40,000 are associated in study groups or societies, which organize rock hunting expeditions referred to as field trips. Some of the better collecting areas are described in Chapter 8.

There are few thrills to equal the satisfaction of personally finding a beautiful agate or other quartz gem and then processing it yourself into a gem of great beauty. There is a fascination in this gem hunting and cutting hobby that no writer has ever succeeded in transscribing to the printed page.

The present day gem and mineral societies are the outgrowth of earlier mineralogical societies. The first of these were founded in 1885, one at the Brooklyn Institute and another at Philadelphia, called the Spencer F. Bair Mineralogical Society. These Societies have long since become defunct, but in 1886 the New York Mineralogical Club was founded and it still continues. The author had the honor of addressing it in 1949. There was little activity in organizing new clubs until the early 1900's, when study groups were organized in the principal cities along the Atlantic seaboard.

Present day rockhounding, and the enormous business it has generated, is really a child of the Depression in the 1930's. Many people who were unemployed tramped the hills and valleys in California in search of more gold, and they brought home with them finds of petrified wood and interesting rocks, which had a ready sale in curio shops where they were marketed as so-called "Indian jewelry." Gradually there came an exchange of information among individuals about localities, and finally groups for study and collecting were formed. Among these early associations was the Oregon Agate and Mineral Society of Portland, Oregon, founded in 1933. The Mineralogical Society of Southern California had been organized two years earlier, followed in 1932 by the Los Angeles Mineralogical Society. Through the 1930's many new clubs were formed along the Pacific Coast, the practice being to name them agate clubs in the Northwest and mineralogical societies in the Southwest.

In 1939 the author became interested in hunting for rocks. Selecting likely-looking finds—a piece of chalcedony and a piece of brown jasper—he took them to a prominent commercial lapidary in Los Angeles to have them cut into gemstones. He was a little shocked when he was presented with a bill for cutting four stones. "For $2.50 each I'll cut my own," he said to himself.

Then began a search for information about how to cut stones. He soon found that all the information about gem-cutting methods then available could easily be placed in a cigar box. The lapidary trade was the most closely guarded craft in the world. No professional lapidary would betray his hard-won secrets and one could not get a job in the trade unless his father or a close relative was in the guild. Almost nothing had ever been written about how to cut gems. However, the author did uncover several people who had information to exchange and the result of these meetings was that a group of sixteen people gathered at a dinner meeting and later, on February 10, 1940, organized the Los Angeles Lapidary Society.

The author became the first president and the Society soon flourished into a group of two hundred persons, at which time the membership was closed. The result of this action was that other sections of the city and county of Los Angeles soon began organizing their own local groups. The author acted as chairman of an organizing committee of the Los Angeles Lapidary Society to organize groups in Los Angeles County.

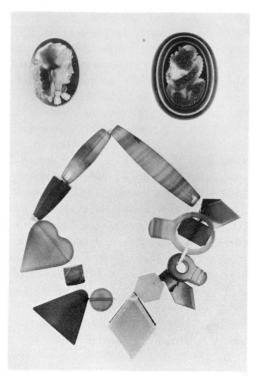

FIG. 3. Cameos made from agate *(above)*. Agate charms as sold to the natives of Senegal *(below)*. *(Photo courtesy of Chicago Natural History Museum.)*

He organized many groups elsewhere, particularly the Lapidary and Gem Society of New York and the Michigan Lapidary Society of Detroit, in 1949.

Today there are more than 900 of these clubs. A revised list of the clubs, with time and place of meeting, is given every year in the April issue of the *Lapidary Journal,* a special issue called the *Rockhound Buyers Guide.*

These clubs differed a great deal from the earlier mineralogical societies in that they did not dwell in their programs on the scientific aspects of mineralogy; they emphasized lapidary and gem cutting techniques and went on field trips for specimens. For a while there was a distinct antagonism between the mineralogist and the lapidary. Those differences have disappeared through the years, however, and now, as clubs are organized, they usually term themselves gem and mineral societies and have a large place in their programs for gem cutting and mineral study, two things that go together like ham and eggs.

In 1941, while President of the Los Angeles Lapidary Society, the author conceived the idea of renting a vacant store and having the members bring the gemcraft work they had done during the previous year, for a display to which they could invite their friends. The idea grew, to become rather ambitious, because of enthusiasm for the project, and the very large quarters of the Los Angeles Olympic Swimming Stadium were secured instead of a vacant store. To the great amazement of the members themselves, more than five thousand persons came to see the exhibition, which filled the stadium with more than fifteen thousand individual items. And thus was born the Society Show, of which there are now about one hundred and fifty a year, drawing hundreds of thousands of people from all parts of the United States and Canada.

For better organization, the Clubs in various sections of the country began forming regional Federations. In the 1940's a great many clubs were organized through the midwest, and in the 1950's Texas and the southern states drew enough interest in gem cutting for many clubs to be organized there. The Federations are the California Federation, the Northwest Federation, the Rocky Mountain Federation, the Eastern Federation, the Midwest Federation, and the Texas Federation. The Federations are in turn organized into the National Federation of Mineralogical Societies. Each one of the Federations holds annual sessions in conjunction with a huge show, and some of these shows draw as many as thirty thousand visitors to the gem and mineral exhibits. The movement is making great headway now in Australia, South Africa, and Canada.

At this point perhaps many readers

will wonder why so much attention is given to detailing the history of these hobby clubs in a history of agates. It is because of the fact that these clubs, through their programs, have returned the art of gem cutting to the people, have restored to them their very first art forms, and have made countless numbers of persons happy in the fastest growing craft hobby in America. The important end result of the whole program is that the amateur lapidaries of America have, in the last twenty years, made more progress in cutting agates and other gems than did the professionals during the last five thousand years. Even the professionals today subscribe to several magazines published for the amateur just to keep up with new discoveries made by these hobby tinkerers. There are thousands of amateurs who possess more skill in the lapidary art than most professionals, for as a rule a professional lapidary is skilled in some phase of gem cutting but seldom covers the field. A professional diamond cutter, for instance, may be a skilled cleaver and unskilled as a polisher. Few diamond cutters have ever produced a diamond from the rough to the cut and polished state. The reason the amateur often exceeds the professional in skill is that he takes the time to do so. The professional is working at a job where every minute is costly; the amateur is only killing time to indulge a hobby, and he therefore takes sufficient time to produce superb cutting and polishing.

In April, 1947, this author established a new magazine devoted to the interests of the amateur gem cutter and silversmith. For, by this time, many of the cutters were also making jewelry so that they could set the gems they had made and, in many cases, supplement their incomes to promote their hobby. This magazine was named the *Lapidary Journal*. Today it is a large monthly magazine, beautifully illustrated and well edited, with hundreds of advertisements in each issue of gem rough for sale and of all the machinery and gadgets needed in the cutting of gems and the making of jewelry. Every April in the large *Rockhound Buyers Guide* issue, nearly all of the Societies in the United States and Canada are listed, with time of meeting and meeting place. From eight hundred to a thousand dealers carry advertisements and nearly every one of about three thousand dealers has his name and address listed. This issue is usually entirely devoted to accounts of trips the reader may take to collect his own precious stone materials. It can be purchased for a dollar a copy postpaid from the *Lapidary Journal*, Del Mar, California. A sample copy of the *Journal* may be secured for 50 cents. If the reader develops an interest in the possibility of finding happiness through the gem-cutting hobby he would do well indeed to send for a sample copy.

As interest in gem cutting grew, it was inevitable that here and there hobbyists would invent ways of doing things and build machines to carry out the ideas. Then they would make machines for sale to others and soon they were in business with a machine shop and a staff. Other stone collectors began to sell some of their surplus rocks and soon opened roadside stands so that the touring rockhound could stop and buy local rocks. Stores began to spring up in the cities, where rockhounds could see the machinery, buy the rocks, and get the necessary mountings, findings, and silver for their jewelry making. Supplying the hobbyist with his needs has become big business and there are now more than three thousand dealers in every part of North America catering to the followers of the lapidary and jewelry making hobbies.

This growing hobby group is a great leveler of people, and in every Society one will find the laboring and professional man, the carpenter and the doctor. About a third of the followers of the hobby are women, who usually gravitate to the jewelry making end of the endeavor. Gem collecting and cutting is a wonderful family hobby. Parents, children, and even the family dog can enjoy the field trips, the vacation excursions, the study of the museums, and the companionship of all working together.

The worker in agate has come a long way in the last five thousand years since making the axhead shown in this chapter. He has made great progress, but most of it has been made in the last twenty years.

Chapter 3

Agate Collecting

THERE ARE many thousands of amateur lapidaries who have large and impressive collections of their work, principally in the field of agates and other quartz gems, who have never had the umatchable satisfaction of "discovering" a gem of their own. Their agates have been acquired through some of the dealers in gemstone rough. These people have missed the most fascinating part of the rock hobby. Then there are those at the opposite end of the hobby, the many thousands who are forever going on rock trips and hauling home tons of rock which they never intend to cut or possibly even look at again. They have only a magpie instinct or their only thrill is the outdoor excursion. They, too, have missed a great deal of the fun of the hobby because they have never had enough curiosity or artistic instinct to process some of their finds into gems of great beauty. They are like the many fishermen who dislike the taste of fish or hunters who will not eat game.

It is true that the hobby is so widespread today that probably half of those interested in it are so situated that they cannot go into the field and hunt their own rocks. They live in sections of the country where gem minerals do not exist. However, for them the picture has changed radically during the last ten years. High speed freeways and toll roads have now made it possible for the resident of New York City to be in agate-collecting country in Montana or Texas in about three days if he drives hard and well. Or he can jet to Portland or Seattle or Los Angeles and rent a car and be in collecting country in from twelve to twenty hours.

As stated in Chapter 1, there is little surface material to be gathered anywhere any more and the rockhound today has to be prepared to do a little digging. However, there are still plenty of locations to be discovered and there is still many times as much agate waiting to be gathered as has been hauled home by the countless thousands during the last thirty years.

If one is fortunate enough to live in a section of the country, like the Pacific Coast, where there are gem and mineral clubs regularly making field trips, the answer is simple. Join a club and attend their field excursions. However, these trips are not as important as they were twenty years ago, for, if it is difficult now for an individual to go out and gather good material by himself, it is many times more difficult for a mineralogical society group of maybe fifty to a hundred people to gather at any spot where each can find a flour sack of good material.

The best way to collect agates is to become an armchair traveler for a while and read about the known locations or the new ones being discovered. This can be accomplished by first subscribing to the *Lapidary Journal*, 12 monthly issues for $4.50 a year, including the big an-

FIG. 4. Camping scene on a club field trip to Mule Canyon in the Mojave Desert, California, by members of the Los Angeles Lapidary Society. (*Photo courtesy of the Los Angeles Lapidary Society.*)

nual April issue of the *Rockhound Buyers Guide*, or to *Gems and Minerals*, $3.00 a year for 12 monthly issues, or to both. The collector will have all the new information on sources of supply, collecting areas, maps, activities of the many clubs, and information about gem and mineral exhibitions.

The armchair collector also now has available a complete library of information that did not exist twenty years ago. It is true that many of the locations discussed in these books are almost depleted of good material or have only material that is hard won by work. In assembling a library of information, it is suggested that the first book the collector should buy is *Gemstones of North America* by John Sinkankas, a massive book of 675 well indexed pages about the gem locations on the North American continent, in Central America, and on many of the islands such as Cuba and Jamaica. This book sells for $15.00 a copy. Another popular book that should be in the library of every collector is the *Field Guide to Rocks and Minerals* by Dr. Frederick Pough, $4.50 a copy. This book is well illustrated in color. The newest book for the collector at this writing is *Gemstones and Minerals, How and Where to Find Them*, by John Sinkankas, $8.95 a copy. Sinkankas writes about the problems facing the collector when he begins taking his trips. He provides the practical information that the average collector looks for and which he may not have been able to get after years in the field and many disappointments. It is also a guide to many other subjects, from planning trips and selecting tools and equipment, to actual methods of digging and extraction.

There are many paperback editions of books on collecting, with maps, available for little money. Among the best of these are:

Midwest Gem Trails by June Culp Zeitner, $2.00

Northwest Gem Trails by Henry C. Dake, $2.00

California Gem Trails by Darold J. Henry, $2.50

New Mexico Gem Trails by Bessie W. Simpson, $2.50

Gem Trails of Texas by Bessie W. Simpson, $2.50

Arizona Gem Fields by Alton Duke, $2.50

The Rock Collector's Nevada and Idaho by Darold J. Henry, $2.50

Colorado Gem Trails and Mineral Guide by Richard M. Pearl, $2.95

Petrified Forest Trails by Jay Ellis Ransom, $2.00

Arizona Gem Trails and *The Colorado Desert in California* by Jay Ellis Ransom, $2.00

Mineralogical Journeys in Arizona by Arthur L. Flagg, $5.50 (hard cover)

Lake Superior Agate by Theodore C. Vanasse, $2.50

There are also available a *Treasure Map of the Great Mojave Desert* for $1.00 and a series of cards with maps called *Arizona Rock Trails* by Bitner for $1.95.

All of these publications are for sale by local gem and mineral dealers or from the magazines mentioned above. If the reader is not near a gem and mineral dealer he can address a request to both of the mentioned magazines and ask for their latest free book list. Both magazines carry a complete stock of all available gem and mineral books. It is suggested that the reader try his local library to see what they have to offer in earth science literature before purchasing any reading matter. Most libraries have some of these books and many libraries subscribe to the magazines.

The *Rockhound Buyers Guide* issue of the *Lapidary Journal* contains many articles on collecting areas. It also contains about a thousand advertisements of gem dealers and craft suppliers from all over the world. Included is a list of the more than 900 gem and mineral clubs in

FIG. 5. Lewis and Mary Humble, of the Los Angeles Lapidary Society, digging sagenitic and moss agate in the Horse Canyon agate field in Kern County, California.

North America, with time and place of meeting and, sometimes, a revised list of museums in America where gem and mineral collections are on display.

Every issue of both magazines gives a monthly list of gem and mineral shows promoted by the various clubs. The reader is urged to try to see one of these exhibitions so that he can learn for himself the results of collecting and gemcraft or lapidary work. Many dealers attend these shows and the show visitor can obtain a good education in gem materials by observing their displays and noting the appearance of popular rocks in the rough before any treatment. Many thousands of slabs or slices of gem rocks are available for purchase and the visitor can determine from these the probable appearance of the rock when it is cut and polished.

The person who never intends to gather rocks or to cut them, but is interested in making a collection, is afforded the choice of many thousands of finished gemstones in both the cabochon and faceted form. The visitor interested in jewelry making can purchase all the findings and supplies peculiar to that widespread hobby and purchase the finished stones for jewelry making. Most of the books and periodicals about the lapidary and jewelcraft hobbies can also be examined at the dealers' booths. A visit to a large show is a liberal education and an unforgettable experience.

It is not my intention to convey the thought that agate and other quartz family gem collecting is wholly confined to the states west of the Mississippi. However, this is the area in which these materials are more abundant and the collector is fortunate in having so much land still in the public domain, where he can feel free to collect. Some of the western states, however, are taking measures to prevent the traveling rockhound from being a rockhog. Nevada, for instance, has a law that prohibits the gathering of gemstone materials or mineral specimens in unreasonable amounts. However, nearly 87 per cent of all the land in Nevada is owned by the federal government and this leaves only about 13 per cent over which the state has jurisdiction, so that no one should be discouraged from collecting in the area. Indeed, the state itself encourages rockhound travel and has published maps for free distribution to rock hunters showing where they can collect. See the section on Nevada in Chapter 8.

The main reason for the popularity of collecting in the west is that the federal government still owns so much of the land, called the public domain, on which any citizen may prospect for minerals and agates. With the exception of Florida, there is no public domain on the eastern seaboard because there never was at any time any public domain in the original thirteen states. A little over 9 per cent of Florida is still owned by the federal government, but the domain is not mineralized. There is no public domain in the District of Columbia, West Virginia, Kentucky, or Tennessee, all east of the Mississippi. There is no public domain in Texas or Hawaii, where all land is owned by someone and collecting is difficult unless arrangements are made with the landowners. There are no quartz minerals in Hawaii. It is amazing that 99.7 per cent of Alaska is still public domain. However, collecting is almost impossible in Alaska because of the lack of roads and for other reasons outlined in the section on Alaska in Chapter 8. In California almost 45 per cent of the land area is still in the public domain, in Oregon over 51 per cent, and in Washington almost 30 per cent.

Just about every state except Hawaii has some area in which agates or some form of quartz gemstones can be found. Hawaii has one location that is only

FIG. 6. The Saratoga Springs area near Death Valley, San Bernardino County, California, a noted agate and jasper locality. Most of the good spots are now private claims. (*Photo courtesy of A. B. Meiklejohn.*)

open to deep sea divers where a fossilized black coral can be found. Florida has one location at Tampa where beautiful agatized coral may be gathered. While gemstones exist in every state of the United States and over much of Canada and Mexico, agate and petrified wood (agatized wood) collecting is principally done in the west for the reasons given above. In Chapter 8 a fairly complete list of the principal agate locations, particularly in the United States, is given. Most of them are discussed rather fully, and presented with maps, in the paperbacked books mentioned earlier in this chapter.

After reading some of the books or magazines, almost anyone will have his imagination fired to the point where he will be planning to take a trip to some collecting area, particularly if he owns an automobile. In planning a vacation collecting trip, it is suggested that the reader try to interest someone else in the project too, so that *two* families in *two* cars can go on the trip together. Not only will such an arrangement result in more fun but it will enable the hunter to visit many spots where it would be dangerous for one or two persons alone in ·one car to visit.

After planning your trip, get a copy of the latest issue of the *Rockhound Buyers Guide* and make a list of the dealers along your proposed route. The *Guide* usually gives the names and addresses of about half of the more than 3,000 rockshops and dealers in North America. You will find that the average dealer will be cooperative in giving local information and you will get to see in the rough or natural state the rocks of any area you may be visiting. And of course you will probably want to purchase some of the dealer's rocks even though you hope to gather your own for nothing. The dealer usually has better examples of the local agates than you are likely to find yourself—and you will not want to be like the fisherman who comes home with

no fish. You will also be able to see, particularly at the larger shops in the large towns or cities, a complete line of lapidary equipment, for you may want to learn amateur gem cutting and continue your fun with your finds long after the vacation is over.

You may wish to visit one of the more than 900 gem and mineral clubs and see how they operate. Their membership is open to interested parties and few special requirements are demanded of the membership. Visitors are always welcome. Dues are small, usually running from $2.00 to $5.00 a year, with the $2.00 fee predominating. These clubs meet regularly, seldom more than once a month, and they have lecture programs on the various aspects of gem and mineral collecting and the earth science studies in connection with them. Some of the clubs lean to mineral and fossil collecting and others toward the craft side of the hobbies, such as gemcraft and silvercraft. The total membership of all the clubs is about forty thousand or about one per cent of the estimated three million people interested in some form of rock collecting, with an interest in agate and quartz gemstones predominating.

The influence upon the hobby of this one per cent, however, is tremendous. They are in the main responsible for our present-day knowledge of gem and mineral locations and for the development of the gem cutting hobby to the point where more progress has been made in the development of gem cutting equipment and methods in the last thirty years than was made by the closely guarded secret guilds in the previous three thousand years. It is from the members of these clubs that the magazines catering to the hobby derive most of their accounts and articles. The societies provide the forums for the exchange of ideas and information. They are not as important as they were twenty years ago and many of the club rosters have declined because they have covered the

Fig. 7. Field trippers in the Montgomery Pass leaving Bishop, California, on the way to Tonopah, Nevada. The area abounds in obsidian (volcanic glass), but also has some agate and jasper. (*Photo courtesy of A. B. Meiklejohn.*)

field several times with lectures on the same subjects and have visited the same collecting spots many times. Because of lack of new members and repetition of lectures and programs, many of the once strong clubs have deteriorated into purely social groups and have lost their early zeal. However, the interested reader is urged to seek out and join one of these societies, even if only for a short while. Nowhere can one find groups that are so diversified in membership, for most of them contain professional men and those engaged in almost every other kind of human endeavor. The gem and mineral clubs are great levelers of human beings.

The *Rockhound Buyers Guide* gives an up-to-date list every year of these clubs, with time and place of meeting, a list too long to be included here and one that changes considerably from month to month. There are clubs in 49 states, all over Canada, and in the Canal Zone. Through close association with most of the clubs, and their federations, through the years as former editor and publisher of the *Lapidary Journal*, the author is well qualified to give a list of some of the more important clubs. This list is based on their past accomplishments through their shows and in other directions. Of course the greatest accomplishments have been made by clubs with large memberships and these exist in the larger population centers. Some of the most important clubs are:

Lapidary Club of Vancouver, British Columbia

Maricopa Lapidary Society and Mineralogical Society of Arizona, Phoenix, Arizona

Gem and Mineral Society of San Mateo County, Burlingame, California

Compton Gem and Mineral Society, Compton, California

Fresno Gem and Mineral Society, Fresno, California

Glendale Lapidary and Gem Society, Glendale, California

Hollywood Lapidary and Mineral Society, Hollywood (Los Angeles), California

Long Beach Mineral and Gem Society, Long Beach, California

Los Angeles Lapidary Society and Southwest Mineralogists, Los Angeles, California

San Fernando Valley Mineral and Gem Society, North Hollywood (Los Angeles), California

East Bay Mineral Society, Oakland, California

Pasadena Lapidary Society, Pasadena, California

Sacramento Mineral Society, Sacramento, California

Orange Belt Mineralogical Society, San Bernardino, California

San Diego Lapidary Society and San Diego Gem and Mineral Society, San Diego, California

San Francisco Gem and Mineral Society, San Francisco, California

San Jose Lapidary Society, San Jose, California

Santa Monica Gemological Society, Santa Monica, California

Delvers Gem and Mineral Society, South Gate, California

Whittier Gem and Mineral Society, Whittier, California

Colorado Mineral Society, Denver, Colorado

Gem and Lapidary Society of Washington, D.C.

Miami Mineral and Gem Society, Miami Mineralogical and Lapidary Guild, Miami, Florida

Georgia Mineral Society, Atlanta, Georgia

Chicago Rocks and Minerals Society

FIG. 8. Menagerie Canyon, start of a trip to Afton Canyon's beautiful material in San Bernardino County, California. Note the lion's head, one of many rock formations in the canyon. *(Photo courtesy of A. B. Meiklejohn.)*

FIG. 9. Another view of Menagerie Canyon, start of a field trip into Afton Canyon, San Bernardino County, California. Afton Canyon is a noted collecting locality and Menagerie Canyon has interesting rock formations looking like animals, one of which is shown in the picture. *(Photo by A. B. Meiklejohn).*

and Chicago Lapidary Club, Chicago, Illinois

Evansville Lapidary Society, Evansville, Indiana

Gem Cutters Guild, Baltimore, Maryland

Michigan Mineralogical Society and Michigan Lapidary Society, Detroit, Michigan

Nebraska Mineral and Gem Club, Omaha, Nebraska

Clark County Gem Collectors, Las Vegas, Nevada

Newark Lapidary Society and Newark Mineralogical Society, Newark, New Jersey

Albuquerque Gem and Mineral Club, Albuquerque, New Mexico

Santa Fe Gem and Mineral Club, Santa Fe, New Mexico

Lapidary and Gem Society of New York and New York Mineralogical Club, New York City

Southern Appalachian Mineral Society, Asheville, North Carolina

Cleveland Lapidary Society, Cleveland, Ohio

Oklahoma Mineral and Gem Society, Oklahoma City, Oklahoma

Eugene Mineral Club, Eugene, Oregon

Oregon Agate and Mineral Society, Portland, Oregon

The Mineralogical Society of Pennsylvania, Philadelphia, Pennsylvania

Mineral and Lapidary Society of Pittsburgh, Pennsylvania

Dallas Gem and Mineral Society, Dallas, Texas

El Paso Mineral and Gem Society, El Paso, Texas

Houston Gem and Mineral Society, Houston, Texas

San Antonio Rock and Lapidary Society, San Antonio, Texas

Mineralogical Society of Utah, Salt Lake City, Utah

Gem Collectors' Club, Seattle, Washington

Wisconsin Geological Society, Milwaukee, Wisconsin

Cheyenne Mineral and Gem Society, Cheyenne, Wyoming

The foregoing list contains the names of about 6 per cent of the clubs. It will be noted that the names of few of the many eastern clubs are given. This is because, while there are many clubs in New England, for example, they do not emphasize lapidary work in their programs. They are largely made up of mineral specimen collectors and traders because these specimens, and not gem minerals, occur in their area. Few of the midwest club names are included because they emphasize fossil collecting and geological study more than they do gemcraft activities. About half of all the clubs in America exist in the three Pacific Coast states and, while the names of but a few are included here, they are all important to the agate collector; they are in agate country and especially in country where active collecting in the field can take place practically any month in the year. The Pacific Coast states are also noted for beach collecting and some of the finest agates in the world have been collected on the beaches of California, Oregon, and Washington. About the only quartz gems that are found on the eastern beaches are the "Cape May diamonds" (quartz pebbles) at and near Cape May, New Jersey, and the agatized coral at Tampa Bay in Florida.

Agate collecting is now being enjoyed as a recreational and craft hobby by several million people in America and the reader is urged to investigate the activity through some of the suggestions given in this chapter, by either joining an associated group, by going on field trips with a group or by one's self, or by reading a few of the many books and publications listed. By seeking out and talking to someone who has followed the hobby for years, one can learn of the many blessings derived from an interest in rocks.

Chapter 4

Varieties and Forms of Other Quartz Gems

So far we have been dealing principally with agates, a form of chalcedony in the quartz family of minerals. Chalcedony in popular parlance in the gemological world is regarded as "clear agate," while agate is regarded as chalcedony with bands of color or shadings of the same color. However, it is difficult to draw such a fine line, and probably unimportant. For instance, one could find wide support for the belief that carnelian is red chalcedony, while others would call it red agate. When such an agate has layers of contrasting colors (resulting in banding when cut) it is called sardonyx, although this term is mostly confined to a red and white variety. A yellow variety is called sard. The black and white variety is referred to as onyx agate and it is from this material that most onyx cameos are carved.

A characteristic of agate and chalcedony in the quartz family of gem minerals is that they are translucent while other forms of quartz gems, except the crystal varieties, are opaque. That is to say, agates will permit light to shine through them, but they are not transparent and cannot be seen through. Other forms of quartz materials, like petrified wood and jasper, do not reflect or give out light and are impervious to light rays. Hence they are not as beautiful as agates and are not as popular with collectors or gem cutters.

While in the gem mineral world no species is more abundant and widespread, more varied or more beautiful, than the quartz gem, the only varieties that are widely commercialized as finished gems are agate and crystal. Agate is not referred to in regular jewelry stores as agate, however, but by the names of agate varieties such as sardonyx, sard, carnelian, and onyx. Indeed, most jewelry salesmen would argue with the customer who referred to these stones as agate, but then relatively few jewelry salesmen have even a good working knowledge of the gemstones they are selling and quite innocently misinform customers about gems. Many jewelry stores continue to sell citrine or yellow quartz as topaz, although some will lean to the side of honesty in retailing and qualify it by calling it "topaz quartz," meaning that it is topaz-*colored* quartz. Almost never does a jeweler call yellow crystal quartz by its correct name of citrine, which is due to its lemon color. Good genuine topaz is usually a ginger-ale color rather than a deep yellow and is much harder than quartz.

When crystal quartz, which is almost transparent when cut, is purple through lavender in color, it is called amethyst. Both citrine and amethyst are faceted like the diamond, and both gems are very popular and very beautiful and the most expensive of the quartz gems.

25

There are all shades of quartz from clear quartz to morion or black quartz. The shades of black bordering into yellow are called smoky quartz and often incorrectly sold as "smoky topaz." A variety from Scotland is called cairngorm, and many people, particularly in the British Isles, believe it to be a distinct gem, although cairngorm is just another name for smoky quartz. All of these varieties of crystal quartz are popular with amateur gem cutters and the faceting lapidary usually begins (and too often stays) with this gem variety in his craft work. Crystal quartz is adaptable to color change through heat treatment.

Rock crystal is a transparent mass of clear quartz from which figurines are carved. This is the source of the crystal ball, examples of which can be very valuable. This material should not be confused with glass, but many people think, when they buy crystal tableware, that it is quartz. It is true, however, that the glass is made from high-grade silica or quartz sands.

Rose quartz also occurs in a massive form and is much used for figurines and other carvings. It is usually pale pink and is so badly fractured that it does not often lend itself to faceting as do the other crystalline varieties. When faceted it presents a milky appearance and is not as brilliant as other crystalline colors.

Several methods have been devised for changing the color of agates. The natural gray and pale shades of some agates are not conducive to enthusiastic appreciation. The most common method of changing the color of agates is by heat-treatment. Since no material is added in this process, the color change must be attributed to a rearrangement of the atoms of the tinctorial agent, according to G. F. Herbert Smith. Some of the crystalline varieties of quartz gems can be changed in color by the application of heat. Amethyst, which is purple quartz, can be changed to orange, yellow,

and green, while smoky quartz can be made yellow.

Varieties of quartz gems other than agate and crystal are seldom seen in regular trade channels, but they are highly popular in rockhound circles and widely sold in the stores of hobby suppliers, both in rough and finished form. Petrified wood, for instance, makes beautiful bookends, and jasper forms are ideally suited for beads. Later we shall see illustrations of the many things that can be made from these lesser varieties of quartz.

Next to agates and crystals, probably the most popular quartz gem variety is the jasper family, followed by the many types of petrified or agatized wood. These are opaque and not as attractive as agate but they are ideal for novelties of all kinds such as ash trays, bola tie settings, bookends, bracelets, beads, ring settings, and ash trays.

Jasper is widely distributed in the western states and appears under many variety names, usually derived from the location from which it comes. Many of these names appear in the glossary at the end of this chapter. Considered by most collectors as among the most beautiful of the jaspers are the orbicular or eye jasper from the Llagas Creek area near Morgan Hill, California, and the Stone Canyon jasper from near San Miguel, California. The latter is a varicolored mottled or brecciated jasper and it is found in large solid unfractured masses, but it is difficult to obtain any large pieces of the Morgan Hill orbicular jasper that are fracture free. Indeed it is difficult to find unfractured pieces large enough for good cabochons.

So closely akin to jasper varieties are the flints and cherts that it is quite difficult to distinguish one from another. If the material appears to be of gem quality it is usually called jasper, although it may actually be chert or flint. The flint from the Flintridge, Ohio, area looks so much like the finest jasper that almost any gem cutter would call it that. This is particularly true of a yellowish variety so closely resembling the Stone Canyon type mentioned above that the two stones are scarcely distinguishable from one another. Many genuine jaspers are often carelessly classed as chert merely because they are unattractive. These three varieties of quartz gem materials are so widely distributed that there are few gravel pits anywhere that will not yield some good specimens.

Sometimes opaque jasper will have sections of translucent agate and the material is then referred to as jasp-agate. Most so-called agatized wood (petrified wood) should more properly be called jasperized wood, as it contains practically no translucent or agate areas. This is particularly true of the wood from the Petrified Forest in Arizona. This very fine jasperized wood contains markings of black dendrites of pyrolusite or manganese. When cut into slabs or cabochons for jewelry, the markings take on the appearance of trees and many gems have interesting "scenes" in them. As jasper is not translucent, it has to depend on these scenes or an interesting color pattern for its intrinsic value.

Flint is a mixture of quartz and opal and may easily be distinguished by its fracture, which is always conchoidal or shell-like in appearance, the same as the opal. Because it is easily chipped and is hard, it has been the favorite material for fashioning arrow- and spearheads since prehistoric times. It is widely distributed all over the world and flint artifacts have been gathered wherever civilization has been found. Because of its usually dull appearance it is not favored as a gemstone.

One of the varieties of agate most appreciated by the collector is iris agate. This is a chalcedony that appears uninteresting until it is cut into very thin slabs and polished on both sides. It then displays all the colors of the rainbow when held before a light and becomes one of the most beautiful of nature's creations. This material is rare and seldom developed unless the lapidary is purposely looking for the phenomenon. Authorities report that possibly no more than one in twenty thousand agates possesses the iris quality. In some areas the average is higher, however, and there is a locality in Mint Canyon, Los Angeles County, California, where the average is reported to be one in six. The rainbow effect is caused by refracted light passing through almost countless bands in the agate. These bands run between twenty thousand to fifty-five thousand per inch. The finest examples come from northern Mexico and sometimes Montana agates produce some fine specimens, particularly the specimens without moss inclusions that are usually discarded by the collector. Most authorities believe that no moss agate ever has the iris phenomenon, but the author has cut an agate he found at Nipomo, San Luis Obispo County, California, that displays beautiful plumes in one half of the cabochon and a distinct rainbow in the other half.

Another form of agate that is seldom seen in collections is the beautiful fire agate of California. This material was discovered in 1946 in the Black Hills of Riverside County, California. Since that time it has been much sought after and some entrancing gems have been cut from it. This chalcedony usually occurs in a form known as desert roses because of their resemblance to a flower. Dark portions of the roses have inclusions of limonite, and when the layer of limonite is barely exposed to the surface by exceedingly careful grinding, the stone has the appearance of being on fire. Some authorities claim that the inclusions are goethite but expert mineralogists find it difficult to distinguish between limonite and goethite, as both minerals are forms of hydrated oxide of iron. The material is also found in Arizona.

A great favorite of collectors of the quartz group of minerals and gemstones is the geode. A geode is usually a hollow ball of mineralized earth, such as rhyolite, into which ground waters containing silica have filtered to form a crystal lining. Sometimes the crystals are colored and good amethyst has been recovered from them, especially in the geodes from Uruguay and Brazil. When the geode is completely filled and the rock is solid, it is called a nodule. The inside portion of the geode often contains layers of agate and when the geodes are cut in half and polished they reveal entrancing patterns and colors, designs, and "scenes." When halved the solid geodes or nodules usually show a definite pattern of the agate inclusions that is almost always in the rough shape of a five pointed star. Sometimes the pattern will include very fine examples of moss and sagenite agate.

There are several areas in Illinois and Iowa where geodes are plentiful, although they are usually on private land where collecting is not allowed. These geodes are small but very attractive. They have little intrinsic value and are not suitable for gem cutting. The midwest geodes are crystal lined and the average size is from that of a lemon to that of an orange.

Probably the most popular geodes with collectors are the thundereggs of Oregon, usually nodules rather than geodes, as the centers of most of them are solid with agate fillings. The name comes from a popular belief among the Warm Spring Indians of Central Oregon that the concretions were missiles from the volcanoes of the Cascade Mountains, thrown whenever the gods inhabiting the mountains became angry. These nodules contain many interesting scenes when sawed in half and polished—as can be seen in the accompanying illustrations. Thundereggs were very plentiful in the thirties and forties and easily available on the surface of the ground.

They are still plentiful, but they are won only by some hard digging. They occur in sections referred to as beds and sometimes a few square yards will yield literally thousands of the eggs. There are privately owned locations where the collector can collect for a daily fee. These locations are bulldozed regularly and fresh areas exposed so that the collector is free of the backbreaking work of digging for them. The locations appear in advertisements in the various magazines catering to the collecting hobby.

The most spectacular geodes, aside from the fantastic amethyst Uruguayan and Brazilian geodes, are found in the Chuckawalla Mountain of Imperial County, California. Fortunately, the area is public land and collectors are free to collect there. It is a formidable land in the summer, however, and collecting in the summer months is not suggested unless the collector is accompanied and the party contains at least two cars. There are no paved roads into the area and there is no water. While the temperatures in the summer are always over one hundred degrees, and most of the time up to one hundred and thirty degrees, the winter months are delightful. In January and February, hundreds of trailers come from all over the United States and campers can be found digging in the various beds. Hundreds more come each weekend from the clubs in Southern California, for the area is about two hundred miles from both Los Angeles and San Diego.

These agate geodes are of no value as gem materials, although fine cabochons can be cut from slices of them. They are strictly curios but to a man with a diamond saw they possess infinite attraction. No two geodes are ever quite alike, just as no two agates are ever alike, and it is impossible to put into words the thrill that comes to a man when half of the geode he is sawing falls off into the splash pan to reveal an interior of sheer beauty, perhaps

FIG. 10. Large beautiful specimen of quartz crystals on hematite. Source unknown, but believed to be England. From the author's collection. *(Photo by O. D. Smith.)*

lined with red or purple crystals. The polished halves make wonderful cabinet specimens for the collector who has the room and the inclination to display such things. Specific information about the various locations in the Chuckawalla Mountain area and many other agate and quartz gem areas in the United States appear in Chapter 8.

Locations in Canada and Mexico are described in Chapter 9.

Authorities always include the opal in a list of quartz gems. However, the opal is a non-crystalline gem and is amorphous. It is composed of silica, the same as the other quartz varieties, but in a hardened jelly form. When it shows a play of the colors of the spectrum it is called precious opal and most gem lovers agree that it is then the most beautiful of all the gems. This deserves a separate account, which is given in the next chapter. The subject of petrified wood or agatized wood is covered separately in Chapter 6.

GLOSSARY OF AGATE AND OTHER QUARTZ GEM TERMS*

Agate jasper
   See Jasp-agate.
Agatized wood
   See Petrified wood.
Aleppo stone
   See Eye agate.
Algae jasper
   A local name for a jasper found in the northern counties of Minnesota. It is bright red with a cell-like pattern.
Amberine
   A yellowish-green chalcedony from Death Valley, California.
Amethyst
   A pale lavender to a deep purple transparent variety of crystalline quartz. It can be cut cabochon or faceted and is a stone of great beauty. It was much preferred by the Romans and is often referred to as the Bishop's stone. The color most preferred is a reddish purple, popularly known as wine color. This material comes from Brazil, Russia, Uruguay, Arizona, and California. It was once the popular belief that, if an amethyst was deposited in a glass of wine, it would prevent the drinker from getting drunk. This belief stemmed from the fact that many Romans had drinking cups made from amethyst and, after they had been drinking awhile, the servants would fill the cups with water, which still looked like wine, and would suppose they were fooling their masters. It is doubtful if anyone was fooled.

*A separate glossary on opals appears in Chapter 5.

Amethystine
   Sometimes called azure quartz and sapphire quartz. This is a color designation meaning violet to purplish, used as in amethystine glass, amethystine quartz, etc. Sometimes incorrectly used as a term for badly flawed cabochon material. This is usually an opaque type of amethyst with mixed shades of color from lavender to purple and is never faceted.
Apricotine
   Trade name for yellowish-red, apricot-colored quartz pebbles from near Cape May, New Jersey. Sometimes occurs as reddish-yellow or apricot color.
Arkansas candles
   Quartz crystals in clusters from Arkansas, being about six times as long as they are thick.
Arkansas stone
   A pure white porous rock containing millions of minute quartz crystals cemented with chalcedony and known to mineralogists as novaculite (Sinkankas). Chiefly used as whetsones. Found near Hot Springs, Arkansas.
Auriferous agate
   An uncommon light red agate containing gold. Occurs as stream pebbles.
Aventurine
   A translucent green quartz containing very small inclusions which produce a glittering sheen and spangled effect. The inclusions vary. Mica inclusions produce a silvery, brassy, or golden glitter called aventurescence. Fuchsite inclusions produce a greenish aventurescence. Hematite or goethite inclusions produce a metallic reddish appearance. Aventurine may be gray, yellow, brown or green, but only the green variety is preferred as a gem and it is always cut as a cabochon.

Banded agate

Agates with colors usually arranged in parallel bands, which are usually wavy. Most of the agate in the trade is this variety but it is dyed or heat-treated. The bands are of differing tones due to their varying ability to absorb the dyes or heat. Sometimes called riband agate.

Basanite

A deep velvety-black variety of amorphous quartz, slightly tougher and finer grained than jasper. The Lydian stone or touchstone of the ancients. Used by jewelers for testing precious metals. Widely distributed and associated with jasper in gravel deposits. The best quality comes from India but good specimens have been found in the vicinity of New York City and along the Delaware River below Easton, Pennsylvania. Not a gemstone. Sometimes erroneously called black jasper.

Bavarian cat's-eye

Quartz cat's-eye from Hof and other locations in Bavaria which produce only a few stones of fine quality. Other qualities usually sold as Hungarian cat's-eye. Quartz cat's-eye from the Harz mountains in north Germany is sometimes sold as Bavarian cat's-eye.

Bayate

A local name for a brown ferruginous variety of jasper from Cuba.

Beckite

The star pattern of coral geodes of Panama. Sometimes spelled beekite.

Binghamite

Named for William J. Bingham of Saint Paul, Minnesota, who discovered the material in quartz veins in the iron ore formations of Minnesota. Crystalline quartz containing replacements of goethite. When polished the gem exhibits a decided chatoyance due to the light reflections of the embedded fibers. Some-times produces fine cat's-eye gems. Reported to be 98 per cent pure quartz. The inclusions appear in straight lines. A similar material is silkstone, but this material is not as nearly pure quartz and the inclusions are not straight.

Black chalcedony

The correct term for black onyx. It is usually a dyed clear chalcedony, the black color being produced by boiling it in a sugar solution. Very popular material for men's jewelry, such as lodge emblem rings.

Blood agate

A very pretty cabochon material from Utah in flesh red, pink, or salmon colors. It is sometimes called hemachate.

Bloodstone

Dark green jasper with blood-like red spots. It is cut as a cabochon and is popular in men's jewelry. The best material comes from India but it has been found in limited quantities at several spots in the American west. The author found some beautiful bloodstone in the Mint Canyon area of Los Angeles County, California. A variety called heliotrope is a chalcedony with red jasper spots.

Blue agate

A rare color in agate. A light sky blue variety comes from near Ellensburg, Washington, and a darker blue comes from the vicinity of Lead Pipe Springs, California.

Boakite

A local name for a brecciated green and red jasper found in Nevada.

Botryoidal agate

Agate having the form of a bunch of grapes. Small spheres of agate resting on a matrix.

Bouquet agate

This name was given by the author to a very fine form of flower agate found near Alpine, Texas, in which the flower-like inclusions resemble arranged bouquets.

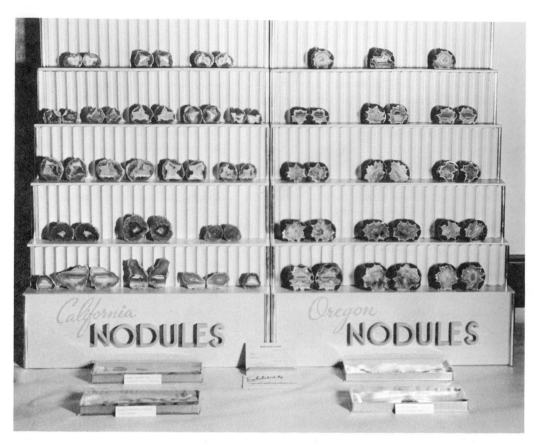

FIG. 11. An interesting and contrasting display of agate-filled nodules from California and Oregon by John E. Gaston, former president of the Los Angeles Lapidary Society. This was one of the exhibits at the first amateur lapidary show held in March, 1941. *(Photo by G. Haven Bishop, courtesy of the Los Angeles Lapidary Society.)*

Brazilian topaz

A misnomer for citrine or yellow quartz.

Brecciated agate

Agate which has been broken into irregular fragments and then cemented together again by silica solutions. Well typified in Stone Canyon jasper.

Brecciated jasper

A reconstituted form of jasper in which the patterns appear as mosaics. Occurrences are widely distributed but a particularly interesting brown and yellow variety occurs near San Miguel, California, and on the beaches north of Ventura, California. A great favorite with ama-

teur gem cutters as material for bookends and spheres. *Also see* Brecciated agate.

Bruneau jasper

Named after the Bruneau River in Idaho.

Burnite

Not a pure quartz gem but a very beautiful sky blue mixture of silicates, oxides, and carbonates of copper. Found near Battle Mountain, Nevada. Sometimes sold as shattuckite and azurite, which it resembles. Named after Frank Burnam, its discoverer, in 1952.

Cairngorm

The Scottish term for smoky quartz and not an individual gem variety.

32

Cameo agate

A little-used term for onyx.

Cameos

Cameos are generally, but not always, fashioned from substances composed of two or more differently colored layers such as the alternate black and white layers in onyx or brownish-red layers in sardonyx. Genuine cameos contain a design produced by cutting away portions of the upper layer to reveal the colored layer beneath. If cut from genuine gem materials such as agate and sardonyx, the cameos are called stone cameos. Shell cameos are cut from shells and coral cameos are cut from coral. Sometimes cameos are molded or pressed and then should be called "molded cameos" or "pressed cameos." Cameos made of two or more separate pieces joined together should be called "assembled cameos." Cameos made of glass or other materials not mentioned above should be called "imitation cameos." (These definitions were prepared and adopted by the National Business Bureau and the American Gem Society.)

Cape May "diamonds"

Small chalcedony pebbles of various hues from white to smoky found on the seashore of the Atlantic Ocean at and near Cape May, New Jersey. They make good clear faceted stones and some shopkeepers in the vicinity are in legal difficulty from time to time for actually marketing the stones as "diamonds." *Also see* Apricotine.

Carnelian

A red, orange-red, brownish-red, or brownish-orange translucent to semi-translucent form of chalcedony. Sometimes yellow or brownish-yellow and when it grades into brown it is called sard. When it alternates with bands of white it is referred to as sardonyx, which

is an alternate birthstone for August. In the jewelry trade carnelian is often sold as sardonyx.

Carnelian onyx

A term used in a broader sense for any true onyx, one or more of the alternating bands being carnelian in color. Differs from sardonyx. *See* Carnelian.

Carved agate

A term applied to agate which has been carved or worked into objects. More particularly applied to the agate art objects carved in the Orient.

Catalinaite

Sometimes incorrectly called Catalina sardonyx. It is found as pebbles on the beaches of Catalina Island, California.

Cat's-eye agate

Due to reflections and colorings, so-called "moonstone" agate will exhibit an opalescence that gives a cat's-eye effect.

Cave Creek jasper

Jasper from the Cave Creek area near Phoenix in Maricopa County, Arizona.

Cer agate

A rare chrome-yellow colored agate from Brazil. Similar to sard.

Chalcedony

Clear and colorless agate without patterns or inclusions.

Chert

So nearly like jasper that it is usually a matter of personal opinion, and they are chemically identical. As a rule the collector will refer all poorly colored or uninteresting types of jasper to the chert classification. Resembles flint. This term is usually reserved for impure chalcedony formed by precipitation of silica from the hot waters associated with volcanic activity, according to John Sinkankas in his authoritative book, *Gemstones and Minerals, How and Where to Find Them.*

Chrysocolla

This is not one of the quartz minerals but it is often confused with chalcedony. It is a soft blue mineral which occurs as inclusions coloring quartz but it only has a hardness of between 2 and 4. Sometimes called chrysocolla quartz although it may occur both as an amorphous or a cryptocrystalline variety. This is one of the most beautiful blue gem minerals. It occurs principally in Arizona copper mines but it is often confused with other blue copper silicates, which are all called chrysocolla erroneously in that area and in California. Pure chrysocolla is too soft for durable gemstones and what passes in the rockhound gem marts as chrysocolla is really chalcedony with chrysocolla inclusions. When it is good quality blue and translucent it is probably the most valuable chalcedony in the world. Good specimens are much in demand at prices ranging from $25.00 to $50.00 a pound. This is $100,000 a ton for agate!

Chrysocolla agate

Chalcedony in very attractive blue-green to bright green colors caused by copper silicate inclusions.

Chrysoprase

A pale yellow-green variety of chalcedony that is rare in a good quality. It is one of the prettiest of green gemstones. It is a misleading term for chalcedony that has been dyed and called green onyx, although the latter is a much darker green. A corrupted spelling of chrysophrase has been suggested for the dyed material but has never found favor. Always cut as a cabochon.

Chrysoquartz

Another name, seldom used, for green aventurine quartz.

Circle agate

A term used for agate with circular markings.

Citrine

A transparent lemon-yellowish to red-orange or ginger-ale colored clear quartz. When it is very dark it is called smoky quartz. It is often sold by jewelers as topaz, which it closely resembles, and sometimes as "topaz quartz." This term does not imply that it is a mixture of topaz and quartz but rather that it is topaz-colored quartz. The term is also used for burned amethyst and cairngorm, which become yellow when heat-treated. Citrine makes a very beautiful faceted gem and is a favorite with amateur gem cutters.

Cloud agate

A name applied especially to a light gray transparent to semi-transparent chalcedony with large spots of darker gray, resembling clouds. Also called cloudy agate.

Concretion agate

A term applied to the agate portion of the interior of concretions.

Coral agate

Any agate resembling fossilized coral but more specifically agatized or fossilized coral. Tampa Bay in Florida is a prolific source of this beautiful material, which is used so effectively in jewelry.

Cornelian

The British spelling of carnelian.

Creolite

A red and white banded jasper found in Shasta and San Bernardino counties in California.

Crocidolite

A fibrous amphibole, also known mineralogically as blue asbestos. Its bluish color predominates in sapphire quartz and hawk's-eye but is altered to yellow-brown or red in its pseudomorph, tigereye. Listed here not as a quartz mineral but to avoid confusion with tigereye.

Crocidolite quartz

This is the same as tigereye.

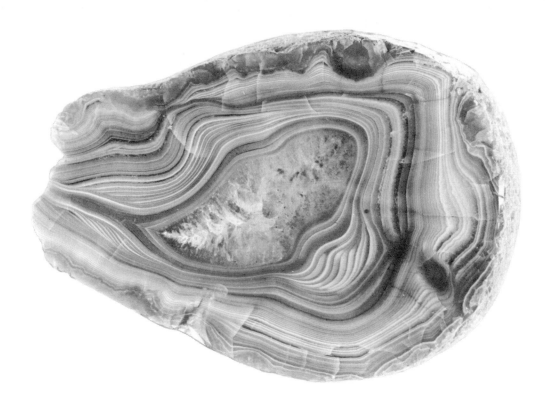

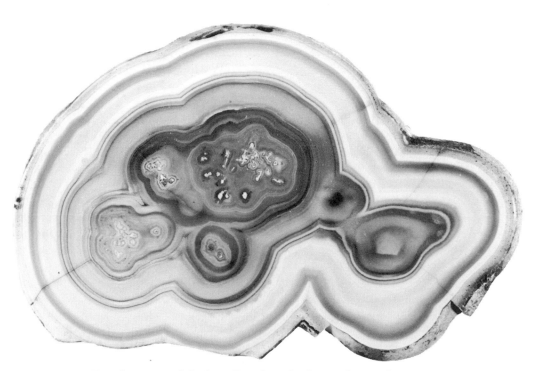

FIG. 12. Two fine agate slabs from Brazil on display in the Smithsonian Institution. (*Photos courtesy of the Smithsonian Institution.*)

Cryptocrystalline quartz

A type of quartz that is indistinctly crystalline. The crystalline grains are not discernible except under the polarizing microscope. The great majority of quartz gems are cryptocrystalline and very few are clear and macroscopic crystals. The opal is amorphous, or without crystalline form.

Crystalline quartz

A term used to distinguish the varieties of quartz that are not cryptocrystalline, such as rock crystal, amethyst, citrine, cairngorm, rose quartz.

Cyclops agate

An eye agate with but one eye.

Delawarite

Aventurine feldspar from Delaware County, Pennsylvania, just outside of Philadelphia.

Dendritic agate

Agate such as the mocha stone and moss agate, having inclusions of iron or manganese oxide arranged in forms resembling trees, ferns, moss, flowers. Usually composed of iron or manganese oxides.

Desert roses

A flower-like flat nodule form of chalcedony that is slightly pinkish, being translucent to opaque. The agates also resemble oyster shells. Dark brown portions of the roses contain goethite or limonite and are cut into gems called fire agates. The material occurs in the Black Hills of Riverside County, California, and in Arizona.

Dinosaur bone

Actual agatized dinosaur bones. Very colorful and attractive when cut into cabochons. Most of the good material comes from Utah and Colorado. Sometimes referred to by rockhounds as "dinny bone."

Dot agate

White chalcedony with round colored spots.

Dryhead agate

A beautiful and colorful fortification agate similar to Fairburn agate. Found along the rims of the Big Horn River Canyon on the northern edge of Wyoming and the southern edge of Montana, an area called the Dryhead.

Dumortierite quartz

A massive opaque variety of aggregate quartz colored by intergrown crystals of dumortierite. Deep blue to violet-blue and sometimes dull or blackish blue. A pink variety is found in Nevada. Sometimes called desert lapis.

Eden Valley wood

Agatized wood from the Eden Valley, Sweetwater County, Wyoming. This wood is not very colorful, the agatized portions being black, but the limb sections are perfect casts of the original twigs and limbs. Highly favored by petrified wood collectors.

Egyptian jasper

An orbicular jasper found as pebbles along the beaches at Joyce, Clallam Bay, and Port Angeles, Washington. Similar to oregonite. Also found in Egypt. Contains white or gray eyes in a red background. *Also see* Kinradite.

Egyptian pebbles

Jasper pebbles, usually from the Egyptian deserts. Same as Egyptian jasper.

Elephant jasper

Dark to light brown jasper with scattered small black dendritic inclusions.

Ellensburg blue agate

A natural pale sky-blue agate from the vicinity of Ellensburg, Washington. Reportedly favored by Tiffany's of New York but this is a myth.

Emeraldine

A coined name for green-dyed chalcedony.

Enhydros

A Greek word meaning "holding water." A term used in describing pebbles of chalcedony containing water. Of value only as a curiosity. Found in Uruguay, Australia, and India.

Eye agate

Any agate with concentric bands of various alternating colors about a dark center. *Also called* aleppo stone.

Fairburn agate

Beautiful and colorful fortification agates from the Johnny Creek area east of Fairburn, South Dakota. Particularly noted for their wonderful natural colors and interesting patterns. Now quite scarce and highly prized by collectors.

Fairhills agate

Fortification agate similar to the Fairburn agate. Found in the Black Hills of South Dakota.

Falcon's eye

Same as hawk's-eye.

False lapis

Bluish jasper, rarest of the jaspers, has been imitated by artificially coloring chalcedony to a deep blue. It is usually sold as lapis lazuli, which it is intended to resemble. *Also see* German lapis.

Ferruginous jasper

Jasper from the Lake Superior region, highly impregnated with iron oxide.

Fire agate

Chalcedony containing limonite which gives an iridescent fire-like appearance when a cabochon is ground so that a very thin layer of limonite is exposed. Some authorities claim the inclusions are goethite. Both minerals are very difficult to distinguish from each other as both are hydrated oxide of iron.

Fish egg jasper

Another term for orbicular jasper.

Fisheye agate

Contains clusters of colored spots. Comes from an area west of Villa Ahumada, Mexico.

Flame agate

Agate with a flame-like distribution of red coloring. From an area west of Villa Ahumada, Mexico.

Flint

A translucent to opaque form of cryptocrystalline quartz in gray, smoky, brown, or black colors. Usually found in nodules in limestone or chalk beds. Has a conchoidal shell-like fracture. The favorite material of primitive peoples for making knives, arrowheads, and spearheads.

Flower agate

A general term for all moss agate although more specifically applied by rockhounds to the varieties resembling flowers. *See* Bouquet agate; Plume agate.

Flower stone

An incorrect term for beach pebbles of chalcedony found on southern California beaches. *See* Flower agate. More specifically a flower jasper.

Flowering jasper

A little used name for orbicular jasper. This should be the name for the so-called flower stones found on Southern California beaches.

Fluorescent agate

Agate and chalcedony free of inclusions and impurities do not fluoresce. Some inclusions, such as uranium salts, cause agates to fluoresce beautifully. Sweetwater agates have a wonderful fluorescence.

Fortification agate

Agates with patterns resembling the drawings of ancient forts; always in an irregular pattern. Sometimes in a crystal center common to these agates there may be an area resembling a castle, which makes the fortification outlines more realistic.

Fossil agate

Any agate where silica has replaced the wood of trees, coral, or the bones of dinosaurs.

Fossilized wood

See Petrified wood.

Frost agate

Gray chalcedony with white markings resembling frost or snow. *Also see* Frost stone.

Frost stone

A local trade name for chalcedony or frost agate found near Barstow, California, in 1912 which contained white inclusions thought to be opal.

Gastroliths

The birdlike dinosaurs that lived a hundred million years ago used to swallow fragments of rock, usually the quartz types, as an aid to digestion, as do our modern fowls. These were ground sometimes to a fine polish and they are found in a pile, associated with the accompanying petrified bones of the dinosaur from which they came. Unless they are found with accompanying bones they are highly suspect, as many pebbles are found on the surface of the deserts that have a desert polish from weather exposure and appear to be gastroliths. Circular scratches and surface markings are evidence that the pebbles have probably been within an animal. Specimens showing straight lines are river pebbles. Widely distributed in the Mountain States. *Also called* gizzard stones.

Geodes

A hollow nodule of rock enclosing agate and crystal formations in the center.

German lapis

Jasper from Nunkirchen, Germany, dyed blue to imitate lapis lazuli.

Gizzard stones

See Gastroliths.

Glass agate

Exceptionally clear agate or chalcedony. Sometimes confused with obsidian or volcanic glass.

Gold quartz

Milky quartz with gold inclusions.

Grape agate

Clusters of small spherical mammillary growths upon a matrix of chalcedony. The clusters are wart-like and resemble a bunch of grapes. *Also see* Botryoidal agate.

Green jasper

The color is ordinarily due to inclusions of iron silicate, chlorate, or chromate salts. Very popular as an ornamental stone. The chief source is the Ural mountains of Siberia.

Green onyx

A term used in the United States jewelry trade to signify dyed chalcedony in a dark green hue. Sometimes called emeraldine. The term chrysophrase (chrysoprase with an h in it) was once suggested as a trade name, but has never been accepted.

Green quartz

Transparent greenish quartz, a term sometimes incorrectly used for green fluorite.

Half carnelian

A term for yellow agate.

Harz cat's-eye

Name sometimes used to mean any quartz cat's-eye but more especially a variety from the Harz Mountains in north Germany. Is usually inferior to the better grades of Bavarian cat's-eye.

Hawk's-eye

Sometimes spelled hawkeye. Transparent colorless quartz containing closely packed, parallel fibers of crocidolite which impart a blue color. In form and sheen it resembles tigereye. Differs from sapphire quartz in which the fibers are not parallel.

Heliotrope

Dark green chalcedony containing spots or patches of red jasper. Sometimes fades to grayish green and spots are earthy hematite. From India and other sources. Less desirable yellow spots also occur. Sometimes called bloodstone although true bloodstone is a jasper. Often wrongly termed purple opal.

Hells Canyon agate

Fortification agate from Hells Canyon in southwestern South Dakota. Very colorful and similar to the Fairburn agate of the same state.

Herkimer "diamonds"

Quartz crystals from Herkimer County, New York. Sometimes called Trenton "diamonds," Middleville "diamonds," and Little Falls "diamonds."

Hornstone

In Anglo-American usage it is a flint-like non-gem quartz. In German usage it is a fine grained cryptocrystalline quartz, grading into but not including jasper and chalcedony. Gray or brown and sometimes green, black or yellow. A clear yellowish red variety is called apricotine.

Horse Canyon agate

Very fine moss agate from Horse Canyon, near Monolith, Kern County, California.

Horsetail agate

Agate with dendritic inclusions of iron or manganese oxide resembling a horse's tail. Common to the Nipomo agate area in California.

Hungarian cat's-eye

An inferior yellowish green variety of quartz cat's-eye from Bavaria and not from Hungary.

Iceland agate

Not an agate variety but a term for siliceous sinter deposited in layers around hot springs. Also used as a term for layered obsidian and for obsidian from Iceland.

Indian agate

A general term for moss agates from India.

Indian jade

An incorrect term for aventurine quartz.

Indivisible quartz

An obsolete term for opal, referring to its having no cleavage.

Intaglio

A carved gemstone, usually onyx or sardonyx, which may be used as a seal because the carving has been carved into the stone and depressed, not raised as in a cameo. The edges of the stone in an intaglio are higher than the design, whereas in a cameo the edges are lower than the design.

Iolanthite

A banded reddish jasper from the gravels of the Crooked River in central Oregon.

Iris agate

A banded agate which exhibits all the colors of the spectrum when sliced in thin slabs. Sometimes called rainbow agate.

Iris quartz

Rock crystal containing thin air-filled cracks which produce iridescence.

Irish "diamonds"

An incorrect term for rock crystal from Ireland.

Jasp-agate

A mixture of jasper and chalcedony in which the jasper predominates. The chalcedony is usually colorless. *Also called* agate jasper.

Jasper

An opaque cryptocrystalline quartz in all colors. It is a variety of chalcedony agate except that it is always opaque, the mineralogical difference between jasper and agate being slight. Widely distributed all over the earth and a great favorite with amateur gem cutters and rockhounds because of its abundance and its great variety.

Jasper jade

A term used by Chinese dealers for jade substitutes such as serpentine, quartz, jasper, or combinations of jade and quartz. Many laymen do not know the difference.

Jasperated agate

Jasper mixed with agate.

Jasperine

A name, not in general use, for banded jasper of various colors and shades.

Jaspilite

A term used for bright red jasper alternating with black bands of specular hematite; from the Lake Superior region.

Jasponyx

An opaque onyx, part or all of whose layers consist of jasper or jasper-like chalcedony.

Kalmuk agate

Not an agate but a banded opal from Kalmuk, near Astrakhan.

Keweenaw agate

Agate from the Keweenaw peninsula region of Michigan.

Kinradite

A trade name for jasper containing spherulites of colorless or near colorless quartz. Much of it is the same as orbicular jasper and the material is found at several spots in Oregon and California.

Lace agate

See Mexican lace agate.

Laguna agate

A very popular and beautiful agate from the Laguna Ranch situated at Ojo Laguna, Chihuahua, Mexico. Reportedly a privately owned ranch where no rock hunting is allowed.

Lake George "diamonds"

Exceptionally clear quartz crystals from the Lake George, New York, region.

Lake Superior agate

Agates from the Lake Superior region; not confined to the shoreline of the lake itself. Sometimes confused with thomsonites from the same region. Many of these agates have been washed down the Mississippi River and are found in gravel deposits, particularly in Iowa.

Lake Superior fire agate

This is not an agate at all but a glass imitation of opal.

Landscape agate

White or gray chalcedony with moss-like inclusions of manganese oxide which form fanciful resemblances to landscapes.

Lavic jasper

Jasper from Lavic, a railroad watering stop and not a town, on the Union Pacific railroad near Barstow, California. This is one of the most colorful of all the jaspers. It is red with white markings of chalcedony.

Little Falls "diamonds"

Another name for Herkimer "diamonds" found in Herkimer County, New York.

Macaroni agate

Streamers of milky quartz in chalcedony. The ends of the streamers have openings which suggest macaroni.

Madagascar amethyst

A very beautiful amethyst from Madagascar. Dark violet with a slight smoky tinge. Sometimes lighter in color with a violet-purple tinge.

Madeira topaz

This is not topaz at all. It is heat-treated amethyst.

Mammillary agate

Small spherulitic forms appearing within an agate but usually on the surface. *See* Grape agate.

Mexican agate

Any agate from Mexico. Several varieties are described herein and agates from Mexico are greatly favored by the amateur lapidaries because of their interesting moss effects and natural colors.

Mexican lace agate

A very popular agate with amateur gem cutters. Has a lacy effect in the patterns. Always cut as a cabochon. Found at several locations in Mexico.

Mexican onyx

Not a true agate onyx but a term loosely applied to a banded, mottled, or clouded travertine (calcite) or aragonite; usually in yellow or green varieties with bands. Most of the material used commercially does not come from Mexico at all but from Argentina.

Middleville "diamonds"

Another name for Herkimer "diamonds" from Herkimer County, New York.

Milk agate

Chalcedony with a milky or cloudy translucency.

Milky quartz

A translucent to nearly opaque white variety of crystalline quartz. Sometimes it has inclusions of gold and is then called gold quartz.

Mocha stone

Another name for moss agate.

Mojave moonstone

Sometimes spelled Mohave moonstone. A gray translucent chalcedony and not a true moonstone.

Montana agate

A term for moss agate from Montana. The Montana variety is widely noted and preferred for its scenic effects. The inclusions make black blotches in a usually reddish background and when cut the slices exhibit unusual scenes. Sometimes called Yellowstone agate when it comes from deposits along and in the Yellowstone River in Montana.

Moonstone

Chalcedony, often erroneously called moonstone, especially when it exhibits a sheen. Genuine moonstone is a variety of orthoclase.

Morgan Hill jasper

Orbicular jasper from Morgan Hill, California.

Morion

Deep black crystalline quartz; an almost opaque smoky quartz. Very striking when faceted.

Morrisonite

A local name for an attractively banded and colored chert which polishes beautifully. It is found near Horse Heaven Mine, 22 miles east of Ashwood, Oregon, near the John Day River.

Mosaic agate

A brecciated agate from Mexico. Often used by Mexican jewelers.

Mosquito amethyst

Amethyst containing tiny scaly or platy inclusions of goethite.

Mosquito stone

Spanish name for quartz with tiny dark inclusions. Variety of moss quartz.

Moss agate

A general term used in North America for any translucent chalcedony, agate, or cryptocrystalline, quartz with inclusions of any color arranged in moss-like, tree-like, flower-like patterns, in fern or leaf designs, and in scenic or landscape designs.

Moss jasper

Synonymous with moss agate and sometimes used incorrectly as a name for banded petrified wood with streaks of translucent quartz. Found in New Mexico and Arizona.

Myrickite

Named after a desert character and prospector named "Shady" Myrick who discovered a white to gray chalcedony with red mercury inclusions in the Death Valley, California, area. An opal variety with red inclusions of cinnabar (mercury), found in the same area, is sometimes called myrickite but should be called opalite.

Nipomo agate

Some of the world's finest sagenite agate and agate with marcasite inclusions from the bean and pea fields surrounding the small community of Nipomo in San Luis Obispo County in California.

Novaculite

Quartz whetstones from Arkansas. *See* Arkansas stone.

Nunkirchen jasper

Light gray to yellow or brown jasper from Nunkirchen, near Idar-Oberstein, West Germany. Dyed blue and sold as "Swiss lapis."

Occidental agate

Poorly marked agate, not very translucent. Opposite of oriental agate.

Occidental cat's-eye

See Quartz cat's-eye.

Occidental "diamond"

Quartz rock crystal.

Ochoco agate

Occurs in nodules or thundereggs containing agate, and plume agate. Found at Wild Cat Mountain east of Prineville, Oregon, and on Stevens Mountain farther to the east.

Ochoco jasper

Found on the beaches of Ochoco Lake above the dam, five miles east of Prineville, Oregon.

Onegite

Light amethyst-colored sagenitic quartz from Lake Onega, north of Leningrad in Russia.

Onicolo agate

A seldom used term for agate with a white layer over a colored layer or layers beneath. A variety of onyx, ideal for cameo carving.

Onyx

This is banded agate in which the bands are always straight and of alternate color. Most common varieties are black and white, black and red to brownish red, white and red to brownish red. When the bands are gray and white the material is more correctly called onyx agate. The term onyx is incorrectly used, but generally accepted in the jewelry trade, for clear unbanded agate which has been dyed black. It is also incorrectly used as a term for other layered gem materials such as marble and travertine.

Onyx marble

Not an agate substance but calcite. The term onyx is used because the material is banded like agate onyx.

Oolitic agate

Agate with small grain-like inclusions resembling oolite, which is a rock consisting of small grains of carbonate of lime cemented together. Similar to grape agate.

Opal

See Chapter 5, which lists all the varieties of opal in a glossary at the end of the chapter.

Opalized wood

See Petrified wood.

Orbicular jasper

Jasper containing round or spherical inclusions, sprinkled and spotted here and there. The "eyes" are usually of contrasting color to the rest of the stone. The orbicular jasper from Morgan Hill, California, is a favorite of amateur gem cutters, though it is hard to get even a small piece for a cabochon that is not badly fractured. The Morgan Hill jasper occurs in many varieties, some with chalcedony inclusions. One variety with red eyes in a yellow background is called poppy jasper. Sometimes called kinradite and paradise jasper.

Oregon "jade"

A local name for a dark green jasper or plasma found in Shirttail Creek, near Durkee, Oregon.

Oregonite

An orbicular jasper. Sometimes called kinradite. Found north of Holland, Oregon. Not to be confused with a mineral variety of nickel-iron-arsenide, which is officially named oregonite.

Oriental agate

Well marked translucent agate; the opposite of occidental agate.

Oriental amethyst

This is not amethyst at all but a violet to purple sapphire.

Oriental carnelian

Deep bright red translucent carnelian—the best.

Oriental chalcedony

Fine translucent gray or white chalcedony. When cut in a cabochon it is sometimes referred to erroneously as a chalcedony moonstone.

Oriental jasper

Another name for bloodstone. Also used as a name for any jasper believed to have originated in some Asiatic country.

Oriental onyx

Not a true onyx but a banded, mottled, or clouded travertine.

Pagoda stone

Agate with pagoda-like markings.

Paradise jasper

An orbicular jasper from Morgan Hill, California.

Pastelite

A very interesting form of jasper occurring in the Mojave desert in California. Noted for its large wavy areas of pastel greens, pinks, reds, and browns. Has a waxy luster.

Petoskey "agates"

Found along the shores of Lake Michigan, particularly at Petoskey, Michigan, and at several other midwest localities. These "agates" are really not agates at all but they are very interesting and popular for use in jewelry sold at the Michigan resorts. The Petoskey STONE, as it is more correctly called, is fossilized coral, not even siliceous in character but composed chiefly of limestone or calcite. However, silicified or agatized "petoskey stones" do occur in Iowa.

Petrified wood

Fossilized wood in which the cells of the wood have been entirely replaced by crystallized silica and thereby converted into quartz or opal. It is easy to identify as it resembles closely the original patterns of the wood. *Also called* opalized wood, silicified wood, and agatized wood. See Chapter 6 on petrified wood.

Pigeon blood agate

A local name for a carnelian variety of agate found near Cisco, Utah.

Pincushion quartz

Clusters of slender quartz crystals from the Collier Creek Mine in the Crystal Mountains of Arkansas.

Pipe agate

Agate with tube-like or pipe-like inclusions.

Plasma

Green semi-translucent, almost opaque, cryptocrystalline quartz, sometimes with white or yellowish spots. When it has red spots it is sometimes erroneously called bloodstone.

Plume agate

A variety of agate with sagenite inclusions resembling plumes. Very fine specimens come from Oregon and Texas.

Point chalcedony

White or gray chalcedony flecked with tiny spots of iron oxide, the whole surface assuming a uniform soft red color. *Also called* point agate.

Polka dot agate

Local name for a type of Oregon agate that has brown spots like circular dots in a cream-like background. Sometimes it has yellow or red spots. As the material is quite opaque it should really be called polka dot jasper.

Pom-pom agate

A sagenite agate from Texas in which the inclusions are arranged in yellow to orange patterns resembling pom-poms or chrysanthemums.

Poppy jasper

See Orbicular jasper.

Poppy stone

See Orbicular jasper.

Porcelainite

Not a true jasper but hard masses of partly silicified or baked clays with dull red or green colors. Usually found in low grade coal deposits.

Prase

Translucent light or grayish yellow-green chalcedony and colored by inclusions of actinolite needles.

Precious opal

See Chapter 5 on opal.

Priday Ranch agates

Plume agate from the Priday Ranch near Willowdale, Oregon. Now known as the Fulton Agate Beds.

Pseudo agate

See Fossil agate.

Puddingstone

A conglomerate in which the pebbles are rounded and cemented together by a finer grained material. This is a brecciated material. Sold as a curio stone in the Lake Superior district, where it is called puddingstone jasper. A favorite material with the Chinese for carving snuff bottles.

Quartz cat's-eye

Light to dark grayish green crystalline quartz with a good cat's-eye effect resulting from fibrous mineral inclusions. Sometimes called Bavarian cat's-eye, Harz cat's-eye, Hungarian cat's-eye and occidental cat's-eye.

Quartz glass

Transparent fused rock crystal, better known as fused quartz. A term sometimes applied, often deceptively, to any glass which, being made from sand, is principally quartz.

Quartz topaz

An incorrect name for citrine. *See* Topaz quartz.

Rainbow agate

Same as iris agate with an iridescent effect.

Rainbow quartz

Same as iris quartz.

Red top moss agate

Montana moss agate with a red stain at the base of the black dendritic inclusions.

Regalite

A green quartz, and white with green veins. Found in Utah and formerly sold as jadeite, which it closely resembles. The name is now seldom used.

Rhinestones

A glass imitation of cut quartz.

Riband agate

See Banded agate.

Ribbon agate

Agate with wide ribbon-like areas running through the agate.

Ribbon jasper

Banded jasper with ribbon-like stripes of alternating colors. Sometimes called riband jasper.

Ring agate

Agate with concentric rings but with less distinct color contrasts than eye agates.

River agates

Agate or jasper pebbles from stream beds.

Rock crystal

Massive pure crystalline transparent quartz. Not to be confused with rock crystal glass, which is not quartz at all except that it is manufactured from silica sand. Used for carving figures, making crystal balls.

Rogueite

A local name for a greenish jasper found in the gravels of the Rogue River in Oregon.

Rose agate

Local name for a gray and rose banded agate from Brewster County, Texas.

Rose quartz

Pink or rose translucent to semi-transparent quartz used for carving figurines and other valuable art objects. Sometimes star quality rose quartz is cut cabochon and backed with blue substances to imitate star sapphires.

F<small>IG</small>. 13. A superb single quartz crystal 7″ long with double terminations. These are hard to find in such perfect condition and divorced from a matrix. Note the characteristic etchings. The crystal is transparent. From San Diego County, California. From the author's collection. *(Photo by O. D. Smith.)*

Ruin agate

Agate with a pattern that resembles the outlines of ruins. The straight bandings characteristic of agate are shattered and arranged in angular patterns consolidated by later inclusions of chalcedony. Sometimes called brecciated agate.

Russian jasper

Red flecked jasper.

Rutilated quartz

Same as sagenitic quartz.

Sagenite agate

Same as sagenitic quartz and a term often misused for various types of moss agate, particularly those types with grass-like inclusions. This is a correct name however for clear chalcedony containing tiny needles of foreign minerals.

Sagenitic quartz

Term used for transparent colorless or nearly colorless quartz containing needle-like inclusions of rutile, actinolite, goethite, tourmaline, or other minerals, regardless of the manner in which the crystals are arranged. Rutilated quartz is the more popular term used to refer to this material.

Saint Stephen's stone

A little-used name for a disputed gemstone called green plasma by some and chalcedony by others. Contains small circular dots similar to polka dot agate.

Sapphire quartz

In the western states the term applied to chalcedony of light sapphire blue to a pale blue color.

Sard

Translucent brown to reddish-brown chalcedony. *See* Carnelian.

Sard agate

Banded agate similar to sardonyx in coloring except the bands are not straight and parallel.

Sard stone

Name variously applied to both sard and sardonyx.

Sardoine

A sub-variety of carnelian usually darker than sardonyx.

Sardonyx

Chalcedony (agate) with straight parallel bands or layers of reddish-brown to brown alternating with other colors. The name is used incorrectly for carnelian, especially in the jewelry trade.

45

Scenic agate

The same as landscape agate.

Scotch pebbles

Any of several varieties of quartz, chiefly cairngorm or smoky quartz.

Scotch topaz

Yellow quartz or citrine; not topaz at all. *See* Topaz quartz.

Seam agate

Agate from a thin vein in layered rocks.

Seaweed agate

Another name for sagenite or moss agate. Resembles a submarine garden when sliced.

Semicarnelian

An old and undesirable name for yellow agate.

Serra stone

Agate from the Serra do Mar mountains in the state of Rio Grande do Sul, in southern Brazil.

Shell agate

Agate containing silicified mollusk-shells. *See* Turritella agate.

Siberian amethyst

A long established trade term for the highly desirable and popular deep reddish-violet or purple amethysts, although amethysts found in the Urals at this time are characterized by a less desirable light violet color. Amethyst of the old Siberian color now comes from Brazil and Uruguay and a little is found at Twin Peaks in Arizona. Reportedly no longer mined in Siberia.

Siliceous malachite

A descriptive name for green chrysocolla.

Silicified wood

A term which includes all varieties of wood that have been converted into silica. This is the correct term for petrified wood where the petrifaction has been caused by silica (quartz) deposits. Contrary to popular belief, all petrified wood is not silicified, for logs have been found that were almost pure uranium.

Silkstone

Crystalline quartz containing replacements of fibrous goethite. Similar to binghamite, but the inclusions are not straight as in that material. Not as pure quartz as binghamite.

Sinopal

An aventurescent quartz with inclusions of a red iron mineral; from Hungary.

Sioux Falls jasper

A decorative brown jasper-like fine grained quartz from Sioux Falls, South Dakota. Used for table tops and interior architectural trim.

Smoky quartz

A smoky black crystalline quartz which is very beautiful when faceted. Much of it is heated until it becomes yellow, when it is sold in the trade as topaz quartz, as distinguished from citrine, a natural yellow crystalline quartz. Called cairngorm in Scotland and morion when it is dense black.

Smoky topaz

A misnomer for smoky quartz.

Soldier's stone

This is amethyst.

Sowbelly quartz

A colloquial name for the amethystine quartz from the silver mines in the Creede District of Colorado. It makes attractive cabochons but is unsatisfactory for faceting.

Spanish amethyst

A term formerly used for deep purple amethyst of an unknown source and marketed in Spain.

Spanish citrine

Citrine from Spain, especially that yellow quartz called Hinjosa topaz.

Spanish topaz

A trade term broadly used for any orange to orange-red citrine. More specifically used as a term for Hinjosa topaz. Sometimes called Madeira topaz erroneously. That variety is usually heat-treated amethyst.

Spectrum agate
A seldom used term for iris agate.

Spherulitic jasper
Jasper with inclusions of spherulites which are usually quartz. If they are a different color from the jasper it is usually an orbicular (eye) jasper.

Stained stone
A stone the color of which has been altered in a number of ways. Quartz is cryptocrystalline and especially adapted to staining— including agate in which the bands become more pronounced.

Star agate
Agate exhibiting star-shaped figures. Not to be confused with agate exhibiting asterism or a star effect.

Star quartz
Asteriated rose and clear quartz which often shows a star by transmitted light and sometimes by reflected light if cut as a cabochon.

State Park agates
Fortification agates found in the Custer State Park area of South Dakota. Very similar to Fairburn agates from the same state.

Stone cameo
A term adopted by the National Better Business Bureau to describe cameos carved from genuine gemstones such as onyx and sardonyx. *See* Cameos.

Stone Canyon jasper
A brecciated jasper from Stone Canyon near San Miguel, California. *See* Brecciated jasper.

Striped jasper
Synonymous with banded jasper.

Sweetwater agates
Dark gray translucent chalcedony nodules containing dendritic growths in star patterns. Found in the Sweetwater River areas of Fremont County, Wyoming. Easily found by the collector on the surface as fresh supplies are uncovered by the weather each year. Small nodules, seldom larger than an inch in diameter and never larger than two inches. Most of the nodules are about the size of jelly beans, which they resemble. These agates make interesting ring settings and are very popular with amateur gem cutters. They fluoresce beautifully, one of the very few agate types that display fluorescence.

Swiss lapis
Jasper dyed blue. *See* Nunkirchen jasper.

Tempskya agate
Agatized tempskya tree fern. Found in the Pacific Northwest and in Bingham County, Idaho.

Tepee Canyon agates
Found in Tepee Canyon in southwest South Dakota. Very similar to the Fairburn agates of the same state.

Texas agate
Any agate from Texas but more specifically jasp-agate from the gravels of the Pecos River.

Thetis hair stone
Crystalline quartz containing inclusions of green fibrous crystals which may appear tangled or wound into a ball. The crystals are hornblende. *See* Venus hair stone.

Thunderegg agate
The agate fillings or interiors of thundereggs or nodules. The fillings produce all types of agate, the thundereggs from Central Oregon and New Mexico being particularly productive of fine agate gemstones.

Thundereggs
Nodules filled with an agate center.

Tibet stone
A mixture of aventurine quartz and quartz porphyry of various colors from Russia. Cut as an ornamental or curio stone.

Tigereye
A yellow and yellowish brown ornamental and gem variety of quartz. Pseudomorphous after crocidolite. Colored by limonite, which probably

turns to hematite when heated. Heating produces a red and brownish-red tigereye. Gray tigereye is produced by an acid treatment. When cut with the flat surface parallel to the fibers, the slightly differing colors produce a changeable silky sheen as the stone is moved. A popular stone for cameos and intaglios. The author once baked a piece of tigereye in a loaf of bread and produced a peculiar pink variety which he named rhubarb agate. Principal source is the Asbestos Mountains, west of Griquatown, Griqualand, South Africa.

Tigerite

Another name for tigereye.

Topaz quartz

The term recommended by the American Gem Society for use in the trade to supersede the use of the terms topaz, quartz topaz, occidental topaz, and other terms formerly used by many jewelers to inaccurately describe citrine, burnt amethyst, or burnt smoky quartz. The term means topaz-colored quartz and does not imply a mixture of topaz and quartz as the term might imply if it were hyphenated. Rules of the Federal Trade Commission specify that it shall not be represented as topaz.

Topographic agate

Agate with fine markings resembling a map. Similar to fortification agate.

Touchstone

See Basanite.

Tree agate

Moss agate with tree-like inclusions. India is the principal source.

Trenton "diamonds"

Quartz crystals from Herkimer County, New York. Also called Herkimer "diamonds."

Tube agate

A rare form of agate containing tube-like inclusions that are sometimes hollow.

Turritella agate

Agate containing silicified mollusk shells. A particularly fine black variety occurs in Wyoming but because of its highly opaque character it should be more correctly called turritella jasper.

Turtle back agate

Clear chalcedony which, when cut in slabs, exhibits a layered effect resembling a turtle's back.

Uruguay agate

Agate from the border between Uruguay and Rio Grande do Sul, Brazil. Usually found in large masses up to twenty-five inch boulders. Material is usually gray but when treated with heat and chemicals it produces many colors which are common in the trade today. Most of the commercial agate used in novelty manufacture, such as agate marbles, ash trays, etc., comes from this source. Most of this agate is dyed and processed in the lapidary shops of Idar-Oberstein, Germany.

Uruguayan amethyst

From the same region as Uruguayan agate. Used as a trade name it denotes amethyst from any area that has a deep violet color and is transparent. Uruguayan amethysts are small and irregularly colored.

Vabanite

A brown-red jasper from California.

Variegated agate

A type of agate in which moss inclusions and coloring are distributed without pattern.

Variegated jasper

A term for jasper in which the markings and coloring are varied. Widely distributed on the beaches in California and elsewhere.

Venturina

Aventurine quartz.

Venus hair stone

Crystalline quartz containing inclusions of reddish brown or yellow rutile fibers which appear tangled.

View agate

This is the same as landscape or scenic agate.

Wart agate

A wart-like or mammillary series of small spherical growths on colored agate. The warts are usually carnelian. Also called grape agate and botryoidal agate.

Wascoite

An interesting and variegated material from Wasco County, Oregon, but not a true agate although it consists in part of agate.

Water agate

See Enhydros.

Water drop quartz

Rock crystal containing inclusions of water and air. A curio stone similar to enhydros.

Wax agate

Yellow or yellowish red chalcedony. with a pronounced waxy luster. Similar to yellow carnelian.

White agate

A term sometimes applied to clear or whitish chalcedony and milk agate.

White carnelian

A term used for white chalcedony with faint tints of red.

White moss agate

Agate containing large areas of white inclusions.

Wolf's-eye stone

A rarely used term for tigereye, especially that which is partly silicified and therefore intermediate between tigereye and hawk's-eye.

Wood agate

Same as petrified wood.

Yellowstone agate

Montana moss agate specifically from locations along the Yellowstone River in Montana. Among the finest scenic agate in the world, it is much preferred in the jewelry trade.

Zebra agate

Black and white striped agate from the interior of genuine onyx or black agate nodules found near Baroda in the state of Bombay, India.

Zebra jasper

Dark brown jasper with lighter brown streaks. From India.

Zigzag agate

A brecciated fortification agate in which the bands have become broken and then cemented together again by percolating waters bearing silica.

Chapter 5

Opal and Its Varieties

IF A consensus could be obtained from rockhounds as to which gemstone offers the greatest thrill in cutting or hunting, the opal would no doubt head the list by a wide margin. And while any cutter can get his thrill by cutting his own purchased opal, the cutters who find their own opal specimens will always be few and far between.

Most authorities agree that of all the varieties of the many-hued opal, the finest comes from the Virgin Valley district of northwestern Nevada. The reader is referred to the Nevada section in Chapter 8 for information about this location. This area is off the beaten path in a forbidding part of America where the cold in winter is fierce and the heat of summer very severe. But one can drive there in a modern automobile and dig in the mines for a daily fee, with almost sure reward for his efforts. And there is a vast area in which he can prospect for his own opal and perhaps find and establish his own claim. The Virgin Valley area is one of the few thrill areas for the rock hunter.

A bad feature of the Nevada opal is that it has a strong tendency to craze or crack, especially when it is subjected to lapidary treatment where heat is generated. This is believed to be due to expansion of the high water content, for all opal contains water, sometimes as high as 20 per cent, although precious opal has less than 10 per cent. Instead of trying to process a find into jewelry

settings, therefore, successful hunters are urged to retain their finds as cabinet specimens, to be observed and admired for their great beauty. Even in this form they are very valuable and the highest prices ever paid for opal rough have been paid for the Nevada opal, especially by museums.

The Virgin Valley opal is the result of the replacement by silica gel of the bark of ancient trees that were buried by volcanic action on a great forest. Many of these trees drifted west on a huge lake in the valley and were opalized at the west end of the lake. Green fire opal, not a replacement of wood, has been found in deposits in the east end of the Valley but it seems to bear no relation to the petrified wood area on the other side.

The reader will hear or read of many methods of "preserving" opal, but after cutting and collecting opals for many years the author believes that the methods are old wives' tales and can be disregarded. However there is no evidence of any harm coming to the opals by having them "preserved" in glycerine, mineral oil, or even water, and these liquids do enhance their showing. The author has had for twenty years a beautiful rough polished half pound opal from Australia, and it has no cracks at all, although it is only enclosed in a cardboard box when it is not being displayed. This opal has been donated by the author to the Smithsonian Institution, and should be on display there by the time this book is published. It is illustrated herewith. The Smithsonian Institution in Washington probably has the largest and finest collection of opals in the world, the largest and best being from the Virgin Valley, illustrated below.

In a communication received while writing this work, the Smithsonian Institution wrote as follows: "The Roebling opal is, and always has been, crazed. The crazing, however, is on the surface and a large central core remains good. Most of our Virgin Valley opal is crazed but some, especially the dark pieces, is unblemished after all these years. Some of the Australian opal is crazed and some is not. The Mexicans are not. Passage of time seems to have little to do with the phenomenon. It seems entirely dependent on the material itself. We do nothing to preserve our opals except for one piece of Virgin Valley which is on display immersed in mineral oil . . . Some is crazed but much is not and we do nothing to control it."

The best of the commercial gem opal being mined today comes from several locations in Australia but principally from Andamooka and Coober Pedy, both in South Australia. The latter is an aboriginal term meaning "white man in ground," for the opal field is dotted with innumerable holes in which the opal miners live. White Cliffs, scene of the first big opal strike, is reportedly now deserted and Lightning Ridge in New South Wales has but a very few miners still

FIG. 14. A 1913 photo by D. B. Sterrett of the Mathewson or Dow opal mine in the Virgin Valley of Humboldt County, Nevada. Opals are found in the light-colored beds on both sides of the gulch. Opal horizon in lower light-colored layers. See another view on this area in Chapter 8. (*Photo courtesy of U.S. Geological Survey.*)

FIG. 15. An early 1910 photo by D. B. Sterrett of an opal mine 4 miles northwest of Enterprise, Owyhee County, Idaho. Two openings are in the light-colored porphyry. See another view in Chapter 8 under the Idaho section. *(Photo courtesy of U.S. Geological Survey.)*

searching for the Ridge's famous so-called black opal, probably the most expensive gem opal in the world when sold by the carat. This entrancing opal is seldom really black but it is always dark in color and has flashing red and green fire. It is so dense that it can be cut in very thin layers and used as a topping for a cabochon cut from opal potch or other gem material. These stones are called doublets and are common in the jewelry stores today.

The opal being mined at this time in Andamooka and Coober Pedy is almost all the opal that is in the market, for the opal sold from other locations is really negligible. Australian opal is highly favored because of its great beauty and because its lower water content decreases the tendency to crack. It

occurs in all colors but the generally preferred type in the jewelry trade is the milky white opal evenly shot through with pinpoint fire.

Shortly before the development of the opal fields at White Cliffs, Australia, in the nineties, opal of comparable quality (and also comparable to the Hungarian opal popular at that time and no longer mined) was discovered in the mountains of Honduras. Interest in this discovery was lost, however, because of the far more prolific field in Australia, and opal has never been commercially mined in Honduras.

There are many opal deposits all over the world containing what is called common opal or silica gel. It is only when the opal exhibits a play of colors that it is referred to as precious opal.

Many people call any opal with color "fire opal" but this is incorrect. The term fire opal should be reserved for the really fire-like opal of Mexico, found exclusively in the state of Queretaro. Fire opal at one time also came from Zimapan, east of Mexico City. In the author's opinion, this is the most beautiful opal in the world. It occurs in limpid nodules, almost transparent at times, and has a lambent beauty. The nodules are enclosed in rhyolite. Well-cut specimens of the Mexican fire opal are among the world's most entrancingly beautiful gems and command very high prices.

In addition to the Virgin Valley, Nevada, locality, Sinkankas in *Gemstones of North America* mentions opal localities in 14 other states in the United States and also in Canada and Mexico where various forms of opal can be collected. Most of these are of the opalized wood variety, not valuable but certainly of great beauty and interest. Idaho and California have several localities where precious opal of good quality has been found in small quantities.

Many rockhounds often wonder why opal is included in the quartz family of gem materials since it is not crystalline but amorphous or without a definite crystal structure. The reason is that opal is made by deposits of silica just as are other quartz gems, although the silica did not take a crystal form. Sometimes crystal areas will occur in opal, however, and this is supposed by some to be the reason for the play of colors. Many other theories also exist as to the reason for the coloring of opal but none is accepted widely by authorities and the author treads a neutral ground on this subject. Almost everyone who writes extensively about opal has his own theory, nearly

Fig. 16. General view of the Andamooka opal field in 1962. Note that high transmission lines have now brought electricity to the fields and roads enable automobiles to travel there. It is still a forbidding land of shacks and heat and requires rugged prospecting. (*Photo courtesy of Australian Gem Trading Co., Melbourne, Australia.*)

all of them sounding plausible, none of them offering proof. When the real cause of the play of colors is determined, then, and only then, will man be able to synthesize opal as he has the diamond, sapphire, ruby, and emerald, for opal has never been successfully imitated by man.

Opal is not as hard as other quartz varieties, being 5½ to 6½ whereas quartz is 7. In print this difference does not appear very great, but in actuality a cut amethyst is many hundred times harder than a cut opal.

At this point it would seem wise to direct a word of advice to the opal buyer, for it is not likely that more than a few readers will ever prospect for opal, although most gem hobbyists buy opal rough, most of which is processed into gems. In buying rough opal, remember that you are buying the most beautiful and the most expensive of the silica gems, one of the five so-called "precious" gems. Do not then expect to purchase for a couple of dollars a piece of opal that will yield a $500.00 stone. The most unpromising looking specimen will sometimes yield a most beautiful gem, while flashing rough can sometimes be greatly disappointing when areas of potch are found within the stone. It takes a lifetime of experience to be able to judge rough opal and that experience seldom comes to the amateur collector or cutter. The best course is to patronize opal dealers with long experience and established prestige. Many of these dealers regularly advertise in the pages of the magazines listed in Chapter 12. A buyer should be well acquainted, too, with the terms used in the opal trade, and to help him there is given below the most complete glossary of opal terms ever compiled.

GLOSSARY OF OPAL TERMS

Abanderado opal

From the Spanish *bandera* meaning banner or flag. The colors are in bands or stripes of blue, red, and yellow, giving a flag-like effect.

Fig. 17. Photograph showing the primitive living conditions at the desert-like Anda-mooka opal field in South Australia. Most miners live underground to escape the intense heat, which often reaches 120°. (*Photo courtesy of Australian Gem Trading Co., Melbourne, Australia.*)

Fig. 18. Opal mining at the Lightning Ridge opal field in New South Wales. *(Photo courtesy of Australian Gem Trading Co., Melbourne, Australia.)*

Agate opal

Opal banded like agate. Some agate has bands of opal.

Agaty potch

Potch colored in parallel bands like agate.

Amatite

A variety of siliceous sinter or pearlite.

Amber opal

Opal having an amber or golden color.

Amber potch

Australian name for Mexican yellow fire opal.

Andamooka opal

Opal from Andamooka, South Australia, 85 miles from Pimba. The field, discovered in 1930, is about four-and-a-half miles long and three in width.

Angel stone

A hard and highly silicified layer of clay or sandstone found just above the opal level. It often contains cracks filled with precious opal.

Aranajados

Mexican name for amber-colored fire opals.

Azules

Mexican name for blue opals.

Belemnites

Opalized parts of prehistoric fish.

Black opal

Opal in which the background color is gray or black. Most of the commercial black opal comes from Australia. Some black opal in the form of opalized wood comes from Virgin Valley, Nevada, but this is practically uncuttable due to a great tendency to crack.

Black potch

Common potch which is used for backing doublets.

Bombay opals

Not a genuine opal but a glass imitation.

Boulder opal

Precious opal found in cracks and cavities in boulders of ironstone in Queensland, Australia.

Fig. 19. Cutting Australian opals at the plant of the Australian Gem Trading Co., Melbourne, Australia.

Cachalong

This is a pale bluish white, opaque or feebly translucent, porcelain-like variety of common opal. It is highly regarded in the Orient but of little gemological interest in the Occident. Sometimes it is found banded with chalcedony and used for cutting cameos. It is a very porous form of opal, absorbing moisture so readily that it will stick to the tongue.

Candlebox opal

Low quality opal not good enough to be sold.

Celestial opal

A misnomer for genuine moonstone.

Ceylonese opal

An incorrect term for moonstone.

Cherry opal

Mexican opal with a bright cherry color.

Chinese opal

A misnomer for tabasheer, chalcedony, or moonstone.

Chloropal

Similar to prase opal, with a green body color.

Chrysopal

Similar to prase opal but with a golden-green color predominating.

Claro opal

Mexican name for translucent or fire opal of a pale color.

Common opal

Varieties of opal which have no gemological interest but mineralogical interest only.

Contra Luz opal

A Mexican name for opals which show colors best when held against the light.

Corencite

Similar to chloropal.

Eisen opal

Another name for hydrophane.

Flame opal

Opal in which the red play of color occurs in more or less irregular streaks.

Flash opal

Opal in which the play of color is pronounced in only one direction.

Floaters

Pieces of fair quality opal found lying loose on the surface of the ground.

Gelite

Opal or chalcedony deposited as a secondary accessory mineral, usually as a bond or cement in sandstone.

Glass opal

Hyalite or Muller's glass, also known as gummisteen.

Gold opal

Opal with a golden or amber color.

Gyrasol

Mexican name for a kind of water opal.

Harlequin opal

White opal with close set mosaic-like patches of color of similar size. Resembling the patches in the clown suit of a Harlequin.

Heliotrope

Wrongfully used term for opal of a purple color. The name is correctly used for other gemstones.

Honey opal

Material like amber potch; honey-like in appearance.

Hungarian opal

A name widely used in the trade for any white opal regardless of where it is found.

Hyacinth

Opal of a red-brown color, but the name is also used for other gemstones.

Hyalite

Colorless common opal. Not gem quality. Similar to water opal or jelly opal.

Hydrophane

A form of opal which shows rainbow colors when immersed in water.

Indivisible quartz

An obsolete term for opal, referring to its having no cleavage.

Iridot

A name for opal coined about 1880, when the real name of the gemstone was believed by some to have unlucky associations.

Isopyre

A very impure opal. Also has other mineralogical connotations.

Jasper opal

An almost opaque common opal in yellow-brown. Resembles jasper in appearance and is jasper in which the cementing material is opal and not quartz.

Jelly opal

Another term for hyalite.

Kalmuk agate

Not an agate but a banded opal from Kalmuk, near Astrakhan.

Lechosos opal

Sometimes called lechos or milk opal. An opal with a deep green play of color. A Mexican fire opal with an emerald-green color play and flashes of carmine and dark violet-blue.

Levin opal

A variety characterized by long, thin, lightning-like flashes.

Light opal

A form in which the background color is pale cream, milky, or white.

Lithoxyl

Wood opal showing the woody structure.

Liver opal

See Menilite.

Menilite

Gray or liver-colored opal found in nodules at Ménilmontant, in Paris.

Mexican opal

Any opal from Mexico but more particularly Mexican fire opal, which is the only true fire opal and

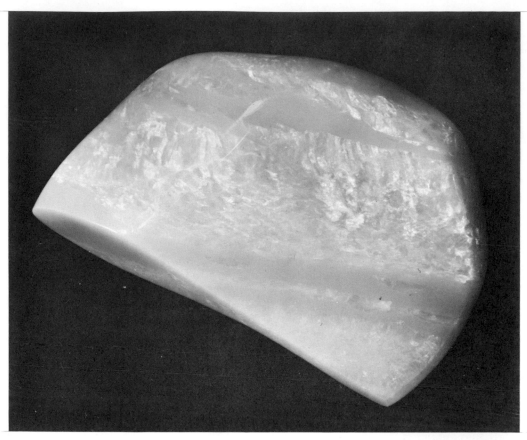

FIG. 20. One of the world's finest opal specimens. This specimen from Australia was polished by the author. The opal is about fist size and weighs a half pound. The fire in an opal defies photography but it shows up fairly well in this photo. The dark patches are blue opal potch with blue and violet fire. The broad patch through the center is a mass of precious opal with red and blue flashes of color. (*Photo by O. D. Smith.*)

the only opal considered by jewelers to be a "precious" stone, although all opal displaying flashes of color is generally regarded as being "precious." Occurs mostly in cherry red or orange colors.

Mexican water opal

A term applied to a translucent to almost transparent opal variety from Mexico with a vivid play of color; yellowish by transmitted light.

Milk opal

A form of light opal in which the background color is pale cream or milky. *Also see* Lechosos opal.

Moss opal

Common opal with black fern-like markings or dendrites resembling black moss agate. Found in Trego County, Kansas.

Mother of opal

Alternative name for prime d'opal. Bright specks of opal in a porous matrix.

Mother of pearl opal

See Kalmuk agate. Layered opal used for cameos.

Mountain opal

Opal found in igneous mountain rocks, in contrast to opal found in the sedimentary rocks of the plains.

Neslite

Opal similar to menilite but slightly grayer in color. It was formerly popular for sword handles and for smaller weapons as well.

Nobbies

An Australian name for a characteristic form of black opal which is probably a pseudomorph. Rounded pebbles of opal resembling nodules, but actually fossils. Splendid pseudomorphs of clams exist in this form.

Noble opal

A term once used for precious opal.

Noodling

An Australian term for searching opal mine tailings or dumps for gem materials.

Onyx opal

Common opal with bandings.

Opal-agate

Banded opal having alternate layers of opal and chalcedony.

Opal matrix

The mother rock in which opal is found and which encloses the opal forming in it. Sometimes used as a term for boulder opal from Queensland. Also used as a term for the finished gem in which portions of the matrix are included.

Opal mother

A dark opal matrix from Hungary.

Opaline

A name occasionally used for opal matrix. Also an old name for Australian opal.

Opalite

A term used for impure colored varieties of common opal. Sometimes used as a term for myrickite. Also used as a term for the black glass used as the backing of opal doublets. Also used as a term for yellow-green potch with black dendritic inclusions.

Opalized bones and shells

Bones and shells that have been fossilized and opalized by silica replacements. The best examples come from Australia.

Opalized wood

Fossilized substance in which common opal and sometimes precious opal has replaced wood. The best examples of this material come from the Virgin Valley in northern Nevada.

Opalus

The Roman name for opal, derived from Sanskrit. This is the oldest term known to civilization for the gem.

Oriental opal

A term used in Ceylon for moonstone.

Painted boulders

Sandstone-quartzite stones impregnated or coated with opal.

Perlmutter opal

An opal variety having a luster like mother-of-pearl.

Pin fire opal

Opal with pin point color flashes smaller and usually less regularly spaced than the patches in harlequin opal. Sometimes called pin point opal.

Pipe opal

Long narrow cigar-shaped opalized fossils. Sometimes called standstone opal. The channels in which they are formed were originally steam vents in the sandstone.

Pitch opal

A yellowish to brownish common opal with a pitchy luster.

Potch

Australian miners' term for an opal which may be interesting but without any play of color. Practically valueless.

Prase opal

Green common opal from Australia colored by chrome. Also from Hungary and Brazil.

Precious opal

Any variety of opal which has value because of its play of colors. A term used by jewelers for Mexican fire opal.

Queensland opal

A term frequently used for boulder opal and named for the Australian province.

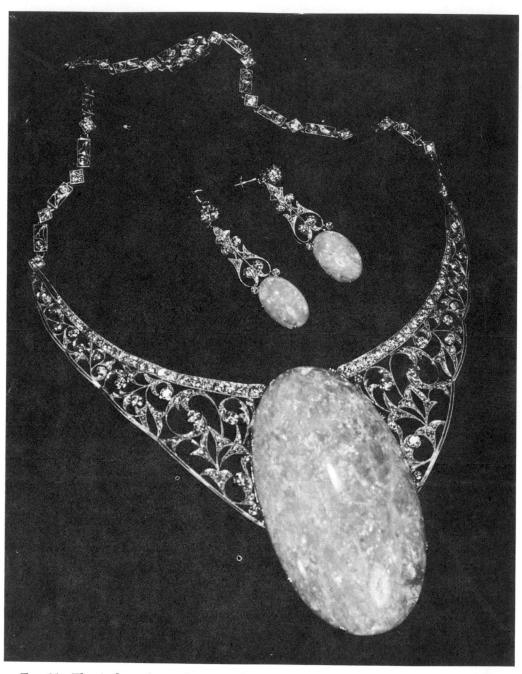

FIG. 21. The Andamooka opal presented to Queen Elizabeth II of Great Britain by the government of South Australia in 1954. This magnificent gem of 204 carats was cut and polished by the Australian Gem Trading Co., Melbourne, Australia. *(Photo by D. Darian Smith, North Adelaide, Australia.)*

Quincite

Sometimes spelled quinzite. A rose-colored common opal.

Radio opal

Common opal of a smoky color caused by organic inclusions or radiolaria in the gel.

Red flash opal

Precious opal with brilliant red flashes which suddenly appear and quickly vanish.

Resin opal

Honey-yellow to ocherous-yellow variety of common opal with a resinous luster.

Roebling opal

An opal in the United States National Museum (Smithsonian Institution) said to be the largest mass of precious opal known. Its weight is 2,610 carats and it came from the Virgin Valley in Nevada. It is opalized wood with brilliant red and green fire. Sometimes called the Roebling black opal. See illustration.

Rose opal

Another name for quincite.

Rough opal

Opal in its rough, unpolished state.

Rubolite

A variety of red common opal.

Rumanite

Opal from Romania.

Sea opal

Not an opal but pieces of a brilliant New Zealand shell (the paua) used in jewelry.

Seam opal

Masses of common opal with bands of precious white opal, from White Cliffs, New South Wales, Australia. Also sometimes used as a name for sandstone opal. Used as a name for white opal found at White Cliffs which occurs in thin flat cakes without adhering matrix.

Semiopal

An undesirable term used for common opal, hydrophane, or any partially dehydrated common opal.

Simav opal

Opal from a mine near the city of Simav on the sea by that name northeast of Izmir (Smyrna), West Turkey. Colorless, milky, or brownish; also orange, yellow, and red varieties, some with a play of color as in fire opal. Sometimes called Simon stone.

Sobrisky opal

Opal from Lead Pipe Springs, near Death Valley in California.

Sun opal.

Another name for fire opal.

Tabasheer

A form of vegetable opal found in the shoots of bamboo.

Tintenbar opal

Opal from Tintenbar district in northeast New South Wales, Australia, which develops cracks on exposure and loses color.

Volcanic opal

Another name for mountain opal.

Wash opal

Alluvial opal or floaters found in dry stream beds where they have been washed down by rain.

Water opal

Same as hyalite. Any transparent precious opal similar to Mexican water opal. Also a misnomer for moonstone.

Wax opal

Yellow opal with a waxy luster.

White cliffs opal

Opal from White Cliffs, Wilcannia, New South Wales, Australia.

White opal

A trade term for precious opal with any light body color as distinguished from a dark background or black opal.

Wood opal

Same as opalized wood but not applied to precious opal pseudomorphous after wood, such as the opal found in Virgin Valley, Nevada.

Yowah nuts

Small nodules of ironstone occasionally containing precious opal.

Chapter 6

Petrified Wood

OF ALL the varieties of quartz gem materials, probably the one in which the average layman is most interested is petrified wood. Few non-rockhounds are aware that it is plentiful and easily gathered or that it can be processed into beautiful cut gemstones and useful and decorative novelties like bookends, table tops, paperweights, ash trays, and many other forms, some of which are illustrated in Chapter 12.

There is a tendency among the meticulous to avoid the use of the words "petrified wood" because, they say, "it isn't petrified and it isn't wood." These people claim (particularly government departments in their reports) that the term agatized wood should be used where the replacement of the wood fibers is chalcedony and opalized wood where the replacement is a silica gel without crystal structure. Both forms can be classified as silicified wood. However, Webster defines the word petrify as to "convert organic matter into stone or stony substance." In petrified wood we indeed have an organic matter that has been converted into a stony substance by having its substance replaced by silica and it seems therefore apparent to this author that the term petrified wood is not incorrect as a term for agatized or opalized wood or silicified wood. The practice of putting quotation marks around the word "wood" whenever it is mentioned seems just as silly as putting quotes around the word "rockhound" . . .

which some writers are still unfortunately inclined to do.

Collecting wood has become so popular that there is fear in some quarters that it may go the way of the carrier pigeon and just disappear, but that is an extreme attitude indeed. However, at this writing (in 1962) the present Secre-

FIG. 22. A cabochon of golden oak from an unknown source. It was in an earthquake and broken and then resealed by further silica infiltration. Note how the growth rings have shifted their alignment. From the author's collection. Enlarged to show detail. (*Photo by O. D. Smith.*)

Fig. 23. The famous Roebling opal specimen from the Virgin Valley, Nevada. Reputed by many authorities to be the finest opal specimen in the world, it has been variously estimated in value as high as a quarter of a million dollars, but it is probably worth much less. The size of the opal may be compared to the penny beside it. This photo indicates how opals defy photography for it looks no better than a lump of coal. It is, however, one of the most beautiful gems in the world, being petrified wood shot through with green and red fire. The opal is on permanent display at the Smithsonian Institution, Washington, D. C., and is one of the museum's most popular exhibits. *(Photo courtesy of the Smithsonian Institution.)*

tary of the Interior, Stewart L. Udall, has submitted proposed legisation to Congress for the protection and orderly removal of petrified wood from deposits on public lands. Providing positive preservation for all kinds of these primitive mineral substances, the proposed law would protect the public recreational values in large deposits but would allow removal of reasonable quantities from other deposits on the national land reserve administered by the Bureau of Land Management. Deposits on lands of the National Parks and National Monuments have long been protected by law and may not be removed. The position of the Department of the Interior is that "petrified wood is not petrified and it is not wood. It is a fossilized mineral substance, a relic, proving the ex-

istence of forests on earth millions of years ago. The substance is formed by silica and other elements that seeped into and gradually replaced the original shape of the wood or trees over a period of thousands of centuries."

Any person may file a mining claim on public lands and petrified wood comes under the classification of minerals, as do other gemstone varieties. Attempts have been made to make abrasive products by crushing the wood in stamp mills. The proposed legislation would remove wood from disposition under the general mining law. All fossilized deposits would be protected, preserved, and utilized under regulations of the Department of the Interior. Large fixed deposits would be set aside specifically for public enjoyment and rockhounds would be permitted to remove limited amounts without charge. While some form of petrified wood exists in most of the states, known *major* deposits of the three kinds of fossilized wood in twenty-six states have been cataloged by the Department's Bureau of Mines and a detailed inventory of other significant deposits on the national land reserve has been started by the Bureau of Land Management. A list of these deposits, in all probability, will be available by the time this book is published.

Wherever deposits of fossilized wood are found today they provide geological proof of the once extensive forest growth that covered most of the northern hemisphere in pre-historic times. Without man to speed the process, the trees died naturally . . . by fires due to lightning storms and active volcanoes, or by the ravages of disease and insects that also existed at the time, as is evidenced by the worm holes found in many petrified logs. In most regions dead and dying trees toppled to the ground and simply rotted away just as they do today. But those falling near stream banks were often carried downstream by floodwaters and dumped in shallow lakes or ponds. Here they were buried under many layers of shifting mud for thousands of years, mud containing volcanic ash rich in silica and other elements. The silica was soluble in surface waters and, under favorable conditions (fully understood by no one), silica, in the form of opal or chalcedony, was slowly deposited as the organic matter of the trees dissolved. The entire process was extremely slow so that delicate structures were retained, allowing recog-

Fig. 24. Photo by N. H. Darton of a group of petrified log sections south of Adamana in the Petrified Forest National Monument, Arizona. (*Photo courtesy U. S. Geological Survey.*)

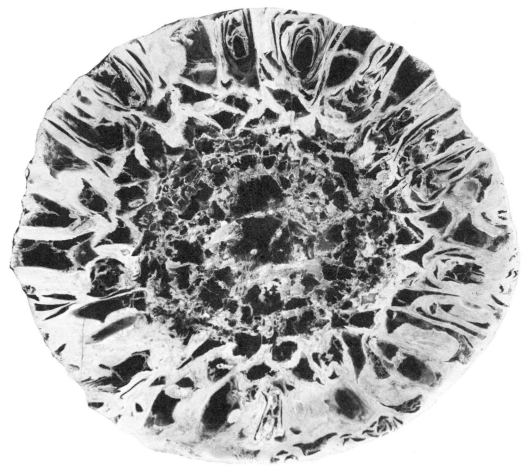

Fig. 25. Section of petrified cycad wood from near the Four Corners region in Utah. From the Morrison formation. Gathered, cut, and polished by Leo D. Berner of Glendora, California, in whose collection it remains. It is 9″ x 9″ and is colored white, black, and brown.

nition of the original form and shape. The various colors and mottled patterns resulted from the mineral impurities present in the ground water and deposited with the silica. Excellent examples of these log jams in former lakes are at the Petrified Forest National Monument in Arizona, where some of the finest agatized wood in existence is found in great abundance, and in the Virgin Valley of Nevada where the world's finest opalized wood is found.

Sometimes a succession of entire forests of many trees was inundated by a tremendous volume of mud and preserved for thousands of centuries. The mountains south of the Lamar River in Yellowstone National Park reveal more than fifteen different forests of sequoia, pine, chestnut, and plane trees, superimposed on each other in successive layers. The Eden Valley wood of Wyoming was such a forest.

There is wide interest among rockhounds in petrified wood but, for several reasons, this interest is confined almost entirely to western rock collectors. The lapidary treatment of wood requires massive equipment . . . saws, lap wheels, etc., and massive equipment requires plenty of space. The finished slabs again require lots of space for display, a spare

FIG. 26. Red, brown, white, and black section of petrified wood from St. John's, Arizona. The slab is 8″ x 11″. From the collection of Leo D. Berner, Glendora, California, who cut and polished it.

FIG. 27. Slabs of petrified wood from near Boron, California. Highly agatized and colored blue, tan, and white. The two larger pieces show worm holes. The largest piece is about 7″ long. From the collection of Carl Lawrence, Claremont, California.

FIG. 28. A magnificent polished slab of Arizona petrified wood 7½″ wide by 6½″ high. This "scene" portrays sunset over Death Valley. Anyone who has ever been there can readily identify in the rich reds, yellows, and white and gray markings the outline of the sunset over the Panamint Mountains to the west, with a dry lake in the center and the shore line at the bottom. One has to see the coloring to appreciate the "picture." From the author's collection. (*Photo by O. D. Smith.*)

room perhaps or a separate hobby shop. Favorable conditions for the development of this branch of the hobby do not exist very often in the east, especially among apartment dwellers. Many collectors never process their finds at all but use them as interesting displays in their gardens. There are so many locations of petrified wood in the Rocky Mountain, Pacific Coast and Southwestern states that few rockhounds in those states live very far from a prospect.

Fossil collectors as a rule are greatly interested in petrified wood as fossils rather than as gemstone material and they have depleted some areas. For instance, there was once an area known as the Shade Creek Petrified Forest near Athens, Ohio, but fossil collectors for more than a hundred years carried away the specimens until now none seems to exist.

The wood from the Petrified Forest National Monument in Arizona is the most colorful of American varieties but the various woods of Washington state indicate the original graining and patterns on the wood probably better than the wood from other locations. Excellent wood specimens may be gathered at many spots in Oregon, California, Nevada, Utah, Colorado, and Wyoming

Fɪɢ. 29. A view of the Wood Pile area near Beatty, Nevada, where petrified wood abounds. *(Photo courtesy of A. B. Meiklejohn.)*

and many of the locations are described under the various states in Chapter 8. Contrary to popular belief, not all petrified wood is silicified. Logs have been found that were almost pure uranium. Anyone really interested in petrified wood should read *Petrified Forest Trails* by Jay Ellis Ransom. See Chapter 12.

While some excellent illustrations of petrified wood are given here, additional illustrations are scattered throughout the book, especially in Chapter 8.

Chapter 7

Where Quartz Gems Occur

THE GREATEST thrill in the lapidary hobby is the actual collecting of gem materials and this is done quite extensively in North America. The United States Bureau of Mines estimates that at least three million people in the United States are rock collectors for some purpose—not always gem cutting of course. A comparable condition occurs in Canada. Agate and quartz gem locations are listed extensively, state by state, in the next chapter and locations in Canada and Mexico are given in Chapter 9.

When one leaves the North American continent, however, the amateur lapidary or agate collector becomes very scarce indeed, practically impossible to find unless one has built up a chain of correspondents. It was much the same in the United States fifty years ago. The lapidary movement in America was developed by the experiments with gemstones of the early mineral specimen collectors and by the fact that many gem varieties were freely available to the collector— and still are. In Europe things are far different, for almost every acre of ground is owned by private individuals, so that there is nowhere to collect except in streams and along the beaches. The author has had correspondence with collectors all over the world for many years and it is difficult to find anyone who has done any serious gemstone collecting except in South Africa and Australia. There conditions prevail similar to our own and a great interest in rock hobbies has developed, with organized clubs patterned after those in North America.

In the British Isles there are many places along the coast where good agates and other types of gemstones have been reported. It appears that cairngorm collecting can be done at many places in the Cairngorm Mountains. Cairngorm is the Scottish term for smoky quartz and most of it is very beautiful when faceted. Agates are not plentiful anywhere and it takes the initiated to be able to find any at all. The beaches of Cornwall and the west coast of Scotland, particularly at Rossshire, are reportedly the best collecting spots. These beaches also yield good examples of carnelian and banded agate.

In Scotland good bloodstone occurs on the island of Rum, agate at Usan in County Angus, and vein agate at Burn Anne, Galston, Ayrshire. Banded agate and fortification agate are reportedly fairly common in Scotland but it is difficult to pinpoint exact locations. Usan, mentioned above, seems to be the best agate locality and Montrose, Ferryden, and Scurdyness, all in Angus County, are reportedly good collecting spots.

Numerous localities are reported in Fife at Balmerino, Scurr Hill, Heather Hill, Luthrie, Newburgh, and Balmeadowside. Jasper is rather common all over Scotland and can be successfully prospected at almost any rocky spot. Aventurine in many colors, except the

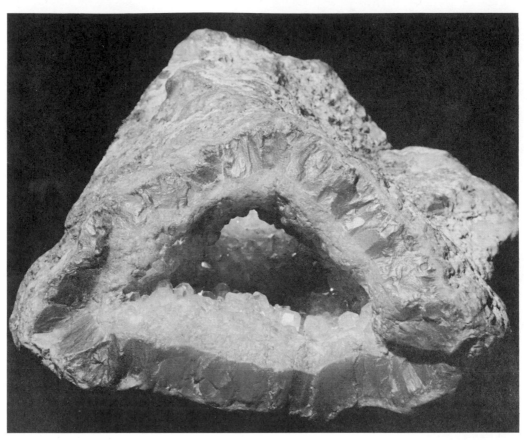

Fig. 30. Red agate geode lined with quartz crystals. This unusual specimen was found in the jungle along the Chilibre River in the Republic of Panama. It is 7″ wide, 4″ high and 9″ long. This specimen is oblong, in contrast to the usual concentric geode. The cavity shown at the front continues through to the rear, where a light has been attached in the natural opening to illuminate the attractive interior of the geode. *(Photo by Paul W. Johnson.)*

fine green of the Indian variety, can be found in the Orkney Islands and in Banffshire on the west side of the Allnack River, about three miles above its junction with the Avon.

Anyone who is really interested in agates and quartz gems will certainly want to pay a visit sometime to the town of Idar-Oberstein in West Germany. This is the oldest gem cutting center in the world and its history is given in Chapter 2. It has been an agate cutting center for more than 2,000 years; today there are over 25,000 people, of the 40,000 inhabitants, cutting all manner of gemstones in about 450 lapidary establishments.

The town is best reached by driving about 200 miles east of the city of Luxembourg, over good roads. There are good hotels and restaurants and the town maintains a wonderful museum in which is displayed every manner of lapidary craftsmanship in gemstones, most of it in agate and other quartz-family gems. Here one can find examples of cut stones in almost every variety known to man and the numerous shops offer everything from diamonds to quartz crystal. Unfortunately, the trade has recently turned to cutting synthetic gemstones, so the traveler should beware when purchasing. The agate fancier has nothing to worry about for there is

FIG. 31. A Brazilian agate with a filled cavity. The specimen is on display at the Smithsonian Institution, Washington, D.C. *(Photo courtesy of the Smithsonian Institution.)*

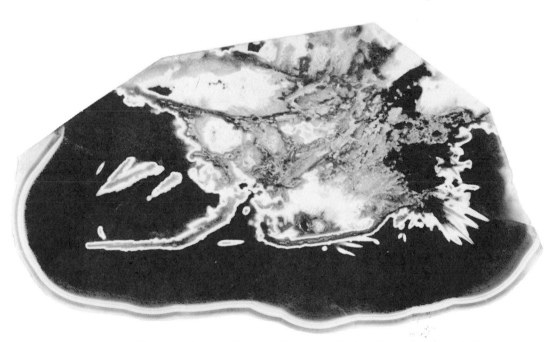

FIG. 32. Agate slab from Brazil, showing that not all Brazilian agate is of the fortification or banded varieties. The agate is on display at the Smithsonian Institution, Washington, D.C. *(Photo courtesy of the Smithsonian Institution.)*

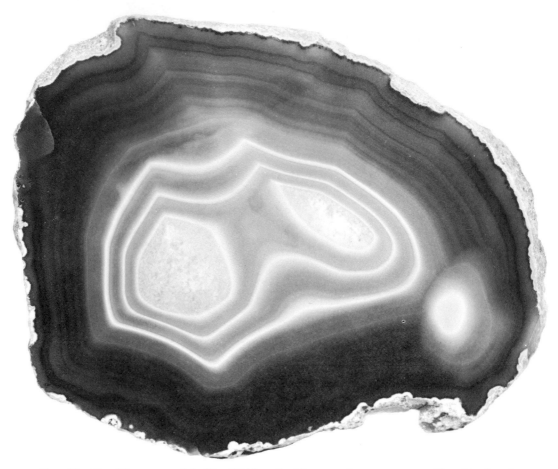

Fig. 33. Brazilian agate slab 8″ x 10″ has double crystal center areas with white bands. Brown agate inside of bands. Outside is blue-gray agate with reddish bands. From the collection of Leo D. Berner, Glendora, California.

no synthetic agate. See illustrations in Chapter 12 of some of the novelty items from Idar-Oberstein in the author's collection.

The author knows of no place in Europe where a collector can gather any agate rough. In a very extensive library of books and periodicals, no references are available on quartz locations there. That they exist is a foregone conclusion, for many thousands of great works in agate occur that were made as long as a thousand years ago, such as the great mosaics and intarsias in the cathedrals of Italy. It must be assumed that the agate materials used in these works came from local sources just as the materials for the ancient scarabs of Egypt and the

Sumerian and other cylinder seals were made from local varieties of agate. The very name of agate derives from the river Achates in Sicily where, reportedly, agate no longer exists. The Sumerians, ancient inhabitants of Mesopotamia (now the United Arab Republic and Iraq), were said to be the first people who used agate as ornaments and it is assumed that the agate was local material, although nothing in the literature tells for certain where the agate came from. Because no great trade routes existed at that time, we must assume that the stones used in Aaron's breastplate and in other references in the Bible (most of them quartz) came from local sources. Probably the local sources

72

were exhausted just as they were exhausted in later years in Idar-Oberstein. When trade routes were opened, we know, according to Pliny, that quartz and agate materials were brought from India, a prolific source and world supplier to this day.

We do know that agate and quartz gem materials exist all over the world but that there is no high interest in them except in North America. Here there is a great variety of easily procured material, with no apparent reason for importing agate from other countries, except from Brazil and India where superior types occur in a few varieties such as the banded agate boulders of Brazil and the bloodstone and tree agates of India.

From long experience in editing the *Lapidary Journal* we learned from correspondents all over the world that they had a sufficient supply of agates locally but that no one was interested in them. People in Australia are interested only in opals and sapphires, probably because they are "precious," but many have written us about the prolific deposits of agate all over that country, which is practically nothing but desert when one gets away from the busy cities of the coastal regions. It is in the desert, of course, that gem materials are exposed for prospecting since, due to lack of moisture, they are not covered with verdure. Field trips are organized every year for American rockhounds to collect opal in Australia but, except for the doubtful thrill of visiting dull and uninteresting opal fields, probably no one ever came away with anything worthwhile unless he bought some opal. Whenever we have asked any of these American visitors if they had seen any agates or other materials, they have all said that many kinds of interesting cutting rocks covered the area but that they did not appear as attractive as their own "home grown" rocks . . . and then, too, excess

FIG. 34. Various cabochons in Brazilian quartz from the author's collection. The markings predominate in red. (*Photo by O. D. Smith.*)

FIG. 35. A large Brazilian agate cabochon cut by the author and in his collection. The agate contains a fair map of South America. *(Photo by O. D. Smith.)*

luggage weight on planes costs a great deal more than the agates are worth.

All kinds of quartz gemstones also occur in great abundance in Africa, particularly in South Africa. However, there is little interest in any of them except the tigereye from Griqualand, a very beautiful stone and a great favorite with amateur lapidaries.

In recent years, in both South Africa and Australia, groups of hobbyist collectors have been formed, who conduct regular field trips. In their explorations they have found many types of agate and jasper and attempts have been made to export them to America, but rockhounds here do not seem to be interested. None of the exporting ventures in those countries has been successful, with the exception of the sellers of the tigereye of Africa and the opal of Australia. Both of these materials are imported by American dealers in huge quantities and are in great demand.

Although the literature does not chronicle the location of agate diggings in China, there must be a great deal of it, as indicated by the many varieties of agate and jasper used in making their

beautiful snuff bottles and other carved objects, some of which are illustrated in color in this work. They appear to have available in great quantities two beautiful quartz materials that are very scarce elsewhere. They are macaroni agate, containing tube-like inclusions resembling macaroni, and puddingstone, which is a beautiful brecciated jasper. The Japanese artisans do not produce anything in agate, probably because they have no local source of supply. Crystal quartz, however, is in plentiful supply and the Japanese have a flourishing crystal carving industry. They also make faceted quartz beads.

Brazil probably leads all countries today in the supplying of agate, especially for the making of novelties, although many of the agate nodules actually come from Uruguay, Brazil's neighbor to the immediate south. All of this agate is banded agate and the nodules are large, so that generous slabs of fracture-free material can be secured. Most of the material is dull in color, however, running to pale blue and gray, but it is pre-heated before cutting so that the colors are enhanced, most of them turning to rich reds, yellows and browns.

There are many fine gems found in Brazil, such as those of the tourmaline group and some of the finest aquamarines in the world. The world's finest diamonds also come from Brazil but not in great quantity. The country is particularly rich in quartz deposits and exports great quantities of the quartz crystal used in the electronics industries of many countries, such as the United States, Japan, and England. The finest rutilated quartz in the world comes from Brazil, in the form of large masses of clear quartz shot through with needles of rutile. This is ideal for the making of spectacular cabochons, beads, and bowls.

Southern Brazil and northern Uruguay have a plentiful supply of the world's most spectacular geodes, many of them huge masses lined with fine dark purple amethyst crystals. These are usually broken into small pieces for sale to mineral specimen collectors. There is a great deal of good amethyst cutting crystal and also a great deal of citrine or yellow quartz. This is usually marketed as "Brazilian topaz." Pale quality amethyst and smoky quartz are heat treated to produce yellow citrine. Morion, or black quartz, is in some demand with cutters and of course there is every shade of smoky quartz in abundant supply. In 1962 a new pink quartz was found which has yet to be named at this writing. This is not to be confused with rose quartz, which is a pink massive quartz and is also in abundant supply in Brazil. The new pink crystals are reportedly clear and well formed but the writer has seen no gems cut from this material, which is still hard to obtain. None is being offered at this writing by any dealers although it may be by the time this book appears.

There is great demand in North American rockhound shops for the quartz materials from Brazil because these relatively inexpensive gems are widely used by the growing number of faceters. Brazil is no place for the rockhound, however, because collecting is almost impossible under very discouraging conditions and there are some of the most difficult export restrictions in the world.

In personal correspondence with many traveling rockhounds through the years, the author has heard that agate and jasper are everywhere but that the natives of other lands are not interested in them. The distribution of petrified wood all over the world is absolutely ignored by every one. If the local gem material is not in the so-called "precious" class where easy money can be realized quickly, the foreigner has no interest in

Fig. 36. A superb example of rough rutilated quartz from Brazil. Note the wide distribution of the rutile needles throughout the clear quartz and the dense spray at the left. From the author's collection. *(Photo by O. D. Smith.)*

FIG. 37. Clear crystal quartz varieties from Brazil used for faceted stones. The large piece at top left is rose quartz, the black pieces are morion, and the rest are yellow citrine. From the author's collection. (*Photo by O. D. Smith.*)

rocks. Having come a long way from the Stone Age, he has no desire to return to it as have so many Americans in their pursuit of happiness. In our next two chapters we shall report at some length on the locations of agate and quartz deposits in North America, where rockhounds can pursue their happiness in the form of recreation and adventure, seeing their country as they have never seen it before.

While most of the agate for novelties comes from Brazil the better types of agate for cabochons, beads, and other jewelry stones still come from India where they are in plentiful supply and have been for more than 2,000 years. Herodotus, writing in 48 B.C., recorded that the sard and onyx used by the

Romans for their agate finger rings were obtained from India. Ptolemy, the Alexandrian mathematician and geographer, wrote in the second century about the agate covered hills of India. Because most of the vast Indian peninsula is covered with lava flows, it follows that it is also covered with quartz gemstones caused by the infiltration of silica into the hollow vesicles of the lava. The types of agate found in India run the gamut of the whole quartz family . . . banded agate, carnelian, jasper, sardonyx, plasma, chalcedony, flint, onyx, aventurine, clear crystal, amethyst, smoky quartz, citrine, and some of the best moss agates in the world. Many of the latter have dendritic inclusions that look like perfect trees and these are

FIG. 38. Small sections of geode linings of amethyst crystal from Uruguay. From the author's collection. *(Photo by O. D. Smith.)*

FIG. 39. Fortification agate *(top)* and two eye agates *(below)* from Brazil. Agates are about the size of large oranges. From the collection of Archie B. Meiklejohn, past president of the Los Angeles Lapidary Society. *(Photo by Bob Forester.)*

called tree agates in the jewelry trade. The world's finest bloodstone also comes from India.

Small attention is paid by the average farmer in India to the agates which usually abound in the plowed fields but he considers the gathering of quartz crystal specimens as an extra crop and regularly prospects every field, after plowing, for specimens of clear quartz, amethyst, and citrine quartz. Many districts are regularly mined for agate, one of the principal districts being at

Ratanpur in the state of Rajpipala. This district was specifically mentioned by Pliny in A.D. 77 and it is probably the place referred to by Ptolemy. Many travelers in the sixteenth century mention the place and identify it with agates. In the nearby country surrounding the ancient diamond mines of Golconda, which is near Hyderabad and at one time was the richest princedom in India, there are good quantities of clear and colored quartz crystal.

The mining methods are the same as

78

those pursued for thousands of years. Mine shafts are sunk into the ground and no machinery is used. The Indians long ago discovered the value of heat in enhancing the color of agate. Selected agates are spread in the sun for several months and then placed in earthenware pots for further baking. The pale colors are darkened in this manner and pale white, yellow, and brown colors are changed into pink and variegated reds, with the rich carnelian color being preferred.

No proper or complete geological survey has ever been made of India but if one is ever made it will undoubtedly reveal commercial deposits that will supply the world demand for centuries to come, providing there is a demand for quartz gems. Many Indian dealers advertise Indian gemstones in the American magazines mentioned in Chapter 12 but the American rockhound buys very little Indian agate because of the prevalence of free agate in North America. Indian bloodstone and aventurine are in good demand, however, because of their superior quality and low price.

A very popular stone with amateur gem cutters is the aventurine or green

Fig. 40. Eye agate from Uruguay. On display at the Smithsonian Institution, Washington, D.C. (*Photo courtesy of the Smithsonian Institution.*)

79

FIG. 41. Two agate slabs from Schlottwitz, Germany, on display at the Smithsonian Institution. The illustration *(right)* shows a fine example of ruin agate. *(Photos courtesy of the Smithsonian Institution.)*

FIG. 42. Two unusual slabs of agate from the old deposits at Idar-Oberstein, Germany. These deposits were used for over 2000 years and became exhausted in the early 1800's. On display at the Smithsonian Institution. *(Photos courtesy of the Smithsonian Institution.)*

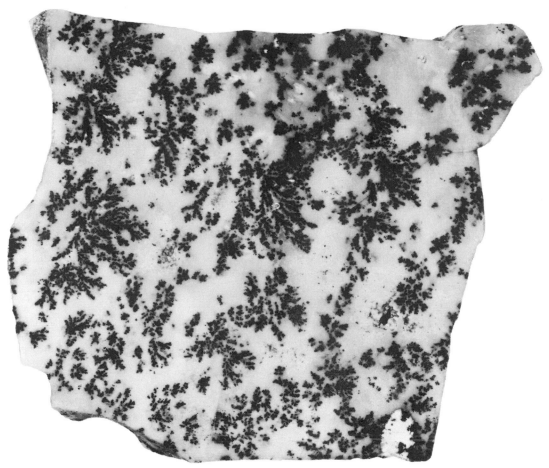

FIG. 43. A slab of dendritic agate from India which is typical of Indian moss agate. (*Photo courtesy of the Smithsonian Institution.*)

quartz which comes from the state of Mysore, a by-product of the mining for iron. This occurs in massive pieces, sometimes as large as 100 pounds. Both green and blue aventurine also come from the state of Jaipur. About 260 miles southeast of Bombay is a mountainous and hilly country containing just about every type of chalcedony except carnelian. From this area come some very fancy agates, pink and green moss agates, variegated jasper, true black agate or the genuine onyx of commerce, zebra agates, bloodstone, and many types of scenic agates. The carnelian for which India is noted is really yellow agate that is heat-treated. This material comes from near Baroda in the state of Bombay. Many other gemstones outside of the quartz family are found in India and are in better demand. Collecting agates in India by the casual traveler is out of the question, however, and should be undertaken only by residents.

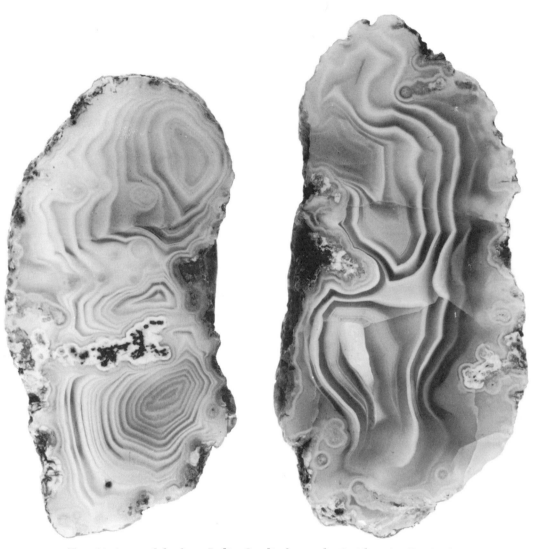

Fig. 44. Agate slabs from India. On display at the Smithsonian Institution.
(Photo courtesy of the Smithsonian Institution.)

Chapter 8

Collecting Areas in the
United States of America

(Arranged Alphabetically by States)

AN ATTEMPT is made at this point to discuss briefly some noted (and some little known) agate collecting areas in the United States. These areas are the places known to the author at the time of the publication of this book early in 1963. As time goes on, it is inevitable that some of the areas will become depleted, others will be barred to collecting because privately owned, or will be set aside by the armed services as test sites and non-public lands. However, it is the custom now among owners of gem-bearing land to permit digging or hunting for a daily fee. Usually such areas are of little value as farm land and the owner is glad to supplement his income by allowing people to haul away his rocks. The collector should be careful to have knowledge beforehand of the land where he expects to collect, for if it is private land, permission should be sought from the owner. Where private ownership of the areas discussed is known, such information will be given. In the east it is no problem for nearly all private land is posted for "no hunting." This also means no rock hunting. But in the west, land that is posted "no hunting" means no hunting of game and land owners seldom object to rock hunters providing no gates are left open or stock harmed.

The best collecting areas are in the west for several reasons. Climatic conditions favor year around collecting, in the southwest particularly. Previous volcanic activity produced the right conditions for the formation of agates and other quartz gems. About half the land surface is owned by the United States government and is therefore in the public domain and free for collecting and prospecting. For instance, in Nevada, a prime collecting area, only 13 per cent of all the land is privately owned and 87 per cent is owned by the United States government. This situation is difficult for the easterner to believe and even many people in the west are skeptical about it when they read of it.

There is not a state among the fifty where some precious stones cannot be found and the collector will, no doubt, wish to be informed about other than quartz gems, such as the jade of Wyoming and Alaska, the diamonds of Arkansas, sapphires of Montana, rubies of North Carolina, or the turquoise of Nevada and New Mexico. Diamonds, sapphires, and rubies can all be collected for a daily searching fee. However, space is not given in this work to anything but quartz family gems, so that several states are omitted only because their importance as quartz gem producing areas is not very great. A complete book on the

FIG. 45. Two slabs of agate from China on display in the Smithsonian Institution, Washington, D.C. Quite unlike any American agate, this is the type the Chinese use to carve their snuff bottles. The veinings are red and green. (*Photos courtesy of the Smithsonian Institution.*)

subject of all the gems in North America is the excellent work of Captain John Sinkankas entitled *Gemstones of North America*. The reader is referred to further information on this and other books on the subject in Chapter 12.

New locations of quartz gems such as agates, jasper, and petrified wood are being discovered practically every month and few of these new locations are kept secret for long. They are revealed to friends, the members of the gem and mineral clubs, and eventually someone writes about them for one of the mineral magazines such as those mentioned in Chapter 12. Month to month information about new and old locations

in the west is usually given in *Gems and Minerals* magazine, in the east by *Rocks and Minerals* magazine. Many of the accounts of new finds are accompanied by maps and many of the "trail" books mentioned in Chapter 12 contain maps, most of them inadequate and poor. Of course no map can tell you the exact spot at which to sink your pick but there are few maps that are not of some help. The annual April issue of the *Lapidary Journal*, the *Rockhound Buyers Guide* issue, is devoted almost exclusively to field trip information, both old and new.

There is one phase of rock collecting that is important—it is a man-and-wife outdoors hobby. Few fishermen or hunters take their wives along on their trips, but the rockhound often does and, surprisingly, the women take to rockhounding like a cat to raw liver. And of course the greatest enthusiasts of all are the rockhound's children. There are many thousands of women in America who collect and polish rocks and they should be considered in any rock hunter's plans.

The following remarks are made in a broad sense and they are the author's personal opinions after long observation. They are subject to diverse opinion but we believe that most rockhounds will agree that, in the main, the observations are true.

California is the greatest state for the collection of gem rocks of many kinds, the quartz family in particular. While great quantities of agate abound at many locations and the variety is great, most people will agree that Oregon is really agate country and California is jasper country. While Arizona petrified wood is the most colorful, the woods from Washington are more varied and interesting. Montana has the most interesting scenic agates while Texas has some of the most colorful agates. The Lake Superior region is wonderful agate country and Iowa and Illinois abound in geodes but they are strictly curiosities and not gem material like the geodes and nodules of California and Oregon. Arizona amethyst is among the world's finest for a rich wine color.

ALABAMA

A fine chert resembling chalcedony is found on a small mountain southeast of Gurley, Madison County, on Highway 72. Chalcedony has been reported in veins in Clarke County. About a mile west of Blountsville, Blount County, and along Highway 128, agates and chert can be gathered in a series of gravel pits.

Few locations have been discovered in Alabama because this is not rockhound country. There are very few collectors in the state and only two clubs. Perhaps the Alabama visitor or reader can obtain good information from the Alabama Mineral and Lapidary Society, which meets on the second Friday of the month in the Phillips Building of Birmingham Southern College.

ALASKA

This is our new empire, our largest state, but reports of agates or any of the quartz gems are very meager indeed. There is little doubt that, because of all the volcanic activity in Alaska's past, great quantities of agate, quartz crystals, jasper, and petrified wood abound. There has been much interest in Alaska's great jade deposits, which have to be brought out by airplane. After all, that is a pay load. But who is going to fly into the interior to explore for agates and then transport any find by airplane? It is unfortunate that this new state has so few roads, because the Government still owns 99.7 per cent of all public land and it would be a paradise for rock and mineral collectors if the weather were not so forbidding and roads for travel were available. It is hardly likely that the roads will develop very soon as they are a great expense for the little time during the year when they can be used, and a state owning only 3/10ths of 1 per cent of its land does not have enough taxable area to promote funds for adequate roads.

About the only highway the rockhound would be likely to use at this time is the Alaska Highway, still called the Alcan Highway by many. About 1,200 miles of this road run through Canada and most of it is still unpaved at this writing. The Alaska Highway begins about 60 miles north of Dawson Creek and runs through British Columbia and the Yukon Territory.

Nearly all of Alaska is covered with a glacial moraine from the last ice age.

The moraine is from ten to a thousand feet deep and about the only place where the traveler can find a spot along the road to look for rocks is in the borrow pits along the highway where material has been removed for road building. The great hindrance to prospecting is the permafrost, soil that is permanently frozen from three to ten feet below the surface. The top of the permafrost thaws in summer, the only time when highway travel is feasible; water is below the thawed section and solid ground many feet below that. This makes most of the country a floating marsh and it is even difficult to walk and explore, for it is, as someone has described it, like walking on a feather bed.

The following information is a recording of known agate locations in Alaska but it is not very helpful to the traveler. Agates and petrified wood have been reported at Nunvainuk Lake and petrified wood at Kujulik Bay. Pale red and honey-yellow carnelian pebbles occur in the gravels of Becharof Lake, on the north shore and near its outlet.

Most of the reported finds of agates in Alaska are at locations on the Aleutian Islands and these are not accessible to the automobile traveler. Attu has small gray chalcedony pebbles on its beaches. Red jasper occurs on the north shore of Adak Island. Tanaga seems well supplied with agate pebbles on its beaches and gray banded agate has been found on Unalaska Island.

ARIZONA

The state of Arizona is great collecting country, for only 55 per cent of the land is publicly owned. There are a great many flourishing gem and mineral clubs, with a wide interest throughout the state in gem and mineral collecting and gemcraft. Some of the best gem and

FIG. 46. Petrified wood, 4″ x 6″, from near Yuma, Arizona. Mostly gray with light rings. Some red, yellow, and black shot through the piece. Well silicified, showing fine banded structure. From the collection of Leo D. Berner, Glendora, California.

mineral shows in the United States are held every winter in Phoenix and Tucson, the dates of which are usually announced in the magazines listed in Chapter 12.

The roads and highways are among the nation's best. In Southern Arizona particularly there are mile after mile of highways through desert country that invite the traveler to park at the side of the road and go prospecting afoot in adjoining areas where agate, jasper, and petrified wood are not too difficult to find. The reader is reminded that this is one of the hottest areas of the United States in the summer, temperatures of 130° occurring at times. The traveler should never permit himself to get beyond sight of the main road in the summertime. Summertime is also snake time and the Arizona desert regions are no place for tennis sneakers or wedgies. The visitor should have high topped leather boots or at least heavy soled shoes. As with all field trips the rock hunter should have a first aid kit and a snake bite kit in his car.

A mecca for all rockhounds is the Petrified Forest National Monument 19 miles northeast of Holbrook in northern Arizona. This is 22 miles south of U.S. Route 66, the main highway across northern Arizona, and the spot should certainly be visited by anyone traveling in the area, for it is one of nature's greatest wonders. There is a 50 cent charge for each car entering the Monument. It is open from 7:30 A.M. until 5:30 P.M. in the winter and from 8 A.M. until 6 P.M. in the summer.

No collecting is allowed and this rule is rigidly enforced. It was estimated by the Monument authorities in 1947 that if each visitor took a ten pound piece there would be no agatized wood left by 1970 despite the estimate at that time of seventy thousand tons of it exposed. Even at 10 cents a pound, the price charged outside the Monument at that time, this would have been fourteen million dollars worth of wood. There is a fine museum containing many examples of the polished wood. The huge petrified logs abounding in the Monument are most interesting to observe for this is probably the finest and most colorful variety of agatized wood to be found anywhere in the world. Most of the wood is a brilliant red, containing areas of chalcedony and dendritic inclusions. When sliced, the slabs often have scenes and when cut into cabochons great use can be made of them in costume jewelry or so-called "Indian jewelry." The material makes superb bookends.

While no collecting is allowed in the Monument, there is plenty of wood to be found at many locations in northern Arizona and many shops along the highways sell the wood in the rough and in the form of the jewelry. No visitor passing through this section of our country will want to leave without taking by purchase or personal search some of the colorful wood. The author has traveled over most of northern Arizona, particularly in the Navajo country, and many times has stopped to explore and prospect at likely spots. Each search was always rewarded with specimens of petrified wood, although none of the beautiful red variety was ever encountered. The wood, which abounds all over the area as silicified wood, is characteristic of the Triassic sediments of which northern Arizona is formed. The red wood of the Monument is not so easily found, however.

Hundreds of Arizona gemstone locations have been reported in the literature on the subject and a list of the books and magazines in which these accounts have appeared is given in Chapter 12. Most of these reports are still available at this writing. Some of them have been abstracted here— enough of them so that the reader can plan a two or more weeks vacation that will cover the whole state.

Mohave County contains many locations of quartz gemstone, although most of it is reported of poor quality. Agate and chalcedony are easily found along the east side of the Colorado River near its exit from Lake Mead, particularly at a spot about 3 miles south-southeast of Hoover Dam. Five miles north of Topock on old Highway 66 a wonderful agate locality extends over the low hills to the left for about 2 miles. About 2½ miles further on, on the road to Oatman, numerous quartz varieties may be gathered on the east side of the road in the exposed gravels. Going south from Kingman and about 6 miles before reaching the ghost town of Goldroad one can find examples of fire agate. This location is near Sitgreaves or Meadow Creek Pass, about 22½ miles from Kingman. The fire agate is found in flat, grapelike growths up to five inches across. These "desert roses" and other chalcedonies can easily be recovered by digging in the top soil. Nice banded agate has been found on the Kingman-Phoenix route, Highway 93, in the vicinity of Burro Creek. This area is reported to be one of the best agate fields in the state.

The Eagle Tail mountains are south of Salome and this is an almost virgin area for the collecting of moss agate, chalcedony and carnelian. By taking the Tonopah road south and southeast from Salome one comes to the Saddle Mountain collecting area, long popular and almost depleted. Storms keep washing out new material, however, and the hunter can usually find some fire agate, brown and white banded agate, and carnelian. The area around Martinez Lake, north of Yuma, is reported to be good agate collecting country. The best agate fields are found on the California side of the Colorado River. Palm Canyon is north of Martinez Lake on Highway 95. Agatized wood abounds here, particularly palm wood. The canyon is on the west side of the Kofa Mountains and similar materials are re-ported on the east side of the mountains also.

Nearly every gem collector visiting Arizona wants to get some chrysocolla for this is the most beautiful of all the varieties of chalcedony. It is chalcedony stained with inclusions of copper silicate or chrysocolla, usually very transparent and a heavenly blue in color, although it sometimes shades into green. While the material is sold as chrysocolla it should properly be termed chrysocolla-stained chalcedony.

Most authorities report that the real chrysocolla is found only at the Inspiration Mine at Miami, but many copper mines have yielded good quality specimens. This is not a material that can be gathered by the rockhound as it is recovered from mining ventures. It appears as a layer near the top of the mine, a few hundred feet below the surface. When the layer is exhausted new supplies are seldom found further down.

The traveler will have to depend on purchase if he wants a supply and it is best to investigate the stock of roadside rockshops, a list of which can be found in the *Rockhound Buyers Guide*. It is suggested that purchases be made by mail after consulting the advertisements that appear regularly in the magazines. By purchasing through the mail the buyer is usually well protected, for he can return for refund unsatisfactory material. There is a great deal of blue colored rock offered as chrysocolla that is not worth 10 cents a pound. Chrysocolla-stained chalcedony is the most beautiful and the most expensive chalcedony in the world and good quality bright blue translucent specimens are much in demand at prices ranging from $25.00 to $50.00 a pound. That is $100,000 a ton! Therefore the reader can see the value of purchasing carefully and in only small lots of a few ounces at a time. Cabochons cut from chrysocolla make beautiful ring settings, pendants, bola tie mounts, and bracelet stones. It

Fig. 47. A large polished slab of Arizona agate, 13″ across by 9″ high. The agate is richly marked in carnelian surrounding the fortification quartz crystal center. A magnificent display piece from the author's collection. (*Photo by O. D. Smith.*)

is one of the few quartz gemstone varieties deserving a gold mounting for it offers a beautiful contrast with gold.

Gila County is chiefly noted for chrysocolla, where it has been found in generous quantities at copper mines in the Globe district. The Live Oak Mine and the Keystone Mine, 6½ miles west of Globe, have yielded fine material. The Inspiration Mine at Miami has been the leading producer.

In buying one should look for pure blue translucent material, which commands the highest price. If the translucency is marred by cloudy formations or if the shade tends to be on the green side, it is not so desirable, although it is still beautiful. It is more expensive to buy chrysocolla in the slab form at so much a square inch, for only then can the buyer see what he is getting. On this basis, several dollars a square inch is not too much to pay for the first class material. The price is not a problem so

much as finding a source of supply, for good chrysocolla is always in high demand while the supply is very meager indeed.

Maricopa County, in which Phoenix is located, has large deposits of bright red jasper occurring on both sides of Camp Creek, about 19 miles north of Cave Creek. It is reported to be one of the finest jaspers in North America. Orbicular or eye patterns in contrasting shades of red are a feature of this jasper.

A very important type of amethyst crystals also occurs in Maricopa County in a large deposit in the Four Peaks about 45 miles east-northeast of Phoenix, and almost 10 miles west of Roosevelt Dam. The deposit is at the western base of the second peak at an elevation of about 6,500 feet. The mine is reached by a Forestry Service road from Roosevelt Dam and thence by foot trail. This is a trip for only the hardiest of rockhounds for it involves a long hike, reported to be 18 miles by one authority. Crystals occur in pocket walls or loose in the pocket dirt. This amethyst ranks with the very finest in the world and the author has cut two magnificent faceted stones of about thirty carats each from this material. It resembles Siberian amethyst in its rich red-violet color. Siberian amethyst, long regarded as the world's finest, has not been mined for many years. A characteristic of this particular amethyst is that it turns green when heated at high temperatures. The purple color occurs at the end of the crystals.

Sinkankas reports an interesting locality for cat's-eye quartz 10 miles southeast of Quartzite in the Plomosa Mountains of Yuma County. This is reached by turning east from Highway 95, 9 miles south of Quartzite, and then proceeding east for another 7.2 miles. The quartz crystals at this spot often contain silky inclusions, and unusual cabochons and cat's-eyes have been cut from this chatoyant quartz. The quartz crystals are colorless with pure white inclusions.

A colorful chert is also found in Yuma County 4½ miles west of the junction of Highway 95 and the road which leads from the highway to Cibola. The chert is wrongly called opalite and occurs on the side of a hill.

Scores of locations of quartz gemstones have been reported in the literature listed in Chapter 12 and the reader is urged to purchase some of these accounts if planning a collecting trip to Arizona. In addition to some of the prime locations mentioned earlier, a brief mention is now offered of scattered collecting sites in the state.

On Highway 95, 19 miles north of Blaisdell, a windmill and some ranch buildings mark the turnoff to Martinez Lake. One mile north of the windmill on this paved road one comes to a road cutting sharply westward toward the Yuma Test Station. Permission must be granted to hunt rocks but this is easily obtained, especially for Sunday hunting when no testing is being done. About 3/10 of a mile along this tank road lies a low sand mound. Almost anywhere along the road below the mound, material can be gathered, principally yellow jasper. This is the area, too, that yields a curiosity the traveler may want to take home, for this is the location of the sand spike, a stem with a ball on the end resembling a petrified war club. Some weigh as much as ten pounds and others are only finger size. This is also an area of petrified iron wood, sections of which ring like a bell when struck with an iron instrument. It is not very colorful when cut, however. This is a great collecting area and, for a distance of about a hundred miles along the river, one may gather many forms of agate and jasper. Petrified palm root can also be gathered below the sand dune. When slabbed the saw cuts through the root fibers and this makes an eye-like appearance in the slab from which interesting cabochons can be cut.

Southeast of this Martinez Lake location are the Muggins Mountains. In the foothills to the south, between Ligurta and Wellton, is a rhyolite formation containing agate veins. Very little of it is gem quality, however, although some of it contains green plume and golden moss agate. There are some black and yellow geodes. Great quantities of agate are scattered over the hills and draws and Ransom reports that all the rockhounds in the Southwest could not remove the surface material in a century, but do not be surprised if the area is cleaned out by the time you reach it. The best route to this field is Highway 80 east through Yuma. Some 4 miles east of the small community of Ligurta and about 5 miles west of Wellton, turn on a dirt road going north. The dirt road ends about 3 miles from the paved highway at the abandoned Johnson Ranch. About 3 miles east of the abandoned ranch there

Fɪɢ. 48. Brown and black section of petrified worthia (pine) wood from the Chinle formation in north central Arizona. Slab is 9" x 11". From the collection of Carl Lawrence, Claremont, California.

is a left turn in the old trail that begins at the ranch. A very rugged road leads from the turn into the foothills and at 1⅓ miles above the turn are the remains of an abandoned bentonite mine. It is recommended that cars be parked about a half mile below the mine and the rest of the journey be made on foot unless one has a four-wheel-drive vehicle. It is a good hike of about 2½ miles above the mine to an iron survey post marking four sections of land. The collecting area is north of the post, mostly in seams that must be dug out with picks and rock hammers. About 3 miles north of the town of Bouse, variegated and colorful agate has been reported.

Driving north on Highway 95 for 37.8 miles, one comes to an almost un-noticeable dirt road trailing west. This is the old freight road from the Castle Dome lead and silver mine. Proceeding 1.9 miles west along the old road, a fork branches north. From this fork until the end of the branch 2.5 miles further on, there is an extensive agate and geode field. Millions of small geodes are reported in this area, from the size of a pea to the size of a potato, very unattractive in appearance but often yielding banded and fortification agate when opened. This trip is rough going for modern cars.

The area around Cibola on the Colorado River, about 100 miles north of Yuma, is good rockhound country. There are practically no inhabitants in the area now and no accommodations for travelers, but there is plenty of good rock hunting in the surrounding hills and in the river gravels. Great varieties of chalcedony, agate, jasp-agate, jasper, and chert abound. Aside from the rock

FIG. 49. Two cabochons, both in a rich sky blue, cut by the author from Arizona chrysocolla. The top cabochon has green inclusions of malachite. From the author's collection. *(Photo by O. D. Smith.)*

interest this is a very colorful trip for the rockhound.

About 3.3 miles north of the Weaver Pass side road to Cibola, and approximately 64 miles north of Yuma, there is a dirt road marked Palm Canyon. After turning east toward the Kofa Mountains and proceeding for 5.4 miles, one comes to a good campsite. About a mile southwest of the campsite, between two low ridges, lies a good geode field with some geodes reported as big as a foot in circumference. The larger geodes are found by digging about a foot into the sand. This is very interesting country geologically, and there are many mines in the area.

Anyone making a collecting trip to Arizona will, no doubt, be interested in the hundreds of copper and other mines, for Arizona is one of our leading mining states. These mines are discussed in books about Arizona mentioned in Chapter 12. Some of the most colorful mineral specimens in the world can be recovered in the mine dumps.

One of the most interesting mining towns in America is Jerome, situated in the geographical center of the state and perched high on the side of a mountain. It was once the third largest city in Arizona but, with the shutdown of copper mining operations in 1952, it has since become a ghost city. A visit to the fantastic town is still an unforgettable experience and the area abounds in quartz mineral localities. Leaving town and driving north on the Perkinsville road, one passes many agate locations. Near Perkinsville, there is an interesting deposit of chert erroneously called pink agate.

The Colorado River is the western boundary of Arizona, separating it from California. It is across the river in Imperial and Riverside counties of California that one of the best agate collecting fields in America is located, and the Arizona visitor is urged to include that locality, which is only a few miles away from the spots mentioned earlier in this account. These areas are described under the California section in this chapter.

Recommended reading: *Arizona Gem Fields, Arizona Gem Trails, Mineralogical Journeys in Arizona.* See details in Chapter 12.

ARKANSAS

There is very little of gemological interest in Arkansas, but it is a rewarding locality for the mineral collector. At Magnet Cove there is a concentration of a great variety of mineral specimens and this is a favorite spot with mineralogists. Collectors passing through the state may wish to visit the diamond mine at Murfreesboro, where you can collect genuine diamond crystals (if you are lucky) for a small fee. These crystals occur on the surface and many really fine diamonds have been found there.

Arkansas is widely known for the great quantity and quality of its quartz crystals. While these are uninteresting as cutting material, since no colored crystals are found, they do have interest for their great beauty, and the souvenir hunter likes to collect them for use as paperweights, doorstops, and for rock gardens. These crystals are found in the mountains throughout western Arkansas; there is a great concentration of them in the Ouachita Mountains around Hot Springs National Park. As with all national parks, no collecting is permitted within the park boundaries. The best place to collect is along the ridges of the mountains, which seldom reach a height of three thousand feet and are fairly accessible at most spots.

Arkansas crystals are noted for occurring in great clusters. Always six-sided and pointed, they occur in all sizes from pincushion quartz, a variety of needle-like crystals in clusters, to candle quartz, which is a larger variety with crystals usually six times as long as they are thick.

Visitors to the state will, no doubt, be interested in Arkansas Stone or novaculite, used in making whetstones or honestones. This material is a flint-like rock consisting of millions of minute quartz crystals cemented with chalcedony. When compact and stained by iron and manganese oxides, it reportedly makes an attractive cutting material in various shades of red, yellow, orange, gray, and green. This material occurs in the Novaculite Mountains in Hot Springs county.

CALIFORNIA

California ranks with eastern Oregon as one of the two best places in the United States for the rock collector for obtaining a great variety of quartz gem specimens. This is particularly true of the desert sections of counties in Southern California — Kern, San Bernardino, Riverside and Imperial. This region is known as the Mojave Desert in the northern part and the Colorado Desert in the southern part.

The state is third among all the states in land area and almost 45 per cent of the land is still owned by the United States Government. This includes four National Parks, more than any other state, where rock collecting is not allowed. These are Kings Canyon, Sequoia, and Yosemite National Parks in east central California and Lassen Volcanic National Park in Northern California. The state also has eight National Monuments, which do not include much of the land area, except for Death Valley National Monument. The state Division of Mines reports quartz crystal minerals in 26 of the state's 58 counties and chalcedony in important quantities in 23 counties, and in some quantity in practically every county. The state is well provided with more miles of good paved roads than any other, over which travel is always good except for a few snowbound roads in the High Sierras in the winter, where little rock collecting is done at any time.

Fig. 50. Cluster of clear quartz crystals about 11″ wide from Arkansas. These are called Arkansas candles, the crystals being about six times as long as they are thick. The largest crystals in this group are about 4″. From the author's collection. *(Photo by O. D. Smith.)*

The gem bearing areas of California are so many and so well documented that to detail all of them would require a volume much larger than this one. Reference is made to the books listed in Chapter 12, but particular attention is called to the books *Gemstones of North America* and *California Gem Trails*, and to the magazines *Lapidary Journal* and *Gems and Minerals*, which give new locations almost monthly.

We shall start our journeyings at the Mexican border and work north 770 miles to the Oregon border. This is a distance on the west coast that would compare roughly to the distance between Philadelphia and Jacksonville, Florida, on the east coast, which will give the reader some idea of the great length of the state. Imperial County is in the southeastern corner of the state, west

of the Colorado River and opposite the city of Yuma, Arizona. Anyone rock-hunting in this section should also include the Arizona territory on the other side of the river. This area is adequately detailed under the Arizona section. The reader is again reminded that this is real desert country, no place for tennis sneakers and wedgies but for good stout shoes. The four deadliest creatures in the United States all live at this one spot and only at this one spot do they dwell together—the rattlesnake, the Gila monster (an enormous poisonous lizard), the poisonous scorpion, and the black widow spider. An encounter with any of these can result in a painful bite or sting and even death. The Gila monster is very scarce now in California, but the other three dangers are indeed present in great numbers. The rock-

94

hound will find plenty of company in the fall, winter, and spring months, and will seldom be far from other campers, but the summer is a dangerous time to hunt rocks in the usual 120° temperature in a waterless land. One should never go alone into this country in summer but should be accompanied by at least one other car. Death on the desert is a yearly occurrence in this territory.

Travelers from the east will enter the state on the principal southern transcontinental highway, Highway 80, which runs from Savannah, Georgia, to San Diego, California. One may wish to visit Mexico while in this vicinity and it is suggested that a stop be made at the bustling modern city of Mexicali, across the border from Calexico, California. It is not the usual border town, but a large, modern city of 172,000 people (in 1960). There are many fine motels in the towns of Holtville, Brawley, and El Centro, where one can establish headquarters for trips into the desert gem country. There are three ranges of mountains in northeastern Imperial County and in Riverside County to the north. They are the Chocolate Mountains and Palo Verde Mountains in Imperial County and the Chuckawallas in Riverside County. All of them are a vast storehouse for an apparently inexhaustible supply of a great variety of quartz-family gems. The Little Chocolate Mountains just over the northern border of Imperial County are noted for their deposits of the largest and finest geodes, with centers in red and amethyst crystals as well as clear quartz and many with colorful chalcedony-filled centers. Illustrations of these types are given here.

Probably the most sought after gem in this area is the now famous fire agate which was discovered in 1947 by two prospectors who were looking for new geode beds. At many spots in the area one may find pieces of chalcedony resembling oyster shells and locally called desert roses. Some of these roses contain brown spots and when these are carefully ground they reveal all the colors of the rainbow, fire-like flashes of color resembling the opal. These agates (really fine chalcedony) have been named fire agates and they have been used in countless beautiful rings, pendants, cuff links, bola tie mounts, and other items of jewelry. Fire agates cannot be cut and polished in the conventional way for cabochons, for too much grinding and shaping makes the fire disappear. The fire is caused by limonite inclusions near the surface and the brown sections should be sawed from the roses and then lightly ground to carefully reveal the fire.

There are several routes to the original diggings. Leaving Highway 80 on the south, proceed to Ogilby along a road that connects with Highways 60-70 at Blythe, California. This road is usually in good condition. About midway between Ogilby and Blythe is a well of water called Midway Well. Five miles north of the well is Milpitas Wash. On the north side of the wash is an old army road that goes for 23 miles in the northwesterly direction to an area known as Coon Hollow. The Coon Hollow road is a mile beyond a road that leads left to the famous Hauser geode beds. It veers to the right for 2 miles to the camp ground. Or one can come in from the north by leaving Highways 60-70 and proceeding a few miles south of Wiley Well to the Coon Hollow road. The Coon Hollow location is just over the Riverside County line in the Mule Mountains and is the best location for fire agate.

One of the greatest collecting spots in America is close by. This is the famous Hauser geode beds, named for Joel Hauser of Redlands, California. Coming south from Highways 60-70 and about .8 of a mile beyond the Coon Hollow road, one comes to what is known as the Black Hills road, which goes to the Hauser beds. Here in the Black Hills

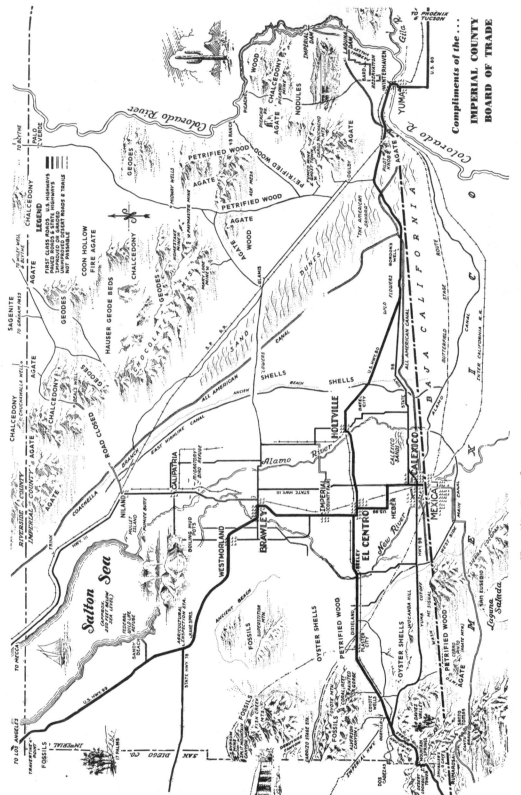

FIG. 51. Gem deposit map of Imperial County, California.
(Courtesy of Brawley Chamber of Commerce.)

96

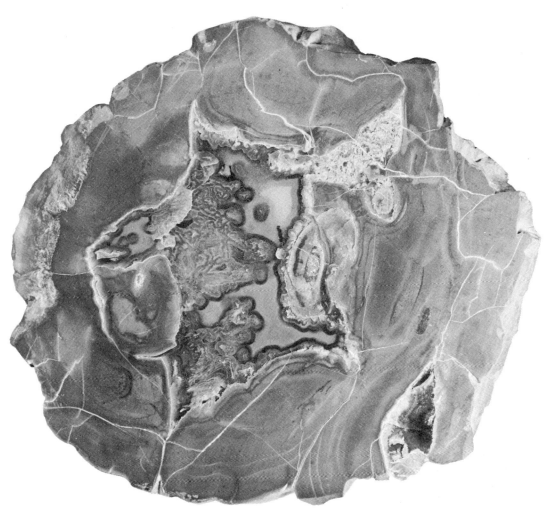

FIG. 52. A polished half of an agate nodule 8″ across from the Beal's Well district of the Chocolate Mountains in Imperial County, California. The rich brown matrix surrounds a solidly filled agate center containing very fine yellowish moss inclusions. From the author's collection. (*Photo by O. D. Smith.*)

are many locations known to the rockhounds of the Southern California clubs as the North Field (3.7 miles), the Long Beach beds (4.3 miles), the Hauser Beds, and the Potato Patch. Except in the hot summer months, it is almost impossible to go into this area and not find many collectors, some of whom are very well informed about the various beds. Friendly inquiries will reveal much information that books do not give. If you are driving east on Highways 60-70, check your mileage at Desert Center and turn off on the right at 30.9 miles, just after crossing bridge number 56-18,

and continue on a rough desert road for 12.1 miles to the Coon Hollow road, going to the left about another mile to the Hauser Beds road, going to the right. In this general area, known as the Wiley Well district, one can find practically every type of agate and chalcedony that can be found elsewhere in America, except that moss agate is scarce. Petrified wood of many types can be gathered at many spots in the eastern part of Imperial County.

East of Imperial County is San Diego County, and while this county is said to be the third largest gem bearing area

FIG. 53. A large 7″ geode from the Chuckawalla Mountains in Riverside County, California. The markings outlining the characteristic star pattern are a rich amethystine border next to a carnelian outline. The interior is beautiful quartz crystal. From the author's collection. (Photo by O. D. Smith)

in the world, it is not important to the quartz collector as the gems are in the pegmatite group—aquamarines, tourmalines, garnets, topaz, kunzite, and some rose and clear quartz. This is very important country gemologically but there is very little for the agate collector. While very fine quartz crystals occur in this county, such as pale straw yellow and very fine smoky crystals, they are found only in privately owned mines and are not available to the collector except by purchase.

North of Imperial County is Riverside County which contains many locations, none of them important. North of Riverside County is the largest county in America, San Bernardino County, with more than 20,000 square miles, the

greater part of it desert and most of it strewn with gem materials of all kinds. This county is just half the size of Ohio, and larger than the combined areas of Massachusetts, Maryland, Rhode Island, and Delaware.

To the west of Riverside county is the coastal county of Los Angeles, which contains more than 4,000 square miles of scenic coastal, mountain, and desert regions, about as large as the state of Connecticut, an area with a population of more than 6½ million in 1962. At one time the coastal towns of Redondo Beach and Hermosa Beach used to be very popular for the collection of agates and "moonstone," which is really chalcedony, but few good gemstones are found on these beaches today because the building of breakwaters and boat harbors has changed the tidal action that once cast these gems upon the beaches, especially during winter storms.

In the northwestern part of the county, adjacent to San Bernadino County, is a large desert region containing many good collecting spots. One of the best known spots is Mint Canyon. Going northeast on Highway 6 one comes to a little place called Solemint with a quaint general store that sells just about everything. East of the store 6.5 miles there is a dirt road to the right that leads into the canyon and to Tick Canyon beyond it. On the surrounding hills there are clear chalcedony nodules about the size of a lemon that yield slices of beautifully banded agate, and occasionally one finds a small piece of really fine bloodstone with small blood spots that is as good as the bloodstone from India.

One can easily spend a week in the Barstow area of the Mojave Desert in San Bernardino County and barely scratch the surface of the quartz gem deposits in the district, all within a radius of Barstow where there are plenty of good accommodations. One of the author's favorite collecting spots years ago was at Lavic, which is not a community but the name of a service stop on the Union Pacific Railroad. Driving east from Barstow on Highway 66 one soon comes to milepost number 113, a white post with black lettering. Stop the car here if you are traveling in a newer car that you do not wish to expose to desert hazards. The surrounding desert is filled with some of the best and most colorful jasper in America and a little picking with a rock pick in the sides of the banks of the gullies will uncover a great deal of material. The abundant

Fig. 54. An early photo by D. B. Sterrett of a rose quartz mine near Mesa Grande, San Diego County, California. The mine has many other gemstones. White mass on the left side of the tunnel is feldspar. Darker mass farther to the left is massive gray and rose quartz. Dark essonite garnets are in front of the man in the tunnel. Large tourmaline crystals are at the left of the picture.

Fig. 55. An interesting cabinet of nodules from California locations, most of them from the Chocolate Mountains in Imperial County. The nodule at bottom left is from Opal Mountain and the one directly above it is from Mule Canyon. Note the clock mount made from Death Valley "onyx," or travertine. From the collection of Ray Kruger. *(Photo courtesy of the Los Angeles Lapidary Society.)*

surface material that formerly existed here has long ago been gathered. Farther on, at milepost 115, there is a turnoff road into an area that is still more prolific in material. The area in the vicinity of milepost 114 is reported to have a plentiful supply and the miles beyond it should be explored. This whole area for many miles, traveling east, rewards the explorer, and it is easy hunting for there is no hill climbing or hard digging required. It is a good spot for the rockhound to explore who is not prepared by dress or equipment to go far from the beaten paths or who does not want to take the car off the macadam. Two illustrations of Lavic jasper are given here. The farther away one walks from the road, the more good material will be encountered, and those who walk as much as three miles south of the road will be rewarded with surface material even today.

To the north of Highway 91 and the city of Barstow are the Calico Mountains, a very colorful series of low mountains which are a paradise for the mineral collector. Here were some of the greatest silver mines in the country. The visitor certainly will want to visit them and see the ghost town of Calico even if no material is gathered. There are many varieties of mineral specimens that can be gathered but we shall keep to our agate story. Before getting to Calico, a poor road goes to the right to Mule Canyon and Tin Can Canyon. By negotiating a few miles of this road and going through the canyons, one comes to a basin called Calico Basin where many kinds of agate, jasper, and petrified wood abound if one digs for it.

Throughout this chapter and in Chapter 6 are illustrations of petrified palm root. This is one of the most interesting and beautiful types of petrified wood for gem cutting, for when the material is sliced through the root fibers it produces "eyes" that always give interesting patterns in colorful browns in a white to gray and cream background. When these slices are cut into cabochons they can be made into unusual rings, pins, cuff links, and bola tie slides. A large chunk makes an extra fine pair of bookends, a conversation piece in any home or office. Petrified palm root can be found at many of the wood spots in the southwestern United States, but the type in the Calico Mountains is the best of all for patterns and color. The material exists all over the area and is usually uncovered by a little digging in the sides of the hills. However, the best type is found near the town of Yermo, 12 miles east of Barstow on Highway 91. Go east through the town to the Agricultural Checking Station and proceed for another 1.3 miles. Turn left and follow the power lines until a series of confusing trails leads off in all directions. Almost any one of them will lead to wood diggings, but try to have the thrill of uncovering one of your own.

For anyone having a four-wheel-drive car, one of the most interesting trips in California is to Afton Canyon. Because of the difficulty of getting into it with ordinary cars, it is still rather virgin territory where there are many kinds of agate, jasp-agate, jasper, chalcedony, and wood. Go east from Barstow on Highway 91, the road to Las Vegas, Nevada. About 48 miles east there is a service station called Barbara's Service Station at this writing, but the name could change at any time. It is the turning off point to Afton Station, just a service stop on the Union Pacific railroad. At the station take a dirt road to the right and follow the better defined road, avoiding the side roads, until you come to the Mojave River which you will have to ford. After fording the river, it takes an expert driver to fight the sand and gravel and narrow trails into Afton Canyon in the Cady Mountains. One passes Menagerie Canyon, which is really only a small but very colorful ravine. Here are fantastic erosions resembling animals.

FIG. 56. Silhouette of Walter Kohn, well-known California agate collector, as he selects a chalcedony pebble from the beach stones at Moonstone Beach in Redondo Beach, California. *(Photo by Kenneth Reeves, Oakland, California.)*

There are many more collecting trips that can be made from Barstow, but the reader is referred to the more comprehensive trail books for additional information. The author might mention at this point that, to the right of Highway 91 on the way to the Afton Canyon trip, the hills and gullies are covered with agate and jasper float and are visited by very few people, as they push on to the well collected and documented spots. Before you start up the grade to

F<small>IG</small>. 57. Slab of Lavic jasper from San Bernardino County, California. Note the dense moss inclusions at the right and upper edges. This is one of America's most beautiful jaspers. From the author's collection. *(Photo by O. D. Smith.)*

Barbara's Station, there is an old station called Midway, approximately 45 miles from Barstow. Here you can drive off the road across the railroad and onto the mesas above the Mojave River. The author gathered his first gemstones at this spot, only small pebbles but they produced his first cabochons and some of the best in his collection.

To the north of Highway 91 there is a vast collecting area but much of it is closed off at this writing because the government will allow no collecting in the test areas they have set aside, the United States Ordnance Test Station and the Camp Irwin Military Reservation. It is in the N.O.T.S. area, at Lead Pipe Springs, that the famous blue chalcedony-filled nodules occur, one of which is illustrated here. Check when

you are in the area, for the Station may be opened again to collectors, particularly on Sunday, as it used to be.

By going 70 miles west over Highway 466 one comes to the town of Mojave, which can be the headquarters of two very interesting trips. Going north toward Reno, Nevada, on Highway 6 one comes to an entrance area to the left of the highway at about 27 miles, called Red Rock Canyon. This is one of the most scenic sights in California, with bright red eroded canyons of terrific antiquity filled with all manner of gemstones, including beautiful agate and wood. If one is lucky he may find a good opal. One of the most beautiful opals the author has ever seen was found in this canyon. If you are interested in petrified wood, one of the best collecting

FIG. 58. Block of red and white Lavic jasper with rich chalcedony markings. Found near Barstow, California. From the author's collection. *(Photo by O. D. Smith.)*

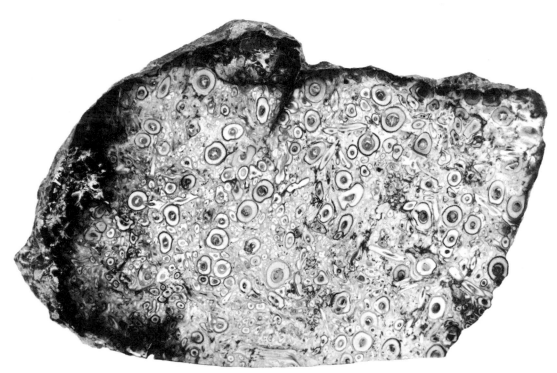

FIG. 59. Slab, 10″ x 6″, of petrified palm root from Mule Canyon, near Yermo, San Bernardino County, California. White roots with dark centers and a reddish border. Collected in 1940 by Leo D. Berner, Glendora, California.

areas in the United States is in Last Chance Canyon, especially for petrified palm. Many opals have been found here too. Just before you get to Red Rock Canyon (or you can double back a mile or so after visiting the Canyon), you turn right on a road to Randsburg, an important mining center even today. It is 5 miles to the community of Saltdale where a dirt road to the left is taken into Last Chance Canyon. The tops of the ridges in the canyon are almost solid petrified wood at many places.

Only a few miles from Mojave is the great Horse Canyon agate field in the Tehachapi Mountains. This is still one of the greatest agate collection spots in America, although the surface material has long since been gathered. Sometimes a fee is charged and sometimes no one bothers the collector. People have been shooed off, but don't be alarmed if someone attempts to do this. Pay any collecting fee if proof is shown by a collector that he has authority. Some people have grazing rights to the area and think they can, therefore, prohibit rock collectors, but grazing rights are not mineral rights and this is government land, open for prospecting to all. The area is called Horse Canyon because fossilized remains of prehistoric horses have been found here.

Going west on Highway 466 out of Mojave for 18.6 miles one comes to a road off to the right along Cache Creek. This is a desert gravel road for a mile or so and then it becomes a sandy trail after passing through a gate. This trail crosses and recrosses the creek 17 times before the canyon is reached at an elevation of approximately 1 mile and about 7 miles from the highway. The area has cold nights but always warm days. There is no water in the canyon.

The character of the country is indicated in the photo shown on page 107. There are now many holes dug by former hunters and one can just continue prospecting in any hole with good proba-

Fig. 60. Three cabochons cut by the author from petrified palm root found at the famous site near Yermo, San Bernardino County, California, described in the text. (*Photo by O. D. Smith.*)

bility that new material will be uncovered. There are many types of agate here, but it is all classified as moss agate with almost every type known in this classification . . . plume, fern, flower, moss, icicle, lace, tubes, and sagenites. Almost any day in the year one will encounter other collectors at this famous spot. If you wish to drive to Horse Canyon directly from Los Angeles, take Highway 6 for exactly 100 miles to Mojave and proceed from there.

Most California rockhounds will, at some time in their lives drive north on Highway 101 between Los Angeles and San Francisco, and certainly visitors from out of state should do so. North of Los Angeles 165 miles on Highway 101 is the very pretty city of Santa Maria with plentiful and fine accommodations, and 4 miles north of Santa Maria is the little town of Nipomo. This is the center of a vast agricultural region given over principally to the raising of beans and peas and known to California rockhounds as the bean fields. This area was once very prolific in agates, but they

105

Fig. 61. Nodule 7″ across from the Lead Pipe Springs district in Kern County, California. The matrix is red rhyolite with a crystal center of deep blue chalcedony, one of the rarest colors in agate. From the author's collection. (*Photo by O. D. Smith.*)

Fig. 62. Geode, 7″ x 6″, from the blue agate field near Lead Pipe Springs, San Bernardino County, California. Red matrix surrounding blue and white agate border around the hollow center, lined with chalcedony stalactites and a botryoidal structure background. This is the first rock ever cut by Leo D. Berner of Glendora, California, for his famous collection, which is well represented in this book.

FIG. 63. A general view of the Horse Canyon agate field in Kern County, California. The area is pockmarked with pits where rockhounds have been digging some of the finest sagenitic and moss agate in the world. *(Photo courtesy of Carl O'Baugh.)*

have become more scarce every year until now they are rather rare. It has always been the author's favorite collecting spot for two reasons: the variety of beautiful and naturally colored agates found here cannot be equaled anywhere in America; and the area is so pleasant for all-year collecting, being near the sea and mild all year, with no rugged tramping or hill climbing or digging.

This is not an all-year collecting spot, however, for no one can collect while crops are growing. Some people do once in awhile and they should be shot . . . and probably will be. There are and always will be thoughtless people who would almost commit murder for a fine agate. In bygone years the local farmers were very hospitable to the rockhounds, but a profound antagonism has arisen toward rock collectors among many of them. The farmers have now found that they have a valuable side crop in the agates they plow up each year, and many of them have agates for sale but will allow no collecting. They are almost the only ones who do have Nipomo agates for sale, for they seldom reach a dealer's shelves. Other farmers will allow collecting for a fee but will allow no collecting while crops are growing. There are always hillsides, however, where no crops are planted. The best time to collect is in the spring when fresh plowing has been done and in the fall when crops have been

Fig. 64. An early 1913 photo by D. B. Sterrett of the F. M. Myrick bloodstone mine about 45 miles northeast of Johannesburg, Kern County, California. The bloodstone occurs in the dark ridge beyond the light area and in front of the second light streak shown at the left, about the middle. The area is the same today, but the bloodstone is scarce. *(Photo courtesy of U.S. Geological Survey.)*

harvested, spring in this instance being February and fall being late August, far advanced over the eastern seasons. Collecting can be done all winter and it is particularly good during a rain, although it is vastly unpleasant because of the tendency of the gumbo to stick to one's shoes until walking is just about impossible.

It is a myth that all the agates are east of the highway, for the author has gathered beautiful material west of the highway toward the ocean. Peculiarly though, this material contained no sagenite or marcasite, characteristic of Nipomo agate. It was a unique peach color or lemon yellow (sard). On arriving in Nipomo, turn east at the little

white church and collect anywhere on the farms running back to the hills. The best collecting is done on the farms bordering the hills.

The advice is offered that any piece of agate that is picked up should be taken home. It is impossible to assay the gem value of an agate while in the Nipomo fields and any agate found there offers so much in possible beauty that it is wise to haul it home. The agates are small, seldom being larger than a lemon and most of them no larger than an almond . . . just large enough for a cabochon. Few agates are so large that they will ever require sawing. All of the agates are pieces that have broken off the formations in the hills and have been

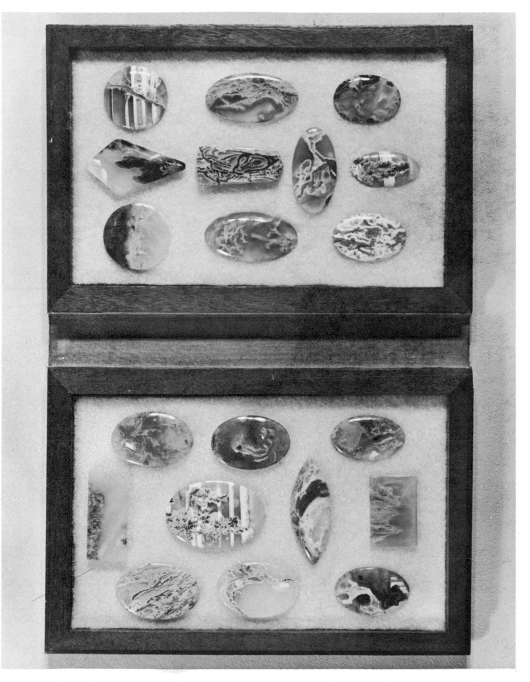

FIG. 65. Collection of superb Horse Canyon agate cabochons. The material is from Horse Canyon, Kern County, California, an area described in the text. This material was gathered and polished by Herbert L. Monlux of Fresno, California. Monlux has long been noted as one of the best amateur lapidaries in the state and has written several fine articles on cabochon cutting. If the page is turned around it will be seen that the collection is mounted in a book-like frame which does indeed fold and gives the appearance of a book. Monlux has made these "books" of materials from nearly every important location in the west and has quite a "library" of gemstones, all cut and polished by himself. *(Photo by O. D. Smith.)*

Fɪɢ. 66. Two of the finest pieces of sagenitic agate the author has ever seen. The top polished slab is 4½″ wide and contains strawberry-colored sagenitic inclusions in yellow agate with a rainbow strip of iris agate across the top. The polished slab at the bottom is 5″ wide x 6″ high and contains masses of beautiful sagenitic sprays in black and brown. The bottom is filled with marcasite inclusions. Such specimens today sell for at least $20.00 a slice if you can find any for sale. This makes the agate worth about $100 a pound, but few pounds have ever been discovered! The agate is from the bean fields around Nipomo in San Luis Obispo County, California. From the author's collection. *(Photo by O. D. Smith.)*

FIG. 67. Examples of Nipomo agates from the bean fields surrounding Nipomo, California, an area described in the text. These cabochons were cut and polished by the author from material he gathered there. They show the great variety of agates from one locality. *Number 1* is a lemon-yellow banded agate with a sagenite bud. *Number 2* is a cream-colored chalcedony with sagenite sprays. *Number 3* is a sagenite scene. *Number 4* is half peach-colored agate and half clear chalcedony, separated by a rainbow of iris agate with pink sagenitic sprays in the left half of the agate. *Number 5* is banded chalcedony. *Number 6* is deep yellow agate with red veins. *Number 7* is bluish-gray agate with sagenite inclusion. *Number 8* is a cream-colored agate with horsetail inclusions. *Number 9* is clear gray chalcedony. *Number 10* is an agate filled with marcasite inclusions. *Numbers 11 and 12* are chalcedony. *Number 13* is a high cut cabochon so filled with sagenitic inclusions that they are scarcely discernible in this photo. *Number 14* is clear peach-colored chalcedony. *Number 15* contains star-like inclusions of sagenite. *Number 16* is a yellow agate. *Number 17* is a blue agate with sagenite inclusions, one of the most beautiful agate cabochons in the author's collection. *(Photo by O. D. Smith.)*

111

FIG. 68. A very fine large cabochon of sagenitic agate from Nipomo, San Luis Obispo County, California. Found and cut by the author and in his collection. Note the dense sagenites at the right and the white spicules at the upper left. *(Photo by O. D. Smith.)*

washed down to the valley through the centuries. Only one place has been found where the agate existed in situ and that place has long ago been quarried out. It yielded great blocks of agate filled with marcasite and plumes, two slices of which are pictured here. Also pictured is a photograph of 17 types of Nipomo agate in cabochons from the author's collection.

Almost everyone going to Nipomo looks for agate with sagenitic sprays in it and if they are not discernible the agate is tossed aside. This is a great mistake for there are countless agates with no sagenitic sprays that contain beautiful marcasite, or the coloring is a rich peach shade or yellow with fortification markings. Even the white agates are attractive. Information and circumstances change from year to year, but at this writing, Frank Middleton at Nipomo has a museum and can give the latest collecting information. Dan Sheehy, Peter Melschau, and Fred Louis, ranchers, can be reached by local telephone for collecting arrangements for a small fee.

San Luis Obispo is 24 miles north of

Nipomo, and at this point the rockhound traveler will probably wish to hunt for a little California jade. Here the rockhunter can go left on Highway 1 for a scenic trip up the Pacific Coast to Monterey, probably the most scenic trip in all America. At many places along the rugged coastline are spots for gathering jade. Although most of it has been gathered by now, the sea still spews some up on the beaches from season to season. Locations are described in other books about gemstones, listed in Chapter 12.

It is unfortunate that the traveler cannot visit Stone Canyon, not far east of Highway 101 at San Miguel, 34 miles north of San Luis Obispo. It is on private property and the owners do not encourage individuals to take out jasper; only groups are permitted in from time to time. Travelers would do well, however, to inquire of California dealers for the latest information, as the picture could change at any time and it would

FIG. 69. A superb specimen of a moss agate from Nipomo, California, showing a mixture of moss and sagenite inclusions. Found and polished in a rough form by the author. *(Photo by O. D. Smith.)*

FIG. 70. A polished bookend made from Stone Canyon jasper from near San Miguel in San Luis Obispo County, California, one of the world's most beautiful and interesting jasper varieties. This piece is really jasp-agate with plentiful yellow inclusions in white chalcedony. From the author's collection. (*Photo by O. D. Smith.*)

indeed be unfortunate to miss any opportunity to visit this locality. The Stone Canyon jasper is probably the finest in America. Several examples of this beautiful brecciated jasper are given in accompanying illustrations showing cabochons and bookends.

About 180 miles north of San Luis Obispo on Highway 101 one comes to the town of Morgan Hill. Here the Llagas Creek (pronounced yah-gus) passes under Highway 101. This is 9 miles north of Gilroy or 13 miles south of San Jose if one is driving south. Here occurs another famous jasper locality where the walls of the creek are almost solid orbicular (eye) jasper, called by many other names such as California jasper, poppy jasper, and flower jasper.

While everyone calls it jasper, and

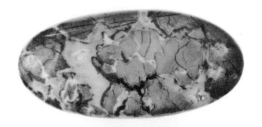

FIG. 71. Good example of the brecciated jasper from Stone Canyon in San Luis Obispo County, California. Cut and polished by the author and in his collection. (*Photo by O. D. Smith.*)

it is so labeled in many museum collections, the material is really a chert. Examples of this jasper can be seen in almost any museum in the country displaying gem rocks, for it was widely distributed to them by the late William Pitts of the California Academy of Science in San Francisco, who dedicated a long life to distributing the material, which he discovered about 1907.

Illustrations of the jasper are given at several points in this book. There are several types that are not illustrated, however. Unfortunately, all of the Morgan Hill jasper is badly fractured and few pieces of really fine lapidary work have ever been made from it. The float material that was in the creek has long been gathered and one now has to quarry rock for a fee to a private owner for every pound taken out. The situation seems to change from year to year and the reader is referred to the current owner of a fine rock shop in the village for latest collecting information. Most California rockshops have both the Stone Canyon and Morgan Hill jasper for sale.

Many of the best favored southern California locations have been covered in the foregoing account. At this point it would perhaps be wise to remind the reader that this area is the most prospected gem area in the land and every year sees a diminishing supply of good material. While none of the mentioned spots have been visited by the author for ten years, he knows from hearsay that practically no one comes home from a trip without material, and countless tons are still gathered every year by the many mineral clubs, particularly in San Bernardino and Imperial counties.

Our journeying has now brought us into Northern California where collecting is entirely different, for here we have heavy verdure north of San Francisco, with great forests and mountains that successfully hide most rock deposits. But the rocks are there, and they have not been exposed to the hordes of thousands who collect in the southern part of the state. The rockhound usually drives as fast as he can between Oregon and the deserts in the south, and completely skips the northern part of the state in his scurrying from one area of open country to another. There are almost countless quartz gem deposits in Northern California, known to local residents but poorly documented for refer-

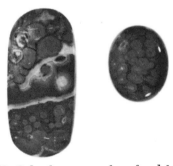

FIG. 72. Cabochon examples of red Morgan Hill jasper from near that location in California. From the author's collection. (*Photo by O. D. Smith.*)

114

FIG. 73. Slab of orbicular jasper from Morgan Hill, near Gilroy, California. This jasper, while very beautiful, is nearly always badly fractured. A gift of William B. Pitts to the Smithsonian Institution, where the slab is on display. *(Photo courtesy of the Smithsonian Institution.)*

FIG. 74. A fine example of the sagenite agate from Nipomo, near Santa Maria, California. Found and polished by Walter Kohn.

Fig. 75. Sagenite agates from the collection of Walter Kohn, who collected the agates at Nipomo, near Santa Maria, and at Horse Canyon, near Monolith, California. *(Photo by Kenneth Reeves, Oakland, California.)*

Fig. 76. An unusual agate from Palo Alto, California, showing a ruin pattern. On display at the Smithsonian Institution. *(Photo courtesy of the Smithsonian Institution.)*

FIG. 77. An early-day photo by D. B. Sterrett of the chrysoprase mine 8 miles southeast of Porterville, California. View looks north along the top of the ridge formed by an outcropping of jasper and chert. The chrysoprase (green chalcedony) has long since given out, but the jasper remains. The Porterville chrysoprase was among the world's finest and for many years was marketed exclusively by Tiffany's in New York. *(Photo courtesy of U.S. Geological Survey.)*

ence. One thing peculiar to them is that where a certain type of agate exists only that type will be found. There is no place in the northern part of the state, for instance, where one can find twenty types of agate float in a few square yards as at Nipomo or where there is as great a variety of agate rocks as in the Wiley Well district.

There is no beach collecting that is worth while in the San Francisco district, although someone is likely to refer you to Pescadero beach. Forget it. The region is surrounded with chert beds if one is interested. Some of it is highly colorful and some has eyes (spherules). Some of it is called kindradite after a local collector, a name which has established itself in the literature. Fine specimens may be had from an outcrop one mile south of Sausalito on the southeast corner of the peninsula just across the

Golden Gate Bridge. Right in San Francisco itself one can gather the spherultic chert one mile northeast of the Cliff House at the beach. The material occurs in red, brown, and green and the eyes are small and evenly distributed so that attractive cabochons can be made of it. On the way to the Northern California beaches one may wish to visit Adobe Creek, about 2½ miles east of Petaluma, and get some petrified wood and jasper.

After an unforgettable trip through the mighty redwoods, the oldest living things on earth, one comes to the coastal region between Eureka and Crescent City, still on Highway 101 after leaving San Francisco. The beach collecting is particularly good in the Crescent City area, for one is not very far from the Oregon beaches with their many miles of good agate beach locations. The agates are the same as the Oregon agates but not in as plentiful supply. One can get fine accommodations in Crescent City and then wander down to the beach at the foot of Pacific Street. The agates here have been described as lemon chrome in color and the shades of yellow seem to predominate. A noted collecting area for this sard type of agate is at Patrick's Hill, north of Eureka. All of the beaches available from the road should be explored for constantly renewed deposits of agate, wood, and jasper, in the 78 mile stretch between Eureka and Crescent City. This is particularly true during the rainy season in the winter, for this region is the rainiest district in the state. That is why the redwoods have survived.

COLORADO

Colorado is a wonderful collecting area because of its magnificent scenery and great variety of mineral specimens. It is a leading mining state. Of all land in the state, 36 per cent is still owned by the government. Agate and jasper can be found across the state and a few of the important locations are detailed here. Further reading is recommended in the book *Colorado Gem Trails and Mineral Guide*, described in Chapter 12. The state abounds in petrified forests, a good account of which is given in the book *Petrified Forest Trails*. Travelers should remember that most collecting in Colorado is done at altitudes from a mile to two miles high and that such collecting is dangerous to many people, tiring to everyone.

The Colorado plateaus west of the Rocky Mountains cover about a third of the state, extending west into Utah, Arizona, and New Mexico. This area, known as the Western Slope, is noted for its production of gemstones, more than thirty species and varieties being in plentiful supply. Because of the high altitude, this is strictly a summertime collecting area, however. The snows come early and remain late and collecting is impossible except in summer.

Good opalized wood can be gathered near the Glade Park, reached after about 13 miles on the Serpent's Trail from Grand Junction or 18 miles from Fruita by Rimrock Drive. About 4 miles from Fruita on the way to the Colorado National Monument is a hill referred to as Opal Hill or Blue Hill. After passing the golf course the first side road to the right enters the Beard Ranch and crosses a creek. Very fine opalized wood occurs here, but it must be dug out now as all surface material has been picked. This wood is reported as being very fine cutting material in various shades of yellow, green, blue, and brown.

The Colorado Plateau area is uranium country and there are many forests where some logs have been replaced with uranium rather than silica. These logs have a high concentration of uranium and other minerals. It is reported that only two logs found near Calamity Gulch enriched their finders by $350,000 but this may be one of the many myths associated with the uranium boom of the forties and early fifties when uranium prospecting was being widely encouraged. Except as curiosities the gem hunter will not be interested in this wood. It can easily be distinguished by its unattractiveness and lack of color because it is the silica content which gives to agatized wood its color and to chalcedony its translucency.

One of the most sought after quartz gem materials is petrified dinosaur bones, called "dinny bone" locally. There is an abundance of it at many spots on the Colorado Plateau and the collector should always be on the lookout for the bright red jasper-like material. A visit to one of the many local rock shops in Colorado will afford an opportunity to observe it in the rough so that the collector can identify it in the field. There are possibly a hundred

Fig. 78 An early-day photo by D. B. Sterrett of the Wild Rose rose quartz mine 5½ miles northwest of Texas Creek, Fremont County, Colorado. This view, looking south, shows the quartz outcrop, which is mostly rose colored. *(Photo courtesy of U.S. Geological Survey.)*

friendly rock shops along the highways and in the small towns of Colorado. The bone structure is clearly defined by the chalcedony replacements, especially in the black variety, and, the cabochons not only make beautiful settings for cuff links and tie clasps, but furnish wonderful conversation pieces with which to amaze one's friends. Anyone traveling through the Plateau region should certainly buy some of the material from a dealer if he is unsuccessful in finding any. Like most other gem materials, it is increasingly difficult to find any good bone on the surface at this time.

Deposits of dinosaur bone replaced by carnelian occur in Moffat County along the Green and Yampa Rivers. Much of this area is preserved for posterity in the Dinosaur National Monument. It extends into Utah where collecting is not allowed. The Monument should be visited, for here can be seen a vast graveyard of the ancient reptiles, some of which are as large as 80 feet long and 15 feet high, their entire skeletons petrified in almost pure chalcedony.

About four miles west of Fruita, Mesa County, dinosaur bone can be found eroding from the sediments of the Morrison Formation on a low bare ridge called Dinosaur Ridge. Bones also appear at the base of the cliffs at Goodman's Point near Cortez and upon the slopes of Ute Peak and McElmo Creek Valley in Montezuma County, according to Sinkankas.

Amethyst has been reported at many locations in Colorado, but little of it is really first class material color-wise. Amethyst is mined in the Red Feather Lakes district of Larimer County. It occurs at several points in Clear Creek

119

Fig. 79. An early 1910 photo by D. B. Sterrett of an agate field in Colorado. This shows the ground strewn with millions of agates, a common sight at that time in many parts of America. Most surface rocks everywhere have long since been gathered. The above field is on Curio Hill, 7 miles due south of Canon City, Colorado. (*Photo courtesy of U.S. Geological Survey.*)

County, particularly in the mines on Red Elephant Mountain in the Lawson-Dumont Mining district. The mine dumps along Trail Creek, emptying into Clear Creek about 2 miles west of Idaho Springs, are also sources of amethyst. Crystals from the latter locations are reported to be of a fine deep color.

A good collecting area is at the silver mines of the Creede District in Mineral County. Creede, at an elevation of 9,000 feet, is on Willow Creek, a short distance from its junction with the Rio Grande. This area includes at least ten mines producing massive amethyst crystals and clusters, and new materials are constantly being tossed on the dumps. According to Sinkankas, good material has been obtained from the Commodore Mine, about 1½ miles from Creede on the west side of the west

branch of Willow Creek, and from the Eunice Mine, high on the west slope of Mammoth Mountain on the east branch of the creek. However, the quantities of good material are small. Amethyst is found as linings and fillings in all of the silver mines, so that whenever the traveler sees a sign denoting silver mines in the area, it would be wise and probably fruitful to investigate the mine dumps. Much of this material is not good faceting quality but it is an amethystine quartz that is very attractive when cut into cabochons. This poorer quality is colloquially known as "sow-belly" quartz.

There are other quartz gem varieties in this area that are easily available. By going north of Monte Vista on the Gunbarrel road about 18 miles and turning west on the La Garita road, going to the

120

little village of that name and then turning north for about a mile, one comes to a small road turning left into the hills. The road leads up a canyon to a closed mine. This locality is known as Crystal Hill and the hillsides and mine dumps yield interesting crystals of quartz. One may find an occasional crystal with a water bubble in it. These are called enhydros.

By retracing one's course to La Garita a good geode location can be reached. Go south along the edge of the mountains for about two miles, where you will encounter La Garita Creek. Turn up a road that follows the creek and go into the hills. About three to four miles farther on is a good geode location on the surrounding hills.

An interesting lace agate location can be reached by following these directions: Go south of Alamosa to Antonito and take the highway that leads up the Conejos River and over Cumbress Pass. Cross to the right bank of the river and proceed through Mogote. About 20 miles above Antonito the highway recrosses the river and goes over the pass. About a quarter of a mile beyond the river, leave your car and climb up to the rocky point you will observe on the left side of the road. A further climb to the rockslide area and you will be ready to search for the lace agate. Some very fine pieces for cabochons can be found, but most of the agate is only suitable for paper weights or bookends.

East of the Rocky Mountains, on the plains leading down to the Mississippi River, there are many great areas of petrified wood, whole forests still standing in some areas. Much of this is good

FIG. 80. An early 1913 photo by D. B. Sterrett looking at the downdraw from the smoky quartz mine of the right hillside. This view is from a half mile north of the old Crystal Peak Gem Co. Camp 6 miles northwest of Florissant, Teller County, Colorado. Copelen Dome is on the left and the Tarryall Mountains are in the distant center. (Photo courtesy of U.S. Geological Survey.)

FIG. 81. Banded agate with quartz crystal center from Colorado. On display at the Smithsonian Institution. *(Photo courtesy of the Smithsonian Institution.)*

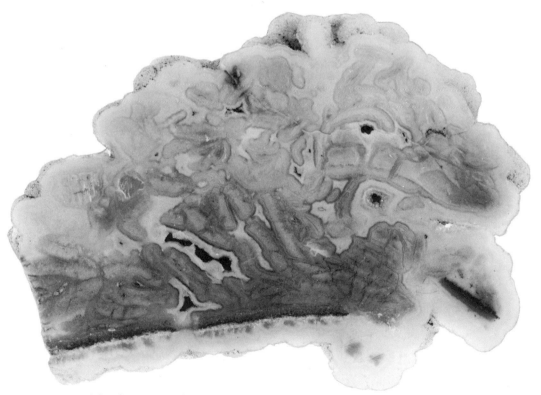

FIG. 82. Slab of an unusual agate pattern from Larimer County, Colorado. On display at the Smithsonian Institution. *(Photo courtesy of the Smithsonian Institution.)*

jasper and opal wood and fine for cutting. Near Florissant is the world's most remarkable group of standing fossilized trees. Inquiry at almost any gasoline station in the smaller communities will usually reveal information about nearby wood localities. A rock shop in any area is a strong indication that gem materials are not far away, for rock shops are usually started where local material is available.

The traveling rockhound in Colorado is urged not to miss a visit to Gem Village, two miles west of Bayfield and in the "four corners" regions of southwestern Colorado where the states of Colorado, Utah, Arizona, and New Mexico all meet. This village is a rockhound's paradise. Now about twenty-five years old, it contains the rock shops of many old timers who have accumulated vast stores of rocks and knowledge. There are motel accommodations and restaurants plus a concentration of rocks for sale in several shops that can be matched at no other locality in the country. Gem Village is on the Navaho Trail or U.S. Route 160. The traveler on popular Route 66 should turn north on Highway 666 at Gallup, New Mexico, and go to Cortez, Colorado, and then proceed 63 miles east on Highway 160. Information on collecting areas is freely available. The Village is a good take-off spot for the Creede amethyst mines mentioned above, about 108 miles east and north on good roads.

CONNECTICUT

(See the special section covering the New England states, p. 139.)

DELAWARE

There are no important references in the literature regarding any kind of quartz gem minerals in this state.

FLORIDA

It is unfortunate that this land of tourists and the retired has little to offer the rockhound, for gem minerals do not exist in Florida with the exception of fossilized coral at Tampa Bay. It is usually a surprise to most mineral collectors to learn that Florida is 28th in importance among the states mineralogically. However the minerals have only commercial interest and produce no spectacular specimens. There is little romance in cement and metallic ores recovered from sand.

The state is a paradise for the shell collector but offers nothing for the gem mineral collector except the coral mentioned above. It is an axiom among rock collectors that the uglier a gem is in outward appearance the more beautiful it is likely to be on the inside. This is certainly true of the agatized coral of Florida, for there is probably no rock that is uglier in appearance than the Tampa material or more rewarding when cut and polished.

Small quantities have been reported at several locations but most of them are not open to public collecting. The principal collecting area is at Ballast Point, located on a small projection of land on the west side of Hillsborough Bay, the northeastern arm of Tampa Bay. This location has been known to collectors since 1825 but it still continues to yield good material to the persistent collector who is content to wallow in the mud and mire of the bay and dig for specimens of these ugly and unimpressive geodes. The geodes are usually about twice as long as they are wide and rarely spherical like other geodes. The average size is 3 to 4 inches across; specimens over 6 inches are rare. The specimens of coral are ¼ to ½ inch thick, and the interiors present a wide and beautiful selection of forms of wax-like translucent chalcedony. They have tiny quartz crystals in brown, gray, and black. Some geodes have several small chambers, some of which are lined with botryoidal concretions covered with an opal-like material.

When sawed lengthwise the polished halves are beautiful and among the most interesting of display specimens, although they are unfit for gemstones. Several important finds have been reported from Tarpon Springs in Pinellas County and at Bailey's Bluff, south of New Port Richey in Pasco County. Other varieties of quartz-family gems do not exist in Florida because there are no large rivers to transport material from other sections of the country and there are no areas of past volcanic activity.

GEORGIA

Many gem varieties are found in Georgia, but it is not a rich area for quartz gems. Diamonds have been reported in 15 counties and sapphires and rubies in 3 counties each. Amethyst is fairly well distributed throughout the state but little of it is of cutting quality and most of it is in private hands. Jasper can be collected in the ditches of southern Bartow County, south of Kingston, and all over the area in the vicinity of Salt Peter Cave.

The most interesting quartz varieties in Georgia are the star quartz and rose quartz found at the Mineral Processing Company's mine, 8 miles south of La Grange and a mile south of Smith's Crossroads on the west side of Highway 219 in Troup County. This material is a pale pink but some of it is flawless and can be faceted or cut into star cabochons and spheres. Many amateur lapidaries cut a star stone from this material, enameling the back of the stone blue, or making a doublet by cementing a piece of blue mirror to the back. The result is a "star sapphire" of great beauty that can fool almost anyone and even a few experts. The author possesses a ring set with such a stone which has caused wide comment on its beauty.

Silicified oolite occurs at Fincher Bluff in Murray County. This is an interesting material in which small spheri-cal concretions in limestone have been replaced by silica. The locality may be reached by a dirt road leading north from Hooker School. Material has been gathered from the road cuts in this area, particularly along Highway 225 between Sardis and Spring Place. Red oolitic jasper occurs in cuts along Tarr Creek near Dalton.

HAWAII

There are no quartz gems in our newest state, indeed no gem materials at all except some very small peridots, and some black coral recovered by divers from an ocean depth of about 200 feet.

IDAHO

If requested to name the one area in which the rockhound would be most likely to find gem materials, the author would unhesitatingly name Idaho because it abounds in gem minerals and has not been scoured too thoroughly by rock hunters through the years. Almost 65 per cent of the land area is in the public domain and open to prospecting. Most rock travelers scoot through the state to get to Montana or Oregon or Washington where the pickings are supposed to be the best. However, no state in the country can top Idaho as a collecting area, and it is particularly rich in the quartz varieties of gem materials. Indeed the state is called the "gem state" and not the "potato state" as many believe.

Collecting is more difficult in Idaho, however, for there are not many paved highways and the best collecting areas must be reached by four-wheel-drive vehicles or the new scooters which are becoming increasingly popular for travel in unpaved areas. By leaving the paved highway and exploring contiguous territory, the hunter can usually find good material at almost any spot in the state. There are hundreds of canyons and almost every one of them yields

FIG. 83. An early 1910 photo by D. B. Sterrett of an opal mine in light-colored porphyry rock located 4 miles northwest of Enterprise, Owyhee County, Idaho. *(Photo courtesy of U.S. Geological Survey.)*

fine cutting material *if* . . . you can find a way to get down into them. There are hundreds of documented gem localities and only a few can be mentioned here because of lack of space. The reader is urged to read the book *Northwest Gem Trails* as a good source of supplemental information. See Chapter 12 for other book titles.

There is one quartz gem that the rockhound will surely seek when visiting Idaho and that is the most beautiful of all—the opal. Good gem quality opal specimens have been found at many widely scattered locations in many counties and Idaho is the most likely prospecting country for opal in all of North America.

Among the many opal prospects reported in Idaho, attention is called to a few that are fairly easy to reach, although in all cases digging is required. There is probably no greater thrill in gem hunting than finding a genuine

opal with all its fiery hues. Opal occurs in a clay-like material a short distance from Marsing. This is known as the Mule Springs deposit and it is reached by going toward Homedale, turning left at the abanded "Y" Inn, an old cinder block building. After reaching Graveyard Point, turn left on the canal road at that place and cross the canal bridge about 2 miles further on, backtracking on the other side about 3/4ths of a mile to the diggings. This opal sometimes contains bars or streaks of red, green, and blue fire. It is reported to cut very well but to be hard won and scarce. Interesting cherry opal in matrix is found near Black Canyon Dam at Emmett. Go toward Horseshoe Bend from Emmett until you pass a small pond with surrounding fruit trees on the left. Follow a trail that passes the pond to the mouth of a large canyon. About a mile up the canyon one comes to the old diggings on the left side. Pieces of opal containing

FIG. 84. Two scenic cabochons cut from gray-green Clearwater picture stone from Idaho. Enlarged to show detail. From the author's collection. *(Photo by O. D. Smith.)*

bright red and green fire, up to the size of a thumb nail, can be chipped from the rock walls. The rock is soft and easily worked.

Another deposit of opal near Marsing is found in a perlite formation. At this writing no one has done much digging in the formation, which is reported to be about 1000 square feet. More specific information about this location is not available except by local inquiry.

A new local material, named Fryite after a local rockhound, contains streaks of fire opal in a black matrix. Follow the north side of the Snake River about 8 miles downstream from Lewiston. The material is found on the weathered basaltic hillsides. Continuing downstream for about another 3 miles, one comes to the gravel pits at Silcot on the other side of the river. Park the car at a stile, climb over it, and proceed on the trail up a steep hill. Several caves are near the top, carved in solid basalt. These caves have yielded some fine opal to prospectors equipped with 16 ounce hammers and rock chisels. Revealed vesicles in the basalt often yield fire opal nodules.

One of the best collecting areas is the canyon of the Bruneau River where the famous Bruneau Canyon jasper can be found. This area is best visited in the fall or the early spring, for the snows in the winter and the heat (and snakes) in the summer prohibit collecting. Reaching the canyons calls for driving over miles of rocky trails. Starting at Mountain Home Air Force base, southeast of Boise, turn off Highway 30 and proceed on Highway 51 south and southeast to get into the Bruneau River country. If you happen to be coming from the east, turn off Highway 30 south of Buhl and go to Castleford, then west across Salmon Falls Creek to Balanced Rock. A dirt road leads west and a turn to the southwest takes you to the river canyon. Local guides can be secured for a modest fee and it is wise to engage one.

Lewiston is sometimes referred to as the gateway to Hell's Canyon, a prolific collecting area. Peculiarly, it has a year-round mild climate. In the vicinity of the junction of the Snake and Clearwater Rivers is one of the best gem hunting areas in the United States. The gravel bars along the Clearwater River between Dent and Lewiston yield a controversial jasper-like material erroneously called gem sillimanite. This appears to be jasper with sillimanite inclusions which give the material a fine fibrous fur-like structure. In the same gravel bars are small boulders of a chert-like material called Clearwater Picture Stone. This is a most unattractive rock in the rough and likely to be by-passed by most collectors. It is gray with black stripes through it. However, when it is cut and polished, it yields some of the most fantastic "pictures" and scenes that the author has ever seen in a gem rock. The scenes are opaque in pastel shades. There are many agates at this spot too, identified by crescent shaped markings on the surface.

While garnet is not one of the quartz gems, it is fairly common almost everywhere. The world's finest star garnets occur in Idaho and no doubt most agate seekers will want to gather some. They not only exhibit the conventional four-ray star, but many of them have a six-ray star. Instructions on how to orient the stars and how to cut them can be found in most books about gem cutting and it certainly seems wise to haul home any garnets that are encountered, for they do cut into very beautiful stones even when stars are not present. The garnets are fairly large and occur as large as 2 inches in diameter. They are easily recognized for their many sides or faces and they are a dark red, almost black in appearance. While they are likely to occur in sandbars along many of the rivers and creeks, they are reported to be fairly plentiful along Emerald and Ruby Creeks in Latah County in the northwest part of the state. Many other locations of garnets,

wood, agates, jasper, and other quartz gems are mentioned in the travel books listed in Chapter 12. Particularly good information can be had in the book *The Rock Collector's Nevada and Idaho,* by Darold J. Henry. None of this information has been abstracted here.

ILLINOIS

Illinois has a fair number of mineral varieties for the mineral and fossil collector but practically nothing for the quartz collector and nothing at all of value to the gemcutter. Chert, formed as pebbles and cobbles, is found in some gravels but it is not gem quality. About the only things of interest to the quartz collector are the geodes found on the Illinois side of the Mississippi River. These are, of course, similar to the Iowa geodes on the western shores of the river but they are not nearly as abundant as they are in Iowa. The shores of Calhoun County yield a fair amount of material when the river is low. The geodes reportedly appear abundantly in the Warsaw formation near Warsaw, Hamilton, and Nauvoo in western Illinois. They are found as round balls eroded from the creek banks and rolled in the stream beds. About 10 per cent of the Illinois geodes are lined with botryoidal chalcedony; rarely a geode will be lined with pale amethyst crystals of no gem value. About 80 per cent of the geodes are lined with

FIG. 85. A petrified wood limb section from near Blanche, Idaho. The interior of the agatized wood is clear milky chalcedony. On display at the Smithsonian Institution. *(Photo courtesy of the Smithsonian Institution.)*

127

quartz crystals and milky quartz but they have no value except as curiosities. They can be gathered for a small fee at a location near Nauvoo.

INDIANA

Indiana is another state that yields nothing for the gem collector. Here and there one may find an occasional agate washed down in the glacial drift, but the only quartz materials available are the geodes. Almost any farmer will tell you if he has these on his farm and, if he has, he most likely will allow you to search for some, particularly at plowing time. Agate and jasper may be collected in sparse amounts in the Fort Wayne area.

IOWA

Silicified or agatized coral occurs in Iowa that is similar in appearance to the "Petoskey stones" from Michigan, except that the latter are calcified and not silicified. While the material is widely distributed, and at no spot very plentiful, it is reported to be rather easily found on farms in the vicinity of Coralville.

Many agates have been found in Iowa, but they are not very plentiful now unless new gravel deposits are opened. The best collecting area is south of Muscatine where a large alluvial flat has been explored for a long time because of its gravel deposits. These agates are of the fortification type and are called Lake Superior agates, as they originated in that area and were washed down the Mississippi River valley. Most of these agates are small, although some have been reported as large as a grapefruit. The average size is about a half inch in diameter. Local inquiry about the location of gravel pits usually develops good information and collecting agates in the Muscatine area is an easy matter compared to traveling in the desert regions of the west. The Lake Superior agates are noted for their con-

trasting colors between bands and are the favorite of many collectors.

Most rock collectors visiting Iowa are interested in the geodes which abound in the region. These are not gem-like but always interesting. The beds occur near Keokuk in a broad area where the Des Moines and Mississippi rivers meet at the junction of the three states of Iowa, Illinois, and Missouri. Many hundreds of tons of the quartz lined geodes have been hauled from the beds by collectors and there seems to be an inexhaustible supply. Most of the geodes are on private land, but permission to hunt for them is usually granted after inquiry at the farm house. The geodes vary in size, but most of them range from the size of a lemon to that of an orange, although geodes have been found that weighed several hundred pounds. They are not all lined with quartz crystals but many have a great variety of other minerals, even oil. Fine geodes have been reported from locations in northern Iowa, but information is vague. It is probably safe to say that geodes occur generally all over the state and local inquiry at gasoline stations and motels will surely uncover some good locations that have not been visited too often.

Fragments of petrified wood are fairly common in the stream gravels. A beautifully banded colored chert occurs in the limestone formations at the southern edge of Mount Pleasant in Henry County.

Any gem seeker passing near West Bend will certainly want to see the Grotto of the Redemption constructed by Father Doberstein over a period of forty years up to the time of his death about ten years ago. The Grotto is still under construction. It is built from very fine mineral specimens, especially crystal varieties, and the Cradle of the Nativity in the Grotto is valued at more than a quarter of a million dollars. Many of the fine quartz crystal groups were gathered from Jewel Cave in South Dakota before it became a National Monument.

KANSAS

Kansas is noted for its beautiful crystal mineral specimens, which are in practically every important museum in America and in many foreign museums. However, the state is poor in the quartz group of minerals and especially poor in gem quality materials. The collector traveling through the state might better push on to more fertile areas but the resident of Kansas can be rewarded by examining the gravels of any stream near him for bits of petrified wood and agate. Chalcedony has been reported in the gravels of practically all of the streams of western Kansas, particularly the Smoky Hill River, the Cimarron, Arkansas, Pawnee, and Solomon Rivers. The best collection area is reported to be along the Smoky Hill River in Trego, Gove, Logan, and Wallace counties. A variety of opal called moss opal has been reported as being found in Trego County, but the location is not known to this writer. It is common opal with black fern-like markings or dendrites resembling black moss agate, and this is the only location known in the world.

KENTUCKY

Nothing of interest in quartz gem localities has been reported from this state.

LOUISIANA

There is little of gemological interest in Louisiana. The collector who lives there can have a lot of fun exploring the creeks and rivers in a boat, and local rockhounds usually have a trailer hauling a small boat so that they can examine the gravel bars of the streams. There are many varieties of agate and petrified wood to be found, but they have all been transported great distances down the rivers and, by the time they tumble into Mississippi and Louisiana, they are so small as to be practically valueless as gemstones. Out of state rockhounds coming west via Highway 80 might better push on across Texas and spend their collecting time in west Texas, New Mexico, Arizona, and Southern California where the collecting is abundant.

MAINE

(See the section covering the New England states, p. 139.)

MARYLAND

Nothing of importance regarding quartz gems in Maryland has ever been reported.

MASSACHUSETTS

(See the section covering the New England states, p. 139.)

MICHIGAN

There are a great many rockhounds and lapidary clubs in Michigan and the author had the great pleasure of organizing the very important and successful Michigan Lapidary Society (Detroit) in October, 1949. There is, however, very little of gemological interest to be found in the state. The quartz group is restricted to the gathering of Lake Superior type agates on the beaches of the Keeweenaw Peninsula. These also abound on Isle Royale but, since this area was made a national park in 1940, collecting is no longer allowed there.

Collectors will hear locally of the Petoskey "agates" found in the vicinity of Petoskey, and they may want to collect some of these interesting rocks, which make beautiful paperweights when polished as is. These "agates" are not agates but calcium formations of petrified coral. They do, however, closely resemble a similar material found in Iowa and elsewhere which is really silicified or agatized.

While searching the lake beaches, collectors should keep their eyes alert for

Fig. 86. Paperweight made from calcified coral from near Petoskey, Michigan. Erroneously called Petoskey "agate." A similar agatized form does occur, however, in Iowa. Enlarged to show detail. From the author's collection. *(Photo by O. D. Smith.)*

thomsonites and chlorastrolites, which are not quartz but are very interesting curio gemstones. In visiting any of the many rock shops in the Peninsula, you should ask to see these stones so that you become familiar with their appearance and can be on the lookout for them.

Geologists claim that about 125 million years ago a volcanic eruption near what is now Minneapolis formed Isle Royale and the Keeweenaw Peninsula. The local agates have been washed out and eroded from this lava flow. The Michigan agates are beautifully marked with fine bands, sometimes as many as 20,000 to the inch, and they occur in all colors. The most sought after are the purple banded agates with thinner bands of clear chalcedony or milk-white or cream. Only a few of these are found each year

at Seven Mile Point Beach. Another rare agate is the black and white onyx found at Black Creek Beach where the creek enters Lake Superior.

All beaches on the Lake Superior side should be prospected. The agates are plentiful, but selection of good ones is desirable. While some agates have been found as large as ten inches in diameter, the average size is less than two inches.

An interesting jasper-like material called jaspilite is found in abundance in the Porcupine Mountains of Ontonagan County. The basic jasper material is laced with bands of steely hematite of the variety known as specularite and it presents a handsome appearance when polished. Fortunately, this material occurs in masses big enough for spheres and bookends.

MINNESOTA

Minnesota is an abundant source of the Lake Superior agates mentioned above in the Michigan account. While some agates as large as fourteen pounds have been reported, the bulk of them are less than 1½ inches in circumference. They vary greatly in pattern and coloring and are high among the favorites with amateur lapidaries, as they make beautiful settings for pendants, rings, bracelets, and pins. There are many specific locations given in the books mentioned in Chapter 12, but locations are not difficult to find, as inquiry at local gas stations and stores will usually establish the fact that a gravel pit is nearby and a visit to it will certainly result in a good supply of agates. As in other localities, stream beds and lake shores are always productive of good material. A fortunate fact about the Lake Superior agates is that, at any one location, one may find a great variety in pattern and color with the fortification type predominating.

A quartz gemstone that is unique to Minnesota is a crystalline quartz replacement of fibrous goethite. This material presents a unique chatoyancy when polished. This is caused by light reflections from millions of tiny fibers embedded in quartz. The material is variously called binghamite (after its discoverer) and silkstone, although binghamite is about 98 per cent quartz and silkstone is somewhat less. Some stones are stained mahogany-red by hematite and some are stained yellow by limonite. When the fibers are arranged parallel, some fine cat's-eye gems can be cut. Both gems occur sparingly as quartz seams in the iron ores of the Cayuna Range near Crosby and Ironton in Crow County according to Sinkankas. The quartz seams are seldom more than 6 inches thick. Material has been found on the dumps of the Arco and Portsmouth Mines.

MISSISSIPPI

While agates and petrified wood can be found in the stream gravel bars, Mississippi is not a good collecting area, although residents can be rewarded by exploring their own area's streams. None of the quartz materials are in situ, but all have been washed down from the north.

MISSOURI

Missouri is a great area for the collector of spectacular and showy crystal mineral specimens but it has little to offer the agate collector. The area around Joplin is the center of the tri-state lead mining district extending into Kansas and Oklahoma. The traveling rockhound passing through the area may wish to purchase some of the spectacular specimens for his own collection or for swapping for quartz materials farther along the journey. Numerous rock shops are along the highways, particularly on Route 66.

The quartz geodes described under the Iowa section occur in the bluffs along the Fox River near St. Francisville and Lake Superior type agates are found in the Mississippi River gravels. According to Sinkankas a compact chert is found in Dade and Benton counties where beds have been exposed by road grading along the tops of a number of low hills at the western edge of the Ozark Mountains. The farms around Doniphan on Highway 160, southwest of Poplar Bluff and just over the Arkansas line, are productive of a gemmy flint in many colors that polishes well. The small streams in the Doniphan area, and particularly the Current River, have much material in their gravel bars.

MONTANA

Montana is the land of a world-famous variety of moss agate known everywhere as "Montana agate." The agate is in the form of gray chalcedony nodules shaped

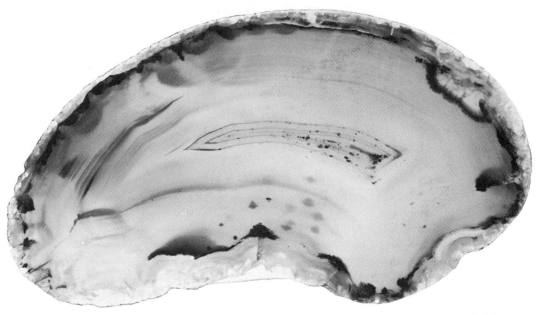

Fig. 87. Half of a large moss agate nodule from Montana. The material is a rich blue chalcedony with dendritic or "moss" inclusions. From the author's collection. (*Photo by O. D. Smith.*)

somewhat like potatoes and about their size. The chalcedony is shot through with manganese oxide and when the agates are sliced they present scenes of black mossy inclusions resembling mountains, trees, ferns, bushes, lakes, clouds, figures, and other objects. These inclusions tend to produce some wonderful scenes. There are dozens of shops throughout the state featuring jewelry made from the agates. Rockhounds who have no cutting equipment can arrange to have their agate finds cut on the spot at many of these shops and then make a selection of patterns to be further cut and polished and mounted in jewelry and sent home. The stones make particularly fine and interesting ring and cuff link settings.

Montana is a very large state and about 30 per cent of it is still in the public domain, but the agates occur in only a very small part of it, principally in the area beginning a few miles west of Miles City on Highway 10 and extending for about 140 miles west along the Yellowstone River to Billings. Some

agate can be found farther along the river up into Wyoming where the river rises in Yellowstone National Park and flows north. Between Billings and Miles City the river is a swift stream because it falls rapidly, and new material is constantly being revealed. The foregoing is the best collecting area but collecting is also good as far as the junction of the Yellowstone River with the Missouri River, just northeast of the North Dakota line. Collecting is also good along the Big Horn and Little Horn Rivers, and the Powder River running north into the Yellowstone.

The place to hunt for Montana agates if the river is too swift for wading on the bars is in the dry washes and in the hills bordering both sides of the river. A particularly likely area is the section north of the river and east of Fallon, where agate has been plentiful in the past in the side streams of Hatchet, Crackerbox, Whoop-up, and Sand creeks. The agates there are now reported scarce, but when found they are of the best type. The best time of the year to

132

hunt is in April before the grass grows to cover the agates exposed on the hill-tops during the previous winter's storms. In the summer few agates will be found on the bare south slopes of the hills but many can be found by careful search in the tall grass on the north side.

There is a warty nodule that is plenti-ful and also looks like a potato, but these rocks seldom produce any gem material and many a collector has hauled home a load of this worthless junk. The smoother the agate surface the more likely it is to be good. Almost every type of agate ever heard of, and just about every color, has been found in the Yellowstone Valley, but this is the exception rather than the rule.

Slice for slice, good Montana agate brings the highest prices in the agate market. Many agates have produced slices a few inches in area that have sold for as much as $10.00 a slice. A good sized "potato" will yield perhaps ten slices, which makes the agate worth $100, a good price indeed for any rock. But, remember, that is after the agate is slabbed. Before it is slabbed, it is a bigger gamble than picking a good cantaloupe. If you happen to see a dredge working the river, do try to get permission to go through some of their gravel, for you will undoubtedly get a bucketful of good agates in short order. Be sure, too, to examine thoroughly any new road cutting activity or old road cuts. Do not fail to gather any broken pieces of agate, for these often yield some of the finest gemstones and it is better to have some good broken pieces than miss the boat altogether just because you did not find a whole "potato."

All over Montana, and not necessarily in the agate country, the traveler will find rock shops selling the agates in the rough. Be wary of buying whole agates, for the vendor has understandably high-graded his material and picked the best for his jewelry-making activities. Most of the dealers are busy all winter making

jewelry for sale in the summer and they have their private hunters, usually mem-bers of their families or neighbors, out hunting the streams and hills early in April and on through the summer to keep up a needed supply. These same dealers are anxious, too, to buy your surplus finds if they are good; and most of them, to the author's personal knowledge, are reliable and will not take advantage of the ignorance of the hunter. If you have a surplus for sale, it would be wise to see what the dealer offers and what he charges so that you can more fairly judge any offer he may make, remembering that agates are a business with him and only a hobby with you. He is entitled to his fair profit and he takes a great gamble on your uncut material.

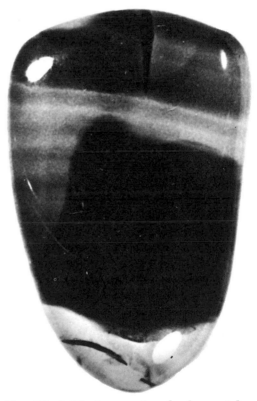

FIG. 88. A Montana agate cabochon cut by the author. A beautifully colored agate, it shows the sunset in red over the Rock of Gibraltar in black dendritic inclusion. En-larged to show detail. (*Photo by O. D. Smith.*)

133

At this point it seems wise to offer some slight advice on the proper cutting of these fine agates in the event that the reader may find and want to process his own agates. Authorities report that the first thing to do is to look into the rocks as far as possible with a strong light to determine which way the moss or banding layers lie. Light cuts taken off an end or a side, at right angles to the layers, will then reveal whether the best scene or effect can be obtained by slabbing from end to end or from side to side. Nearly all of the rocks are cracked, some only a half inch in depth, and these cracks have to be taken into consideration when sawing to get the largest slices with the best dendritic or color effect from the fracture.

Sometimes it looks as if nothing can be salvaged, but by turning the rock sidewise about 90° in the saw and taking a cut or two, some solid material may be found. About the time one is ready to abandon sawing an unpromising rock, one may encounter the fine spray he is looking for, so do not give up too easily. This is particularly true of the milky chalcedony type which one cannot see into. Do not saw the agate through the middle on the first cut, as is usually done with thundereggs and geodes. This would probably ruin the agate because the best sprays lie at the center. Some of the finest scenes and figures are found by sawing through large and thickly formed dendrites. This type of inclusion is usually widely spaced through the rock and in clear material, so that it can be picked out and the saw cuts figured to cut through the dendrites.

In recent years a new agate has been discovered in Montana that has been named Dryhead agate. This is a fortification type agate with alternating red and white bands. It is distributed over a wide area in southern Montana and northern Wyoming in the Bighorn River basin, but the agate areas are in the Crow Indian Reservation and on pri-

vately owned ranches that are only reached by jeeps or four-wheel-drive vehicles, and of course by hiking and horseback. This is one of the most glorious and beautifully scenic areas of the United States and certainly should be visited by those equipped to do so. The area is well marked on any good road map. It is best reached by any of the dirt trails running east from Highway 310, which branches off Highway 10 about 17 miles west of Billings. Good trails go to Pryor and Dryhead. If the traveler visits the Custer Battlefield National Monument, a trail west to Saint Xavier beginning at Lodge Grass, south of the Monument, leads into the Dryhead country and Crow Reservation. The best place to look for the Dryheads is on the tops of ridges, where the agates are reportedly plentiful at spots on the surface. This is exciting rockhunting but only for the avid rockhound who is equipped for adventure and outdoor living.

Montana is famous for its cornflower blue sapphires, some of which may be gathered by paying a collecting fee, but this account is about quartz gems only and the reader is referred to other books in Chapter 12 giving accounts of the sapphire diggings. The amethyst collector, however, will find fine specimens and clear quartz crystals in several amethyst localities in Jefferson County to the east of Butte. Turn north from Highway 10 at Milepost 19 and drive about 5 miles to the Homestake mining district. Commercial amethyst mines have been developed for many years and many fine quality gems have been mined. Many of the quartz crystals in the district are by-products of the gold mines, and the dumps of these mines often yield gem quality crystals. Some of the best deposits are reportedly on the west side of Rider Creek.

Many types of chalcedony, petrified wood, jasper, and chert are generally distributed all over the state, and it is a

Fig. 89. Cabochon cut from Montana moss agate, 1¾″ x 1¼″, showing characteristic scene of snow and trees. From the collection of Leo D. Berner, Glendora, California.

wonderful area for personal prospecting. Sand bars in streams and gravel pits on dry land should be explored wherever encountered.

NEBRASKA

While there are a great many Nebraska rockhounds who can show impressive collections of the quartz gems of their state, the state itself holds little of interest to the traveling rock collector, who is usually anxious to get to the more productive areas of Colorado, Wyoming, or South Dakota nearby. Some of the old Fairburn agate fields of South Dakota extend down into Nebraska and these beautiful agates have been found near Crawford and Harrison. See the South Dakota section for an account of these agates.

One of the best collecting areas is supposed to be about 18 miles south of Omaha where the Platte River joins the Missouri River at Plattsmouth. An area on both sides of the Platte River for about 75 miles upstream is supposed to be very productive of banded and moss agates and chert pebbles in the gravel pits and gravel bars. Agate and jasper are found in the gravel pits near Fairbury and Steele City in Jefferson County and petrified wood is found in the gravel

pits near Johnson, Nemaha County, according to Sinkankas.

At the Agate Springs fossil quarries near the small town of Agate in western Nebraska, fossils are preserved in chalcedony. Other good rock deposits are reported near the towns of Rushville, Chadron, and Crawford in northwestern Nebraska, according to Zeitner.

NEVADA

Nevada offers very great opportunities for the gem hunter, for it is a vast, relatively unexplored, area abounding particularly in petrified wood. In the author's opinion, Nevada produces the most beautiful quartz or silica gemstone in North America—the famous opalized wood of northern Nevada's Virgin Valley. These opals are among the world's most glorious and more money has been spent for museum specimens of Nevada's opal than for any other gemstone found in North America, it is believed by several authorities. The Smithsonian Institution in Washington and Cranbrook Institute at Bloomfield Hills, Michigan, have very rich displays of this fire-like opal that are entrancingly beautiful.

The difference between opal and other quartz gems is that opal is silica in an amorphous form. That is to say, it has

135

Fig. 90. A 1913 photo by D. B. Sterrett of the Mathewson or Dow opal mine in the Virgin Valley of Humboldt County, Nevada. Opals are found in the light-colored beds on both sides of the gulch. Opal horizon in lower light-colored layers. The area looks the same today. See another view of this area in Chapter 5. (*Photo courtesy of U.S. Geological Survey.*)

no crystal structure like the other quartz gems. It ranks as the favorite gemstone with a great many gem collectors. The Virgin Valley type is among the world's best and most beautiful opal although it is the most difficult to cut because it has a tendency to break or crack during lapidary treatment. There are very few important gemstone collections that do not include a specimen of the Virgin Valley opal, as it is called.

The only way to hunt for opal is to go into the fields and camp. There are no towns nearby and practically no water in the Valley. Any prospector is fortunate indeed if he finds enough good opal to fill the palm of his hand in the course of a week's hunt, unless he goes to the known and famous mines where he can dig for a daily fee and almost

certainly be rewarded for any effort expended. But even then it is a long trip to the Valley and several days visit should be planned.

The Rainbow Ridge Mine, which has yielded the world's most spectacular opal specimens, some weighing as much as seven pounds, is open for prospecting for a fee during the summer months. This mine is on the western side of the Valley and the opal is always associated with petrified wood. Opal at the Green Fire Mine, on the eastern side of the Valley, is not associated with wood but occurs in seams. This is the only mine on the eastern side, all the important locations being on the western side. Besides the fire opal there are many kinds of common opal in shades of red, purple, orange, yellow, green, and blue, any of

FIG. 91. A 1913 photo by D. B. Sterrett of the Monarch opal claim of Deb Roop in the Virgin Valley, Humboldt County, Nevada. Roop, in the foreground, is digging around an opalized log. Such scenes were common early in the century, but opal is scarce today. *(Photo courtesy of U.S. Geological Survey.)*

which make attractive specimens but are not good cutting material because they tend to fracture after being cut.

Opal specimens kept intact rarely crack and probably the most valuable specimen in the world, the famous Roebling opal (from Virgin Valley) in the Smithsonian Institution, has been on exhibit for many years without showing any signs of deterioration from its original condition. About five years ago a visitor to the Valley discovered an opal mass in an old mine shaft that has been valued at from $30,000 to $75,000. There is, no doubt, far more valuable opal in the Valley at this time than has ever been taken out. It is a fascinating place for a vacation gem hunt if one is prepared for it and has time. Before visiting the area one should read the

Sinkankas account of the Valley in *Gemstones of North America*, the most complete discussion that has been published on this beautiful quartz gem.

Virgin Valley is reached by unpaved Highway 8A going east from Cedarville, California, or by paved Highway 8A running south from Denio on the Oregon border. The valley is at the end of a road which turns off south of the highway a few miles east of the Summit Lake Indian Reservation road. This country is in the high desert region where the states of California, Oregon, and Nevada meet. It abounds in agates and petrified wood and is greatly rewarding to the rockhound who is prepared with food, water, and supplies to spend a week or two prospecting at almost any spot along almost any byway. It is too

137

cold to prospect in the winter and it is terribly hot in the summer—definitely no place for an overnight campout. There are no accommodations or stores in the area.

Dumortierite quartz is found in Pershing County in both pink and blue varieties, although it is only the blue variety that is much sought after for gemstones, particularly for men's jewelry. Dumortierite resembles lapis lazuli (laypis lazh-you lie), although it is a denser blue and has no pyrite inclusions. It is often referred to in the west as "desert lapis." An extensive deposit occurs in Gypsy Queen Canyon about 6 miles north of Oreana.

Nevada is still a great wonderland for the traveling rockhound and it abounds in quartz-family gem materials all over the state, particularly in petri-

fied wood. Few locations, however, have been pinpointed and documented in the magazines. The most complete account of Nevada locations is Darold J. Henry's book, *The Rock Collector's Nevada and Idaho*. See Chapter 12.

An interesting article entitled *Nevada —The Rockhound Frontier*, accompanied by a fair map showing the gem and mineral locations in Nevada, has been prepared by the Nevada Department of Economic Development and the Nevada Bureau of Mines. Free copies may be secured by sending to one of these bureaus at Carson City, Nevada. In addition to showing locations of agate, petrified wood, and thundereggs, the map also shows locations of other gem and mineral materials the traveler may wish to collect, such as Nevada's famous turquoise, wonderstone, and rhodonite.

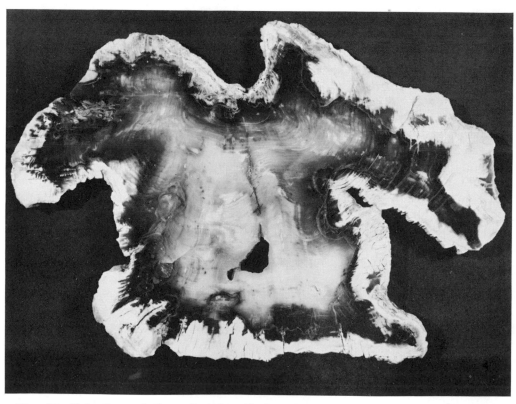

Fig. 92. Slab of petrified wood, 10″ x 7″, from Fish Lake, Nevada. Highly agatized with a white opal border. Center is light brown and gray with some amethystine color and some blue agate. From the collection of Leo D. Berner, Glendora, California.

138

NEW ENGLAND STATES

While the New England states have been a favorite hunting ground for mineral collectors since before the settling of the west, they have always been very poor territory for the collector of quartz minerals. No one has ever attempted to document the area thoroughly and relatively little information exists about agate and jasper localities. From time to time sparse deposits of agate and jasper are found and are usually reported in the pages of *Rocks and Minerals* magazine. Travelers in the area, or residents, would do well to consult members of the many local mineral clubs for information. All of the New England states were among the original thirteen states and, therefore, there is not now, nor has there ever been, any land in the public domain that would normally be open to prospecting. All land is privately owned and this does not encourage collecting.

The whole area abounds in quarries, many over a hundred years old, and they have large dumps for investigation and search. However, few of the quarries produce much quartz although they are often rewarding in a great variety of other mineral specimens. As a general rule, the New England collector is a mineral specimen collector and not a gem cutter. Collecting is limited because of the weather, the lack of public domain for prospecting, and the heavy verdure that hides the signs of deposits. Gemstone finds of any kind are hard won in the New England states and the following meager information is all the author has available on the entire area. Some information is given, however, on each of the six states in the region.

Connecticut

Connecticut is sparse territory for the collection of quartz gems and very little has ever appeared in the literature about locations. The information that is available is very vague. The state *Geological and Natural History Survey* lists several locations by towns, but what is probably meant is "in the vicinity of." These towns are principally in the western part of the state. A few of these are Southbury, a small town south of Waterbury; East Haven, a section of New Haven; West Haven; Milford; and Farmington, southwest of Hartford. Agate, carnelian, jasper, and bloodstone have all been found at these localities. Actual collecting should be preceded by previous contact with local sources such as one of the mineral clubs. Amethyst has rarely been found in the Meriden quarries.

Maine

Because of its pegmatite formations, Maine has quartz crystals associated with other crystal gems such as aquamarine and tourmaline at several locations. Good quality rose quartz occurs at the Scribner's Ledge quarry in Albany Township. The quarry is a mile north of the North Waterford pumping station. Deer Hill is a fine location for quartz crystals, a ton of them being recovered in one pocket as recently as 1956. Deer Hill is 1¾ miles southeast of North Chatham, N. H., and 4½ miles north of Stow, Maine. Oxford County appears to be the only locale for quartz minerals in Maine, agate, jasper, etc. being practically unknown.

Massachusetts

Some of the earliest literature reports fine agates in nodule form found in the basaltic rocks near Deerfield, Massachusetts. The basalts in the Connecticut River Valley contain gas cavities filled with various quartz gemstones such as chalcedony, agate, and some geodes sometimes lined with amethyst crystals, according to Sinkankas. Other agate localities are at Amherst and Conway. No new localities have been reported for many years.

New Hampshire

New Hampshire has several good quartz crystal locations, but there is little knowledge of other quartz gem locations. Good faceting material is scarce but some amethyst stones have been cut up to 40 carats and good amethysts from Berlin Township are in the collection of the American Museum of Natural History in New York. Amethyst occurs loose in the soil and in pockets upon Green's Ledge in the western part of Milan Township, on Diamond Ledges on Long Mountain in the northern part of Stark Township, between North Peak and Square Mountain in Kilkenny Township, and at many other locations listed in Sinkankas' *Gemstones of North America*.

Rhode Island

Diamond Hill in Providence County, the state's most northernmost county, is the best of that state's localities for hunting quartz gems. This barren hill is about two miles northeast of the village of Cumberland Hill. In the pockets of the numerous crevices and cavities, usually lined with small smoky and clear quartz crystals, one can find jasper, agate, chalcedony, and amethyst. On Calumet Hill, about a half mile west of Diamond Hill, fine sagenite quartz specimens were found many years ago when the granite quarries were operating, but now a thorough search has to be made to uncover any specimens. Gravel deposits near Bristol have some jasper pebbles and pebbles of carnelian are found along the shore of Narragansett Bay near Warwick.

Vermont

One of the best deposits of bright red jasper occurs on the Parrott Farm, just off Highway 2, about 9 miles north of Burlington, Vermont. Reports of other quartz varieties in Vermont are practically non-existent.

NEW JERSEY

New Jersey is one of our smaller states, but few realize the great variety of its scenery and geologic formations. South Jersey is even considered a foreign country by the people of north Jersey and vice versa. It is the author's original home and he has lived all over the state and is well acquainted with it. The state has little to offer the gem mineral collector, however. On the Atlantic seashore around Cape May, at the southern tip of the state, chalcedony pebbles occur on the beaches that are almost finished cabochons, so perfectly has nature tumbled them in the sea for countless thousands of years. The pebbles are referred to locally as Cape May "diamonds" and some shopkeepers are in constant trouble with the law in marketing them as "precious" gems. They occur in all shades from colorless through the smoky shades. When they are a yellowish-red or apricot colored, they are referred to in the jewelry trade as apricotine. They facet well and produce some striking stones. There do not appear to be any other beach pebbles worth gathering at the many other fine New Jersey beaches.

While the mountainous regions of north Jersey produce some wonderful mineral specimens, such as at the zinc mines, there is little of gem quartz interest in the area except some occasional poor quality amethyst at some quarries. The jasper collector is well rewarded when collecting in any of the numerous gravel pits in the western part of the state, along the Delaware River, particularly between Trenton, 30 miles north of Philadelphia, to Penns Grove, 20 miles south of that city. Every community along the river has one or more gravel pits, and local inquiry at a gasoline station will usually elicit information as to their whereabouts. All of these pits yield a great variety of jasper pebbles in all colors and occasionally

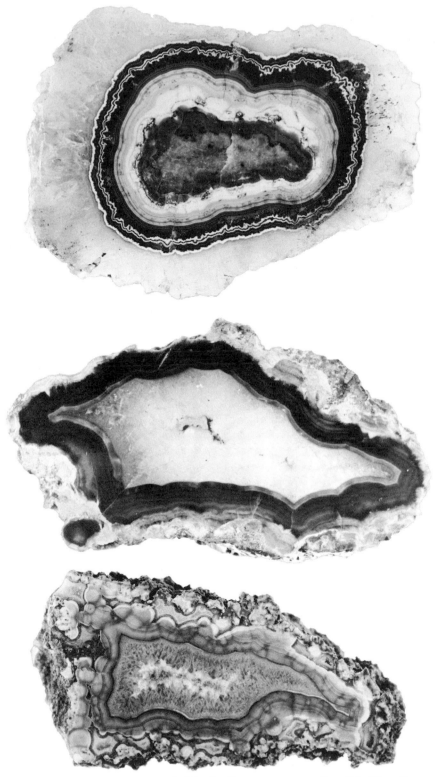

FIG. 93. Three examples of probably the finest agate ever found in New Jersey. The agate comes from Braen's Quarry at Hawthorne. On display at the Smithsonian Institution. *(Photos courtesy of the Smithsonian Institution.)*

some striped clear agate. As a boy of 10 the author used to collect these pebbles in the Delaware River back of the State House in Trenton, where, in the summer, it is possible to wade the river and great quantities of pebbles can be examined, especially on the Pennsylvania side.

NEW MEXICO

After trying to offer something encouraging and interesting on quartz materials in the rather sterile areas of New England and New Jersey, it is challenging to now discuss briefly the wide possibilities for agate collection in the state of New Mexico.

New Mexico has many areas where agate and wood can be gathered the year around. It also has several chert locations where the stone is of gem quality and very colorful. One of the varieties is Pedernal Chert, which is creamy white with stainings of red, yellow, and black. This is found in the Petaca District of Rio Arriba County. This and other locations are described by Sinkankas in *Gemstones of North America*. Very few articles, indeed practically none, have appeared in the magazines regarding New Mexico locations despite a wide variety of quartz minerals existing there at innumerable spots. The best information available at this writing is Bessie Simpson's book *New Mexico Gem Trails*. (See Chapter 12.)

Anyone entering New Mexico via Highways 70-80 in the southern part of the state should certainly pause at Deming, where good accommodations are available. Get Eddie or Bill Lindberg of the Deming Agate Shop to take you to their agate claims and, for a small fee, you will be assured of a plentiful supply of some of the finest agate and agate nodules in America. The claims are regularly bulldozed so that there is a minimum of digging required. At the "big diggins," about 27 miles southwest

of Deming, one can gather banded, plume, and sagenite agate in all sizes from small nodules to agates so big that a hoist is needed to move them. The nodule beds are another 19 miles south of the "big diggins," and here may be found some of the most beautiful agate nodules in existence, from the size of a lemon to that of a cantaloupe, and solidly filled with vividly colored fortification patterns, often in purple and red. Many nodules have a double fortification pattern. Some of the nodules are hollow, and are therefore geodes, filled with crystal linings ranging from clear quartz to cinnamon brown and amethyst. A few have been reported containing blue opal of a poor quality, with an occasional fire opal.

If you pass through Lordsburg, about 60 miles west of Deming on Highways 70-80, be sure to stop at the Triangle Rock Shop and see the famous hooded owl agate, one of the world's most unusual agates. This is illustrated in Chapter 9.

While in the Deming area try to collect some of the good carnelian agate in the Cooks Mountain area where Cooks Peak rises 8,404 feet. This is reached by going north for a short distance on Highway 260, turning right at Highway 26. Proceed for 5½ miles and turn left for another 6 miles. Here, in an area of about 20 square miles, the low hills are covered with float containing small amounts of good carnelian, new supplies being constantly uncovered by storms of wind and rain.

About 12 miles east of Deming, on the way to Las Cruces, is the Spanish Stirrup Ranch where comfortable accommodations with good food are reportedly obtainable at the Spanish Stirrup Guest House. This is a good area for crystal-filled geodes and agate.

There are many quartz gem collecting areas in west central New Mexico. Apache Creek agate is found in an area beginning at the Apache Creek store on

Fɪɢ. 94. An unusual agate from New Mexico, showing an inclusion of travertine. On display at the Smithsonian Institution. *(Photo courtesy of the Smithsonian Institution.)*

Highway 12 about 11 miles northeast of Reserve. Go north about 5 miles on gravel road 32 to the National Forest boundary fence and park north of the fence. On the left, and across Apache Creek, you will see two canyons, Lee Russell Canyon and Kerr Canyon. Hike up Lee Russell Canyon on the north. At first the canyon is wide and agate is scattered around, but after you go through the narrow canyon farther on, you will come out on the north side of the canyon into Turkey Flat and Elk Horn Park, about 4 miles from your parked car. In this area there is agate in many colors and patterns and one should find more than he is willing to carry back to the car. Plenty of time should be allowed for this hike, and water and a little food should be taken along.

Good agate collecting has been reported on Highway 260 going west from Luna. Collecting can be done for about 4 miles on the north side of the highway. Go to Hillsboro, reached by going south of Truth or Consequences (Hot Springs) on Highway 85 to its junction with 180, and then proceeding 18 miles west. Continue through Hillsboro for a short distance to an iron bridge crossing Percha

Creek, where you will find parking space on the left. Agate hunting is reported good on the mountain to the right of the road, collecting being more prolific on the other side of the mountain.

A rugged but highly scenic trip for agate can be taken from Silver City. A short distance east of Silver City, Highway 25 goes north to Piños Altos, beyond which point it is a gravel road across the mountains, through canyons and pine and aspen forests, a magnificent trip although the road is poor at this writing. About 20 miles north of Piños Altos is Sapillo Creek. Here the road is really only for jeeps or the new and popular scooters. Alum Peak is about 8 miles further and here are banded agate geodes and carnelian.

If you are in northern New Mexico in the Albuquerque area, go west on Highway 66 for about 11 miles to the Tepee filling station. Follow the dirt road to the left of the highway, making only right turns for about a quarter mile to where the arroyos lead toward the river. In the banks of the arroyos and on all of the ridges, agatized wood, jasper, and agate can be found, but not in great quantities. This is a spot, however, for

Fig. 95. A very fine 6″ polished agate nodule from near Deming, New Mexico, showing a double fortification marking in rich carnelian agate surrounded by colorful lavender agate with many interesting bubble patterns. From the author's collection. *(Photo by O. D. Smith.)*

the hasty traveler with a new car to have the thrill of picking up a few mementoes of his trip.

New Mexico is like Arizona and Idaho . . . no matter where you are do a little prospecting of your own. It is a rocky land and full of minerals and 35 per cent of it is public domain so that prospecting is practically uninhibited and usually rewarding. No mention is made here of the hundreds and hundreds of good collecting areas for mineral specimens, Indian artifacts, and other materials like turquoise, Apache tears (obsidian), and other gem varieties, for this is not the field of this book. However, even if the reader's interest lies strictly in the quartz area, he should be alert to other good items that he can collect and swap later on for the things he

wants that he did not find. New Mexico is an all-year collecting land, cool in the high mountains in the summer, pleasant in the low areas in the winter . . . and it has some of the grandest scenery America has to offer, truly living up to its state motto of the "Land of Enchantment."

NEW YORK

It is a sad circumstance that the "Empire State" with so very much to offer in the beautiful scenery of its mountain ranges, its lakes, rivers, and seacoast, has so little of interest for the gem hunter or rockhound. Practically nothing in the quartz family of gems is to be found in the state, with the exception of a very fine clear doubly terminated quartz crystal named the Herkimer "diamond" occurring at several spots in Herkimer County, surrounding the towns of Middleville and Little Falls, where the crystals are locally called Middleville "diamonds" and Little Falls "diamonds."

This area is not an open collecting area, as all of the prospects are located on private farms and practically none of the farmers will permit any collecting because they are afraid their cattle will fall in the holes made by prospectors. There are a few farmers, however, who encourage collecting, charging a daily fee for prospecting on their property. Ownership of these farms changes from time to time so that names cannot be given here, with the exception of the Taber Estate near Middleville, where the collecting is reportedly the best in the area. Inquiry at the offices of Chambers of Commerce in the towns in the area will no doubt disclose current information on where one can collect for a fee.

The crystals are small, but unusually clear and brilliant for quartz crystals, the best gems being about a half inch in diameter. Some crystals, particularly the larger ones, contain water and gas bubbles and some contain black carbon inclusions. By visiting the public library in Little Falls, one can see a display of thousands of crystals. Boulders may be loosened and broken by hard work with crowbars, revealing cavities containing the crystals; or the earth may be sieved at the bottoms of the hills for loose crystals that have been washed down. The crystals, once plentiful, are now hard won. There are good collecting areas at Little Falls, a short distance north of the New York State Thruway. One area is within the town limits and is divided into two parts by the Mohawk River running northeast to southwest. Another area starts about 2 miles from the town and goes through Salisbury and Diamond Hill. Probably the best collecting area, and for the best crystals, is Middleville, west of Little Falls and north of the Thruway. One belt begins at Middleville on the north side of the road on the way to Newport, extending in a northwesterly direction. Another goes eastward from Middleville about a mile on the north side of the road to Fairfield. The most prolific spot at this writing is on top of a hill between Middleville and Herkimer, about 3 miles to the south of Middleville.

NORTH AND SOUTH CAROLINA

These two states were among the original thirteen states and they have therefore never had any public domain. This makes gem hunting as difficult as it is in New England. Any serious hunting must be done with the permission of the owners of the land and needed information about this is difficult to obtain.

North and South Carolina compose the leading area in the United States for a large variety of crystal minerals, with the possible exception of San Diego County in California. Rubies and sapphires can be collected at existing mines for a fee and the states abound in varieties of crystallized quartz such as amethystine quartz, rutilated quartz with red rutile crystals, quartz with tourmaline crystals in reddish-yellow, black, and other reported colors. Rose quartz occurs at several unspecified locations and terminated quartz crystals have been found in clear yellow (citrine) and water clear crystals. Amethyst is well distributed in both states but the localities mentioned in the literature are all at least a half century old and information at this time is very vague. Residents of these states who wish to collect, and visitors passing through, must run down their information through local inquiry. The area abounds in streams, all of which have gravel bars usually highly productive of good gem material, and travelers can prospect the streams with little danger of any prosecution for trespassing. No agate locations are known to this author.

NORTH AND SOUTH DAKOTA

One seldom hears the term desert in North and South Dakota, but the term badlands is common to this area. The dictionary defines badlands as regions where erosion has carved soft rocks into intricate and fantastic shapes and where vegetation is scanty. The reader should remember, therefore, that we are discussing desert regions when we discuss the badlands, although, strictly speaking, a desert is an arid place and there is plenty of rainfall and snow in the Dakota badlands. There is a Badlands National Monument in South Dakota consisting of almost exactly 100,000 acres, where no rock collecting is allowed, but when we refer to badlands with a small "b" the reader will understand that the Monument is not under discussion.

In North Dakota only 4.4 per cent of the land is government owned and the state is not highly productive of gem materials except in the stream beds, notably of the Yellowstone and the Missouri rivers in Williams and McKenzie counties where the moss agates found in Montana also occur. These are some of the finest moss agates in the world. The people of this state are evidently not very much interested in rocks for, at this writing, it is the only one of our fifty states where no gem and mineral club exists. Perhaps that is because there are relatively few badlands in the state and it is highly developed as grain growing country.

The situation is far different in South Dakota, where great areas of badlands exist and there are a great many good agate collecting areas. Less than 7 per cent of the state is in the public domain, however. The most famous of the agate areas is the Fairburn area near Fairburn in Custer County. Here occurs one of the world's most beautiful agate varieties, with contrasting bands of colorful red and white and yellowish-brown and white fortifications. The agate occurs as small nodules about three inches across, although some masses weighing as much as 40 pounds have been found. Once very popular, the agate is seldom found now in any quantity despite the great demand for it, and good specimens have a high value. The agates occur in a belt starting at Creston in Pennington County and extending south to Orella in Nebraska. The widest part of the belt is 15 miles at Red Shirt in Shannon County.

There are many other agate locations in southwest South Dakota where the agates are so similar to the Fairburn type that few are expert enough to tell them apart. In the Custer State Park area east of the town of Custer, there are agates on the surface that greatly resemble the Fairburns, but collectors refer to them as State Park agates. South of Custer and starting at the town of Pringle, there is a wide area branching south and west where a new type of Fairburns is being gathered at this writing, when the location is fairly new. These agates have been named Fairhills agates by June Culp Zeitner, an authority on Dakota gemstones, and the name is likely to stick since it is a place name. The land in the Fairhills district is privately owned by ranchers and permission must be secured to hunt there. Directly west and north of Custer are Tepee Canyon and Hells Canyon, accessible from Highway 16. These canyons abound in agates similar to the Fairburn variety but they are individually called Tepee Canyon and Hells Canyon agates. The Tepee type nodules also occur around Rapid City and Pringle. Most of these areas are in the Black Hills region where the mountains are not hills nor are they black, and the agates are usually found in the limestone plateaus between the "hills."

If the reader happens to travel to this area, plans should be made to visit the Scott rose quartz mine near Custer where the quartz can be purchased at reportedly reasonable prices or collected

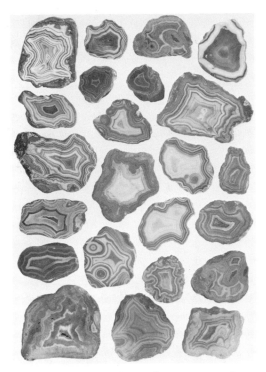

FIG. 96. Group of Fairburn agates from South Dakota. Now scarce, they are one of America's most colorful and beautiful agate varieties. Their reds and yellows and rich browns closely resemble the Mexican agates shown on the cover. *(Photo courtesy of the Museum of Geology, South Dakota School of Mines and Technology.)*

for a small fee. Visitors should get permission at the Scott home on the south side of Highway 16A as you drive east out of Custer. Piles of rose quartz in front of the house will identify it.

The Scott rose quartz comes from a huge vein; the mine has been operated by the Scott family since 1881. It is consistently the best quality of rose quartz from any of the world's localities and for several generations it has been sent to carving mills all over the world and returned to America as beautiful carved ornaments and figurines, lamp bases, beads, and ring settings.

There are several areas where rose quartz may be prospected, but the quality of the quartz is inferior to the Scott quartz. It is hardly likely that any-

one would be in this area without paying a visit to Mount Rushmore to see the carved heads of some of our greatest Presidents. One of the rose quartz locations is the gravel road behind Mount Rushmore leading from Highway 16A to Highway 89. Quartz is reported at spots all along this route. Another spot is a few yards to the left of Highway 89 northwest of Custer. Rose quartz occurs at many other spots in the state; in the Black Hills, near Pringle, and in Custer and Pennington counties. Incidentally, do not believe the old wives' tale you will probably hear that in order to preserve the color of rose quartz it must be wrapped in brown paper.

Amethyst lined geodes occur along the banks of Whitewood Creek near the town of that name in Lawrence County. Similar geodes may be hunted in Spearfish Canyon near the town of that name.

Moss agates similar to the Montana variety may be found in the gravel of the tributaries of the Little Missouri River in Harding County. A jasper conglomerate in quartzite is quarried at the Dells of the Sioux River north of Sioux Falls in eastern South Dakota. This material is widely used for ornamental purposes and the making of novelties. It is known in the trade as Sioux Falls jasper. Agate and chalcedony are widespread in the gravel pits of the eastern portion of the state, but the agates are not nearly as attractive as the Fairburn types found in the west.

There are almost innumerable places

FIG. 97. Chalcedony geodes from the badlands of South Dakota. They are quite small and come in orange and pink with beautiful crystal interiors. *(Photo courtesy of June Culp Zeitner, author of* Midwest Gem Trails.*)*

Fig. 98. White quartz with aquamarine inclusions. From South Dakota. *(Photo courtesy of June Culp Zeitner, Zeitner Geological Museum, Mission, South Dakota.)*

for agate collecting in South Dakota but space does not permit the detailing of these places of lesser importance here. Readers may also be interested in the pegmatite minerals of the state, such as the tourmalines and aquamarines, an account of which can be secured from the books listed in Chapter 12. There are many rockshops along the highways of the state. They should be visited and their wares studied for information, always remembering that the rock shop owner in all probability has a large assortment for sale of the finer specimens that you are not likely to encounter in your own searching. The best information on South Dakota gemstones is found in the book *Midwest Gem Trails* by June Culp Zeitner who operates the Zeitner Geological Museum at Mission, South Dakota, on Highway 18 in the southern part of the state.

OHIO

The only well known quartz location in Ohio is at Flint Ridge. Few collecting spots in America offer the great variety in pattern and color that is available in the flint of this region, so closely resembling jasper that we believe it should be called that. Much of it resembles the brecciated jasper from near San Miguel, California, known as Stone Canyon jasper. The flint is banded, contains moss patterns with scenes, contains rutile, is sometimes crystalline, and has chalcedony areas. It comes in colors from white to black, pink, orange, red, yellow, and blue. A green variety is rare and the most sought after by collectors. The Ridge was one of the favorite spots in America for the Indians to collect rock for their artifacts and Flint Ridge pieces have been found as far west as the Mississippi River, a considerable distance by Indian standards.

The state of Ohio maintains a state park at the Ridge with picnic facilities, but no collecting is allowed in the park. There are many aboriginal pits in the area where the Indians made their artifacts and every once in a while a collector will find one of these half buried "factories" and recover arrow and spear heads. Any of the farms along the east-west road, running east from the crossroad at the Ridge, is a good collecting spot. Permission to hunt must be secured from the local farmers who own the land. Some of them charge a dollar collecting fee and some will permit no hunting at all. The most likely spots are freshly plowed fields, and corn fields in the fall are reported productive of material. Wood lots are also good spots since they are seldom prospected and the flint is covered with forest debris. This material is ideal for jewelry settings.

The Ridge is 3 miles north of Brownsville on Route 40, the most traveled highway in the state. The turnoff is 9 miles west of Zanesville, 130 miles south of Cleveland, and 156 miles northeast of Cincinnati. The flint formation covers an area in a radius of about 10 miles from the Ridge park.

148

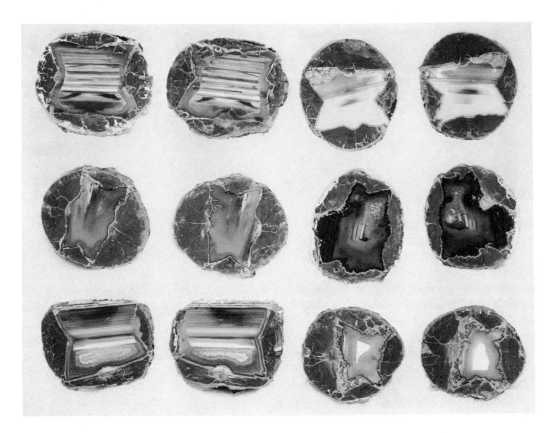

F<small>IG</small>. 99. Box of thunderegg halves from Oregon. These are agate-filled nodules, no two of which are ever alike. Nearly all of them have a characteristic star frame for the picture portion. From the collection of James E. Mueller, Phoenix, Arizona.

OKLAHOMA

Oklahoma has very little quartz gem material. What it has seems to be concentrated in Woods County where petrified wood, jasper, agate, chalcedony, and moss agate appear to be generally distributed. Scattered collecting spots are in Harper, Tillman, Beckham, and Greer counties.

OREGON

Oregon is indubitably agate country and it is here that the original agate clubs started, non-scientific clubs organized for the sole purpose of collecting quartz gems and grinding and polishing them. To properly cover the known collecting spots would produce a volume as big as this one. Therefore, only brief mention can be made here of a few of the more famous localities and for further information the reader is referred to the books listed in Chapter 12, particularly *Northwest Gem Trails*, which has excellent maps. The Oregon Agate and Mineral Society of Portland, Oregon, has for sale at a nominal price an excellent map pinpointing the best collecting areas and giving a good description of the materials at each spot. There is plenty of opportunity for the exploring rockhound to find new collecting spots in Oregon, as many do each year, for the land in the public domain is more than 51 per cent.

Probably the agate item of greatest interest to a collector is the famed Oregon thunderegg, so called because it is a myth of the local Indians that the gods in the mountains hurled them at one another when they became angry. Pony Butte on the old Priday Ranch (called the Fulton agate beds at this writing) is one of the best places to gather the thundereggs. Collecting may be done here for a small fee and the area is regularly bulldozed to uncover new material. These nodules average in size from a lemon to an orange and are frequently filled with beautiful sagenite agate. When a slice is taken from the center of an egg it often yields an area for a cabochon containing entrancingly beautiful plume agate that is unsurpassed in beauty by any agate from any other locality, and probably only matched by some of the Texas sagenitic agate. The Ranch is 17 miles northeast of Madras on Highway 97, near milepost 79.

The Ranch also has a good deposit of polka-dot agate, which is a creamy material with brown freckles that should be more properly called polka-dot jasper, since it is opaque and is not chalcedony. There are many other thunderegg locations, particularly in the Ochoco Mountains around Prineville. Local inquiry can direct you to several beds near Viewpoint where collecting can be done for a daily fee. These beds are productive of eggs with carnelian centers. The Carey Ranch near Eagle Rock, 14 miles south of Prineville, produces some superb plume agate. Collecting may also be done here for a small fee.

While agate exists over much of the state, the principal productive areas of plume agate, petrified wood, and thundereggs are in eastern Oregon in a triangular area bounded by the towns of John Day, Burns, and Bend. Beach agates occur at many spots along the Pacific shoreline right down to the California border.

In the eastern Oregon area there are some favorite collecting spots. The Morrison Ranch near the southern end of the Owyhee Reservoir in Malheur

FIG. 100. Three cabochons cut by the author for his collection. The top two cabochons are Oregon moss agates with red moss inclusions. The bottom cabochon is a moss agate cut from an Oregon thunderegg. (*Photo by O. D. Smith.*)

County has a beautiful jasp-agate called morrisonite. In the same vicinity, along Sucker Creek and south of Adrian, beautiful thundereggs abound containing banded agate. Moss agate, jasper, and petrified wood are plentiful in the rim rocks, over the hills, and in the creek beds. Going northwest in the same area to the Greenhorn Mountains around Baker, one can find good agate around Whitney. In abandoned mine dumps around Greenhorn, good specimens of petrified tree fern (tempskya) may be gathered.

At Warm Springs reservoir find milepost 171 while going east or west on Highway 20. Turn south and drive on a dirt road 14.2 miles to a reservoir on the left. Here there is black dendritic agate and white plume agate along the lake and on the surrounding hills. Opal filled nodules are found in the buttes southeast of Heppner in Morrow County. Thundereggs, moss agate, and jasper are found in the mountain areas of Steens Mountains in Harney County. First quality precious opal has been found at several locations on the west rim of the high peaks of the Hart Mountains in Lake County, and agates, nodules, and a fine jasp-agate similar to morrisonite are scattered in the canyons of the same mountain range.

There is some of the country's finest petrified wood at Nigger Rock in the Sucker Creek country of Malheur County. The area is about 9 miles northwest of the Owyhee dam. Whole trees are buried in rhyolite powder about three feet under the gravel conglomerate. Very fine blue and yellow limb casts can be dug from this hillside deposit. Crook County in Central Oregon has many deposits of wood and moss agate west of Bear Creek and on both sides of Crooked River. Digging is required to recover good material.

One of the best collecting areas for very fine moss agate is the country around Prineville in north central Oregon. Large boulders of moss agate in red, blue, green, and yellow have been found here as well as quartz lined geodes and masses of botryoidal agate. This is ranching country and much of it is closed to collectors but some ranchers give permission to collect. To the east of this section is the Clarno Basin where some of the best fossils have been found. There are mammal bone beds but these have been reserved for exploration by qualified scientists. The rockhounds may gather the fossilized nuts, however, locally called Clarno nuts.

Baker County in eastern Oregon is a very prolific source of good gem agates. A dark green jasper, erroneously called Oregon "jade," is found in Shirttail Creek near Durkee. Large geodes containing quartz crystals are reportedly found loose in the soil near milepost 393 on Highway 30, near Huntington. The foregoing brief accounts of col-

lecting areas in central and eastern Oregon include but a few of the very many recorded prospects. Many traveling rockhounds will not get into this area, however, particularly if they are coming from east of the Pacific coast states and attempting to cover Washington, Oregon, and California. These people will be traveling Highway 99, the main north and south artery through the state. While they will find no thundereggs along this highway there are many collecting spots for fine agate that are not far from the main highway.

Medford in Jackson County at the California border can be used as headquarters for several trips into surrounding country. One noted locality is at Eagle Point, 10 miles northeast of Medford on Highway 62. Fine carnelian moss agate has been collected throughout this area for many years. On the heights above McCloud on the Crater Lake highway (62) quartz crystals can be gathered, some of them spectacular compact masses of acicular radiating crystals up to 8 inches in length. A green and white jasper called medfordite is found at Big Butte and bloodstone is found at Big Falls.

Certainly anyone traveling in this section will want to visit Crater Lake, one of the most beautiful lakes in all the world and probably the bluest. The whole area around the lake is good prospecting country. In the next county north (Douglas), there are many localities where agate, iris agate, moss agate, jasper, carnelian, and bloodstone may be collected. The area is also productive of several gemstone varieties other than quartz.

When one gets into the northern part of the state, between Eugene and Portland, the Willamette River is seldom far from the highway. This is an important river and in the summer, when the water is low, great gravel bars are exposed that yield some of the most beautiful agates in the world. This is

151

true of most of the rivers and streams flowing into the Pacific, and the summer time is the best time to explore them. Where the streams enter the Pacific ocean there is always a good possibility of recovering good material, as the waves are constantly tumbling new agates onto the beaches. However, wading is dangerous at spots where streams enter the ocean.

In the northwest part of the state Clear Creek flows into the Nehalem River southwest of Vernonia. The creek yields good carnelian and plume agate and jasper. The creek may be waded with boots or one can dig in the banks on both sides. By taking Highway 20 southeast from Albany, or going east on Highway 228 from Highway 99 south of Corvallis, one comes to the Sweethome and Holley petrified wood area. This is the most extensive prehistoric forest in the state. There is an abundance of fossilized wood, beautifully colored with well marked graining and ring structure. Ames Creek and the Calapooya River have reportedly yielded some of the finest specimens. Banded agate and crystal lined geodes may also be found.

Probably the easiest rock hunting in America is along the Oregon shores of the Pacific; easy because all you have to do is walk along the beach and pick up the stones washed up by practically every wave. The most productive time to collect, however, is when the weather is at its worst in the winter months, when the fierce winter storms create the big waves that bring in new quantities of agates, but more importantly wash the beach sands away temporarily to reveal tons upon tons of stones that have been buried for countless centuries. When the storms subside in the spring the sand gradually levels the beaches again, and agates are scarce in the summer months.

A visit to a few of the agate shops found in almost every coastal town will reveal the variety of material that can be gathered on the beach. The agates are easily identifiable in beach collecting as they are usually wet and therefore more like the polished state. They have also been tumbled by nature so that their interiors are well exposed and their colors are more easily apparent than in agate masses found in the deserts and other collecting areas. It helps to walk the beach with the sun to your back so that the glint of sunlight on the agate surface is more easily discernible. It also helps the back a great deal if one is provided with a stick, such as a shortened broomstick, in which some wires have been affixed at the end to form a claw. This eliminates a lot of stooping and saves a lot of time, for several stones can be picked up at a time. Estwing, manufacturer of the best rock pick and hammer, also makes a gem scoop of aluminum which is sold in rockhound supply stores. This tool has many uses and is highly recommended.

If you travel Highway 101 from Astoria south to the California border, you will see almost 400 miles of the most beautiful scenery in the whole world, a Riviera of the mountains and blue Pacific Ocean with great forests of huge trees and tumbling streams rushing to the sea. The streams have brought the agates through the long centuries and the sea has tossed and tumbled them about through countless thousands of years so that every wave spews new beauty on the beaches all along the Oregon coast, the only spot where the agate supply is relentlessly renewed every year. The traveler is urged to explore for his own collecting spots, for the fun of discovery is very satisfying. However, there are several well-known locations that should be visited because of a known supply and because of available accommodations.

The northern beaches produce more bloodstone and jasper than agates. This

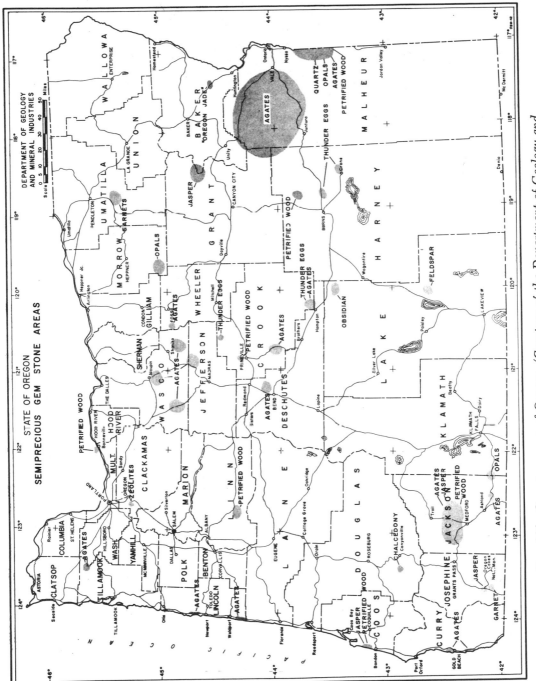

FIG. 101. Gemstone map of Oregon. (Courtesy of the Department of Geology and Mineral Industries of the state of Oregon.)

153

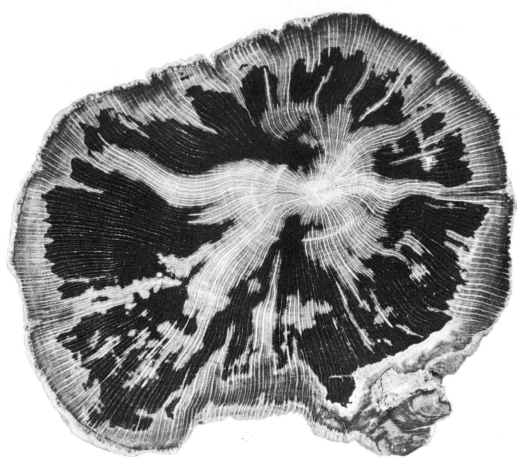

FIG. 102. Section of petrified sycamore wood, 4″ x 5″, from southeast of Prineville, Oregon. Cut and polished by Leo D. Berner, Glendora, California.

is true of Tillamook. Proceeding south to Oceanlake, the beaches between there and Newport all provide good collecting. One then comes to Agate Beach, a very famous collecting spot; although the agates are usually very small, they are also very fine. From Yachats on south to Florence the agates usually contain sagenite inclusions, but other agates, petrified wood, and jasper are in plentiful supply, particularly during the winter storms. The southern Oregon beaches, particularly around Coos Bay, are not visited as much as the northern beaches. They are noted for fine specimens of petrified wood.

PENNSYLVANIA

Pennsylvania is one of our richest states, mineralogically speaking, but not in minerals of gemological interest, the principal minerals being oil and coal. Minerals of the quartz group seem to be confined to the eastern counties and many good amethyst localities have been reported in Delaware, Lancaster, and Montgomery counties (Sinkankas), but most of these reports are from early in the century and the locations would be difficult to find today. All are on private property (there is no public domain in Pennsylvania) and permission to collect is not likely to be granted, especially on farms. Eastern Pennsylvania abounds in quarries, however, and nearly every community of any size has its local quarry. These quarries contain many interesting mineral specimens but quartz gem materials are seldom among them.

Bucks County is the author's home county and reference is made to the New Jersey section where details of jasper collecting along the Delaware River are discussed. In the Delaware River (very shallow for wading in the summer) at Morrisville, and opposite Trenton, N. J., jasper pebbles can be found. Jasper pebbles can be found in practically all of the sand pits that exist in nearly every community along the Delaware shore between Morrisville, 30 miles north of Philadelphia, to about another 20 miles below Philadelphia. Petrified wood exists in the same county in Neshaminy Creek west of Newtown, about ¼ mile southeast of Roelof's Station and at many other spots along the creek. Jasper occurs at many localities, but agate has not been reported.

Quartz crystal localities are reported to be fairly plentiful in western Pennsylvania, particularly in Bedford County where the farmers are said to be very friendly, usually saying in their characteristic Pennsylvania Dutch, "The rocks from my farm you want you can have by the wagonful." One of the best collecting areas in Bedford County is the area around St. Clairsville, reached by leaving the Pennsylvania Turnpike at the Bedford Interchange and taking Highway 220 about 6 miles north. At St. Clairsville, make a right turn eastward over Brumbaugh Mountain. On the other side of the mountain is a valley called Morrison Cove, an area of about 10 square miles. Here one can find Herkimer "diamond" type quartz crystals (see section under New York State) or large doubly terminated single quartz crystals weighing as much as two pounds. Single amethyst crystals also occur. The Cove has many other interesting specimens too, particularly calcite. About 3 miles west of Ligonier on Highway 30 is a very large quarry more than a half mile long, said to be full of quartz crystals and limestone fossils.

RHODE ISLAND

(See the New England states, p. 140.)

SOUTH CAROLINA

(See North and South Carolina, p. 145.)

SOUTH DAKOTA

(See North and South Dakota, p. 145.)

TENNESSEE

Information is lacking on this state.

TEXAS

Texas is a mighty big place, but remember that it was an independent country before it became a state and there is not an acre of public domain in the whole state. The United States Government did acquire over 700,000 acres in 1944, which it set aside as Texas' only national park . . . Big Bend National Park at the big bend of the Rio Grande, the western boundry of the state that separates it from Mexico. No matter where you collect in Texas you are on somebody's land, and nowhere in America is land more jealously guarded than in Texas. A Texas rancher (never call him a farmer) has a holy zeal about his land and his rights. However, the majority of ranchers are usually agreeable in giving permission to hunt on their land when they are requested to do so. All through Texas the wire fences have coyotes and bobcats hanging on them. Don't let your Levis be displayed marked ROCKHOUND.

When one thinks of Texas he immediately thinks of Texas plume agate, for this is some of the world's most beautiful agate and certainly Texas' finest quartz gemstone. And when one thinks of plume agate he immediately thinks of the Woodward Ranch, although not all of the plume agate is on this ranch by any means. Anyone who is seeking for agate, however, will certainly want to visit the Woodward Ranch and collect

Fɪɢ. 103. Surf scene in a Texas agate. The agate pictured above was cut by J. D. Churchill of Dallas, Texas. It came from Reaves County, Texas, in 1943. "No indication of any pattern was on the outside," writes Mr. Churchill, "and I was in a quandary as to how it should be cut. The size of my equipment decided for me that I should cut it across the narrow way rather than lengthwise. I cut several slices and the pattern was practically the same. My cousin told me that a friend of his had some nice looking rocks in her flower bed. I asked him to see if she would let me have some and then he sent me this agate." The surf scene is a faithful picture of the surf as it rolls in front of the author's home in La Jolla, California.

several types of sagenitic agate for a small fee in a locality that has plenty of wonderful material.

The Woodward Ranch is on Highway 118, 16 to 17 miles south of Alpine, which is on Routes 67-90. It is 243 miles southeast of El Paso in west Texas. Free campsites are provided and a charge is made by the pound for all material taken. Agate is for sale if you do not wish to collect your own. The best agates on the Woodward Ranch are the unlikeliest looking. They are about 2 to 3 inches across, seldom weigh more than an ounce or two, and look for all the world like a well baked brownish red biscuit, being only about an inch thick.

When these agates are sliced right through the middle they produce two slabs usually containing some of the most beautiful sagenite agate in the world, magnificent plumes in red and black in clear to creamy chalcedony. While most of the agates are small, some very large ones have been found, one of them weighing 225 pounds, worth a small fortune when sectioned and sold by the slice. Mr. Woodward also conducts field trips for a fee to other claims he owns in west Texas and the reader planning such a trip should make arrangements by mail in advance so that he can be included in a party going on a trip at the time he expects to visit the

Fig. 104. Some interesting New Mexico and Texas scenic agates. The agates pictured above were found in Texas by J. D. Churchill of Dallas, Texas. Mrs. Churchill picked up the agate pictured at lower left. It has a cactus-like plume below an excellent fortification outline. The other two agates were found on the Baker Ranch in New Mexico. The dog at the top (look carefully!) is a brownish color with a red collar around its neck. Churchill advises that the map of the United States, at lower right, was evidently subjected to a sand storm over Texas, New Mexico, and Arizona while it was forming.

area. Address the Woodward Ranch, Alpine, Texas, although this situation may change from year to year.

No collecting is allowed in Big Bend National Park but the Woodwards lease land adjoining it on the north which is filled with agate and jasper. Here is found the now scarce but beautiful pompom agate, a clear chalcedony with yellow pom-poms or chrysanthemum-like sagenite bursts. In other parts of this county (Brewster), and in Presidio County to the west and Jeff Davis County to the north, agate and jasper are plentiful and arrangements can be made with other ranchers to prospect their properties. Much agate, chalcedony, and jasper are found west of the Glass Mountains.

There is another type of agate, now very scarce, which the author named "bouquet agate" in 1949. This is clear chalcedony with clusters of plumes in various colors that resemble arranged bouquets of mixed flowers. Sometimes there are as many as four colors in one small cabochon size piece of agate. To reach this collecting area go west from Alpine on Highways 67-90 for 19 miles and turn right on Highway 169. Go about 18 miles to the Bishop ranch gate on the left. At the ranch house, over the hill, permission can be secured for a small fee to hunt the bouquet agate. The turnoff road is 7 miles south of Marfa if one is driving from El Paso. There is a 59 mile stretch on Highway 67 of good agate hunting country between Marfa and Presidio, the hottest town in Texas, and perhaps anywhere, which is on the Rio Grande. One can take a toll bridge over the river and do a little collecting in Mexico, although the roads there are not paved.

If one is traveling Highway 80 to get to the New Mexico, Arizona, and Southern California collecting locations, one should take the time to collect in this west Texas area, for it is a richly rewarding one or two-day side trip. By leaving Highway 80 at Van Horn it is only 73 miles to Marfa on Highway 90 and another 34 miles to Alpine. The area between Van Horn and Marfa is the Lobo Valley. It is the oldest agate collecting area in the state, but an area where rockhounds are unpopular because of past depredations with trucks, the cutting of wire fences, and in general behaving like rockhogs instead of hounds. Some ranchers permit collecting, however, and will even direct one where to go.

Midway between Van Horn and Pecos on Highway 80 there is a paved road (Highway 290) that runs southeast for about 20 miles to Balmorhea. Here there is a state park and a lake. On both sides

Fig. 105. An unusual agate slab from material found near Del Rio, Texas. On display at the Smithsonian Institution. *(Photo courtesy of the Smithsonian Institution.)*

Fig. 106. Slab of petrified palm wood, 6″ x 15″, from near La Grange, Texas. Cut and polished by, and in the collection of, Leo D. Berner, Glendora, California. Light border with a black center and white sprays.

of a road running around the lake on the north side there are agate nodules containing blue banded agate with an occasional plume agate. Eighteen miles west of Pecos on Highway 80 is the small town of Toyah. Take any one of the numerous ranch roads running out of Toyah and agate collecting can be done on either side of most of the roads. Petrified wood can also be gathered in this area. If you get to Alpine, continue through the town on Highway 90 about 6 miles south until you see a concrete water tank across the railroad on the right. Beyond the tank there is a valley between the hills that contains fine agate and geodes. Some digging may be required by the time you read this, so take a shovel with you when you park on the highway and hike in. It may save you a trip back to your car.

If you are interested in petrified wood, there is plenty of it in Texas, but not in the area we have been writing about. One area where it reportedly still abounds at this writing is in the Madisonville district about 95 miles north of Houston on the way to Dallas via Highway 45, the Dallas-Houston Thruway, or about 141 miles south of Dallas. By taking farm road 978 to Normangee,

one crosses the railroad to Highway 39. Between Route 39 and the railroad, all the way south to Cross, there is good wood collecting. Highway 190 can be taken back to Madisonville. This whole triangle contains a lot of wood.

In another triangular area bounded by the towns of Giddings, Somerville, and Caldwell, and a few miles east of Austin, the capital, there is an area that abounds in petrified palm wood and other agatized types of wood. Follow any of the numerous ranch roads and investigate the bottoms of the many creeks you will cross, for the wood is well scattered in this section of the state. Twenty miles south of Giddings is La Grange, center of another wood collecting area. Information may be secured from almost any local service station operator. This section of Texas is known as the Catahoula formation and petrified wood abounds in a large area beginning on Highway 35 at Cotulla, 87 miles southwest of San Antonio and going east to Three Rivers, which is on Highway 37, and then northeast through Gonzales and on to La Grange. The Formation extends eastward into Louisiana and some wood can be found in almost any portion of it by examining the

159

streams for stumps which look like big petrified onions. These yield large slabs for tabletops, if you can handle them. The Rio Grande valley, especially around Laredo on the Mexican border, is great agate country. Examine the river bed at almost any point and all washes leading into it for agate of all kinds.

The traveler is reminded that all of the country we have been describing is hotter than the equator in the summer months and more uncomfortable than the desert regions of Arizona and southern California because of the high humidity. On the other hand, it is pleasant hunting country during most of the rest of the year and the area is not snowbound. Having visited practically every important city and a great many towns in Texas, the author can testify that the people are among the friendliest in the United States and the members of the thirty-odd gem and mineral societies in Texas are very friendly, too, and extremely cooperative with traveling rockhounds. *Gem Trails of Texas* by Bessie W. Simpson (see Chapter 12), is a good paperback book about most of the locations discussed here, in addition to giving locations for the gathering of fossils and artifacts and Texas' most famous gem—the beautiful Texas blue topaz. It also has many other agate locations and fairly good maps of the best known mineral and gem locations.

UTAH

Here is a great state where the public domain is almost 70 per cent of the land area, and much of it is practically unexplored desert country abounding in all manner of interesting mineral and gem varieties. While much collecting has been done in this state, almost nothing has been written about it. The collecting areas are remote enough to be too far for field trips of the gem and mineral clubs in the other western states, and Utah has few clubs, most of them in Salt Lake City. This means that there is still much float material waiting to be picked up and digging is seldom required at this writing. The area is still "unspoiled" by great group collecting or prolific rockhound activity.

Most of the collecting that we have ever heard about is confined to southeastern Utah, north of the Arizona border and west of Colorado, a vast desert land in which there are few paved roads. This area is one of the greatest scenic wonderlands in America and the preserved beauty spots should all be visited, as they are not very far apart: the north rim of the Grand Canyon, Zion and Bryce National Parks, and the Cedar Breaks and Capitol Reef National Monuments. No rock collecting is allowed at the national preserves, but then nothing of gem value exists at any of them except that agate is reported plentiful in the Cedar Breaks National Monument.

There is an old saying that gold is where you find it. As far as agate in Utah is concerned, it also is where you find it, and that is practically all over the southeastern Utah area, in Wayne, Garfield, Emery, Grand, and Kane counties served by State Highways 54, 117, 95, 24, U. S. Routes 89 and 70, and several others. Travel in the extreme southeastern part of the state is discouraged because this is part of the Navajo Indian Reservation. The area should not be visited at all without guides.

About 25 miles north of St. George, in the southwest corner of the state, one can take State Highway 18 north for about 24 miles to the community of Central, where very fine blue banded agate nodules can be dug out of the surrounding basalt formations. Some of the nodules weigh as much as 60 pounds. This agate is very similar to the Brazilian agate boulders and is reported to take dyes well. One can continue north on this road to its junction with

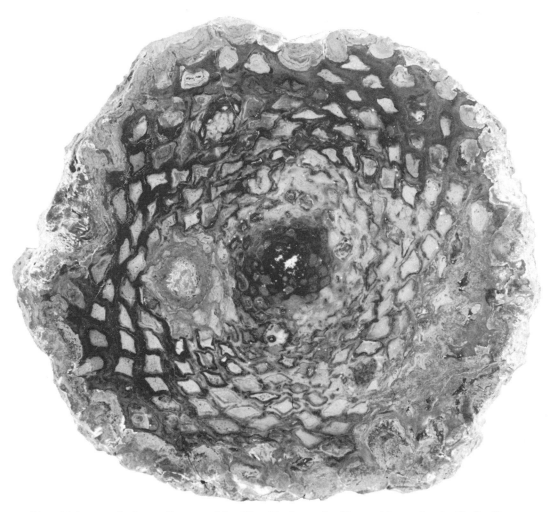

FIG. 107. Petrified cycad agate slab, 9″ x 8″, from the Henry Mountains in Utah. One of the finest that has ever been collected. The diamond-shaped spots are light yellow surrounded by red and green, with a red center and a greenish-yellow border. Found in 1945 and cut and polished by Leo D. Berner, Glendora, California, in whose collection it is today.

State Highway 56 and turn right to Newcastle, about another 6 miles. Or one may drive west on Highway 56 about 28 miles from Cedar City to Newcastle. Geodes can be collected here that are as large as two feet in diameter. They are not good cutting material but are spectacular specimens.

Leaving Salina on Highways 70-89, about the center of the state, take State Highway 10 east into Emery County. A big reef is to the left of the road as you travel east and this should be explored, for good dinosaur bone exists at many places, with good agate and petrified wood. This material is agatized dinosaur bone (locally called "dinny" bone) and slabs cut from it are sometimes as large as 8 inches in diameter in a blood red color. Cabochons made of it make very colorful and interesting jewelry mountings and of course they are always great conversation pieces. The desert area between Castle Dale and Green River is not well supplied with roads but there is a great deal of agate and bone there, the material usually found in the dealers' shops.

161

In the hills along the Colorado River near Cisco, 47 miles east of Green River on Highway 70, there are agatized clams as much as 5 inches across. This is also a good area for dinosaur bone, jasper, and petrified logs as big as 12 inches in diameter. Going southwest 30 miles on Highway 24 from Green River, one comes to a section known as the San Rafael Swell. This whole district has plenty of agate, jasper, and bone, but it is lonely desert country and unsafe in the summer unless two or more cars are traveling together. About 25 miles farther south is Hanksville where small but fine agate pebbles are scattered over the ground about 3 miles west of the town.

All over this southeastern section there are many gem materials other than quartz that the rockhound may wish to take home . . . flowering and other obsidian, septarian nodules for fine bookends, and the enormous fossilized ammonite shells.

VERMONT

(See the New England states, p. 140.)

VIRGINIA

There is practically nothing in the meager literature on quartz in Virginia to indicate that this is collecting country. There is no public domain in the state and, while there are many reports of amethyst crystals on farms, seldom were the finds more than a handful of indifferent crystals and the reports date back to the early years of the century. It is entirely probable that streams and quarries will yield some jasper and crystals as they do in the other Atlantic seaboard states.

WASHINGTON

Washington is another state in the west that has a lot of land area still in the public domain (almost 30 per cent). Most of it is loaded with quartz gem materials, particularly with petrified wood of many varieties, with the wood replacements in chalcedony well defined. Not as colorful as the Arizona wood, it is more recognizable as wood, as is indicated in the accompanying illustrations.

As in Oregon and California, the rockhound flourishes here. There are 66 clubs in the state catering to the interests of rock collectors and polishers, making the state second only to California in the number of clubs. These clubs, with time and place of meeting, are listed every year in the *Rockhound Buyers Guide* (see Chapter 12), and travelers are urged to arrange to attend a couple of meetings to get information and make new rock friends. It is good to have some acquaintances in a place like Washington so that you can swap rocks and correspond when you get back home. As with other sections of the country, rockhounds are always welcome at club meetings. A big gem and mineral show is usually held in Seattle during September, information about which can be secured from the gem cutting magazines.

While Washington state has many agate and jasper locations, the traveling rockhound is usually more interested in the many varieties of petrified wood. Most of this account is given to telling of a few of the more important locations. All Washington quartz locations have been well documented in the rockhound press, for the native Washington collectors like to share their information and rocks with fellow Americans from other parts of the country. Unfortunately, this cannot be said for the residents of all the states, as will be assumed by many readers of this book. Washington still has enough surface wood because some of the logs are as much as six inches in diameter, too big to be hauled away. Much of the wood is also too far from a road to be packed out, for it is very heavy, especially the desirable chunks that one would want for bookends, ash trays, and other novelties.

Probably the most popular collecting section is Saddle Mountain. To reach this area one should take Highway 90 for about 45 miles east of Ellensburg to the small community of Vantage on the Columbia River. This is approximately 178 miles southeast of Spokane, also by way of Highway 90. New freeway sections now being constructed will probably shorten this distance by several miles by the time this book is published. The area north of Vantage is a state park, preserving much of the wood in Ginkgo Petrified Forest. All travelers should visit the fine museum here and see the polished sections of wood. The park has uncovered many huge opalized Ginkgo logs for the visitor to see. After a visit to the museum, drive over the river bridge to the east bank of the Columbia River and take the dirt road to the right, going south, and proceed to the small community of Beverly. Here you will see sage-covered Saddle Mountain rising 2,000 feet. Its slopes are covered with wood and this is range

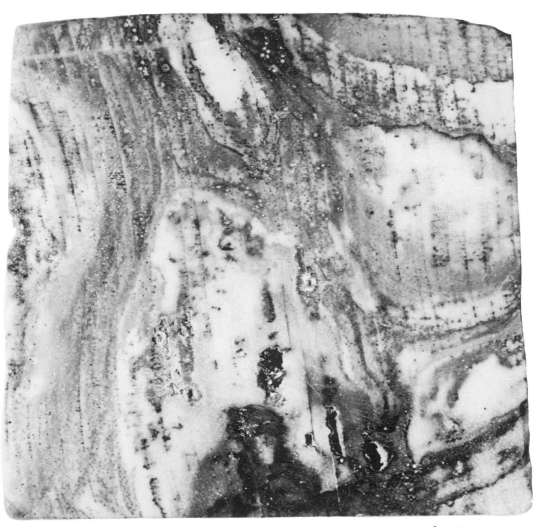

Fig. 108. A block of beautiful petrified wood from Washington State showing many worm holes. The piece has rich coloring in a strawberry and cream effect. From the author's collection. *(Photo by O. D. Smith.)*

FIG. 109. Slab of a peculiar egg-like formation in an agate from near Tenino, Washington. *(Photo courtesy of the Smithsonian Institution.)*

country open to collectors. The forests that have been buried here existed about fifteen million years ago in a very warm climate, as evidenced by the huge size of the trees. As in Arizona and Nevada, the trees would fall and be washed down into lakes and then be blown by prevailing winds to one side of the lake to be buried later by volcanic ash and preserved until ground waters petrified the logs. If one climbs the mountain and goes over to the south side, there are thousands of tons of some of the finest opalized wood material in existence. The big problem is how to get it out of that country with no roads. There is still plenty of wood for everyone, however, on the north side of the mountain. Saddle Mountain is almost in the exact center of a 50-mile-wide belt running from east to west and 150 miles north and south, in which there are many deposits of fossilized wood with countless spots yet to be discovered and with no spot depleted. The very size and weight of the logs and limbs defy the rockhog, so that con-

servative rockhounds should have a plentiful supply of this beautiful material for many years to come. Many of the collecting areas are described in the books mentioned in Chapter 12, especially in the paperback book, *Northwest Gem Trails.*

Washington has plenty of agate and jasper but somehow its collection has never been emphasized by rockhounds, as it has been in Oregon and California. Oddly enough, there are no thundereggs in Washington while there are many beds to the south in Oregon. Probably the most famous agate in Washington is the Ellensburg blue agate which has always been in scarce supply. This is a beautiful robin's-egg-blue clear chalcedony and, when cut in cabochons, it looks exactly like good quality star sapphire without a star. Nothing has been written, to the author's knowledge, about the exact location of this material and, as editor of the *Lapidary Journal* for many years, I was never able to get directions to this deposit . . . if there is a deposit. The so called Ellensburg

FIG. 110. An unpolished slab of an unknown variety of petrified wood from Washington State. The wood is brown and yellow with white chalcedony markings. From the author's collection. (*Photo by O. D. Smith.*)

blue agate is probably some of the blue agate found near Cle-Elum, a town 19 miles northeast of Ellensburg on Highway 90 and east of Seattle about 79 miles on the same highway. At Cle-Elum take Highway 97 going north to the right. The junction of Highways 90 and 97 occurs about 4 miles east of Cle-Elum before you get to the town, or 4 miles beyond it if you are coming from Seattle. About 2 miles from the junction there is an old logging railroad. Park the car and walk up the railroad track for about 1¾ miles to an old skid road. Here there are large masses of blue agate but not the quality of Ellensburg blue. If you visit a rockshop in Washington, and there are many, ask to see an example of the Ellensburg blue and get information about it, if you can. Proceeding north on Highway 97 beyond the railroad a series of canyons will be encountered, all of which are good agate collecting areas. Examine all rock slides for blue agate. A few miles farther on is Mineral Springs Camp, where one can take a dirt road to the left for a 5-mile trip to Crystal Mountain where geodes may be dug, the surface deposits having been gathered long ago.

Fig. 111. Paperweight of petrified cypress wood from Washington State, showing the growth ring lines in brown and white bandings. From the author's collection. *(Photo by O. D. Smith.)*

Shortly after leaving the Mineral Springs camp one will encounter Medicine Creek road on the left. Travel for several miles until you can go no further. You will then have to park and climb up the long trail to the summit of Red Top Mountain at 5,300 feet elevation. This is a long hard trek but you will be well rewarded when you get to the top of the Teanaway Ridge, for here there is much blue agate and geode material. There is more than enough to be had because it is such an arduous journey one is not likely to be able to carry much down the mountain or make more than one trip in a day. The whole area along the way has good agate collecting, however, and there is

166

even good agate at the car parking area at the foot of the trail. Some very fine agate has been collected in the bed of Medicine Creek, which you will follow to get to the Red Mountain area.

Beach collecting in Washington is not very productive of good material; most of it is jasper and very little of it really fine agate like the material found on the Oregon beaches to the south. The area around Chehalis in western Washington has produced some fine agate and notable carnelian, especially in the gravel bars of Lucas Creek where collecting is best in late summer when the creek has little water in it. About 5 miles south of Chehalis on Highway 99 one can turn east to Forest and explore the gravel bars of North Fork Creek. This is about 70 miles south of Tacoma and 88 miles north of Portland, Oregon. This is an area right by the paved highway and is fine for the traveler who cannot climb mountains or dig pot holes. All along the creek for several miles north and south of the bridge there are deposits of carnelian and other agates, petrified wood and bone, and geodes.

There are literally countless places to collect in Washington state and every community has its local rockhounds. Inquiry at any service station will undoubtedly reveal the names and home addresses of some of them. From long experience the author knows that these people are invariably among the friendliest in the world. It is amazing to what extent some of them will go to be hospitable, even to the point of dropping everything and taking you to a good collecting spot or giving generously of their own stock. To go to the western states to collect rocks and return home without having made some rockhound friends is as foolish as to go to London and never hear Big Ben or to Philadelphia and not visit Independence Hall. On the other hand, one is cautioned to mind his manners and not be too demanding. One should also be prepared for the unfriendly encounter and know when to back off gracefully and without prejudice to the many who do cooperate.

WEST VIRGINIA

About the best advice the author can give to those seeking information about West Virginia is to say that there is none and to suggest that they turn to the section under Virginia and apply every word of it to this state. West Virginia is great coal country and coal country is rarely productive of quartz-family minerals and gems. There is no public domain in this state.

WISCONSIN

Wisconsin is a great iron state and, characteristically, does not have associated quartz gem materials. It is also covered with lakes and forests, and mineral deposits are well hidden and protected from the rock hunter. The whole state, however, is underlaid with gravel deposits containing the Lake Superior type banded agate and, where these deposits are exposed, as in gravel pits and some stream beds and lake shores, the chance of success in finding agates is good. There are no known agate locations as such, however. In Wood County a red aventurine has been reported associated with sandstone, which yields large masses suitable for making novelties as shown in Chapter 11.

WYOMING

Wyoming is a vast domain for the rockhunter and richly rewarding to searchers, but it is unfortunate that the weather does not permit a very long hunting season . . . only from about late May until late September. While it ranks 9 in size, it is 48th in population, so it is the most unsettled state with the exception of Alaska. More than 48 per cent of the state is in the public domain, or nearly thirty million acres, of which Yellowstone National Park, the largest of our national parks, and Grand Teton National Park take up more than two and a half million acres. Collecting is not allowed in these parks. A small portion of Yellowstone Park is in the neighboring states of Idaho and Montana. There is no doubt that any traveler in Wyoming will want to visit these most interesting of our national parks and see the many wonders, such as the

Fig. 112. Sweetwater agate from Wyoming. These agates are described in the text. Enlarged to show detail of black dendritic inclusions. This is an unpolished agate from the author's collection. (*Photo by O. D. Smith.*)

geysers, canyons, wild animals, boiling springs and mud pots, and the petrified forests. But there is much for the agate hunter outside the parks.

The knowledgeable rockhound will have one thing in mind when he goes to Wyoming . . . jade. Jade was discovered in the mountains north of Lander in 1930 and many tons of it have been gathered from there and other spots since that time. The chances of a searcher finding any today are very slim indeed. However, all rockhounds should be on the lookout for it at all times. Jade has been discovered at many United States locations since 1930 and in British Columbia, too, the discoveries all having been made by rockhounds who were looking for something

else, usually agate. Further reference to jade is made in the books listed in Chapter 12.

Wyoming contains a portion of the 80-mile Dryhead area in which the famous Dryhead agate is found, an agate very similar to the Fairburn agate described in the South Dakota section of this chapter and an agate area described in the Montana section. This is a vast collecting area along the Big Horn River that is practically inaccessible except on horseback or on foot. The agates are very beautiful but the collecting is only for the hardy. This area is in northwestern Wyoming; if the visitor is in that area it is suggested that he explore both sides of the road (Highway 16) about 12 miles east of Buffalo, where agates, chalcedony, and wood can be gathered by those not prepared for rugged travel. Buffalo is 36 miles south of Sheridan on Highway 87.

About 40 miles southeast of Lander, on the way to Rawlins by Highway 287, one crosses the Sweetwater River. The whole area for many miles on both sides of the river and east and west of the highway is noted for the Sweetwater agates. These are certainly not among the most beautiful agates in the world, but they are, nevertheless, very interesting specimens. These agates are waterworn pebbles that look like jelly beans, seldom larger than an inch in diameter. They are gray-to-bluish clear chalcedony and filled with what looks like petrified pepper or black dendrites. Erosion and storms are constantly uncovering new supplies and they are not hard to find. One does not need to confine his collecting to the banks of the river, as the agates are widely distributed over the surrounding country. If one happens to have a small rake he can uncover thousands of these agates.

Another interesting Wyoming agate that is not particularly beautiful but very interesting is the turitella agate, a compact mass of silicified or fossilized

Fig. 113. Section of black and white petrified wood, 6″ x 6″, from the Blue Valley, Wyoming. This wood is similar to the famous Eden Valley wood and is found nearby. Cut and polished by Leo D. Berner, Glendora, California.

spiral shells less than an inch long. The material is found in slabs one to two inches thick and, when sliced, the cross sections provide an interesting pattern in a black matrix. The material is not on a highway, however, and must be hiked after in areas about 15 miles north of Superior and 15 miles southwest of Wamsutter. Local residents or service station operators in both towns can probably give specific directions as to country roads and trails to the collecting grounds and, of course, shops in the area have the material for sale. The author

once bought a chunk of turitella agate weighing about 5 pounds for 25 cents from a dealer in Rock Springs, but that was many years ago and it is doubtful if such bargains are obtainable today. See accompanying illustration of a slab of this chunk on page 170.

Wyoming is indeed a paradise for the fossil hunter and the fancier of petrified wood, for no state has a greater variety of both. The wood is not as beautiful as the Washington and Arizona wood, but the fossils are among the best in the world, the area being exceeded in im-

Fig. 114. Slab of Wyoming turitella agate, showing cross section of ancient fossil shells in a black jasper-like matrix. From the author's collection. *(Photo by O. D. Smith.)*

portance only by the Gobi Desert. No directions can be given to specific collecting areas except to advise that the Big Horn Basin in northern Wyoming is the best collecting ground for the bone hunter. Here the great dinosaurs thrived and their bones abound, the only place in America where complete skeletons have been assembled by qualified scientists. An interesting sidelight for the bone hunter is to find some gastroliths or gizzard stones, which are usually quartz. These stones, ranging in size from a peach pit to the size of a hen's egg, were ingested by the dinosaurs to aid digestion and they became highly polished while being ground around in the stomachs of the animals. These are not regarded as authentic by scientists, however, unless they are associated

with the remains of an accompanying skeleton, so if a reader finds a skeleton he should look for the associated gizzard stones. They are only valuable as curiosities or for trading, and have no gemological significance.

To petrified wood collectors probably the best and most sought after wood is the Eden Valley wood. This wood seldom occurs in great logs but usually in twigs and small limb sections. See illustration. Here, in an area about 40 miles north of Rock Springs in southwestern Wyoming, there once existed a great forest that was completely buried in volcanic ash from some tremendous volcanic eruption nearby. The forest must have been enormously infested with insects, too, for nearly every piece of Eden Valley wood shows worm holes and trac-

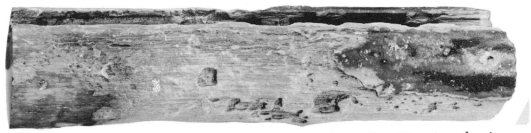

FIG. 115. Limb section of petrified wood from the Eden Valley, Wyoming, showing characteristic worm borings. The limb has been split open and the interior is chalcedony. From the author's collection. *(Photo by O. D. Smith.)*

ings. There is probably no wood that reveals its character as perfectly as the Eden Valley wood. It polishes beautifully as it is perfect chalcedony, but the wood is generally black or gray and it does not add color to a collection. However, any representative wood collection without some Eden Valley material is incomplete. The Eden Valley area is not in the public domain but is principally owned by one family which sometimes allows rockhounds to collect. One should make local inquiry in Eden or other nearby towns before attempting a collecting excursion.

In the extreme southwest corner of the state in Lincoln County are the world-famous fossil fish beds about 12 miles west on Highway 89 between Kemmerer and Sage. This is certainly not a gem material but almost every collector will want to get a fish, the most perfect fish fossils that have ever been found and represented in every important museum in the world. Here is a whole mountain of the best fossilized sea life ever found, and one can easily find a complete bass, chub, pickerel, herring, or sunfish imbedded in sandstone which can be lifted entire in sheets from the soil. A few fish carefully wrapped in newspapers can certainly be swapped along the way for some of the quartz materials you were unable to find or for much better specimens of those you did find. This should give added impetus to your collecting.

There are thousands of good locations for agate and jasper in this big state, which is just one big collecting ground with few fences, but few of the locations have been documented except for those mentioned here. While the minerals that have been mentioned possess tremendous scientific interest, there is really little in Wyoming that possesses gemological interest or great beauty outside of the jade.

Chapter 9

Collecting Areas in Canada and Mexico

CANADA (Covering the Provinces from West to East)

British Columbia

THE GREATEST rockhunting area in North America at this time is the province of British Columbia in western Canada. A hundred years from now the surface will barely be scratched. There is profound rockhound activity there and it appears that British Columbia will soon be the second largest area in North America in the number of gem and mineral clubs. Only one Canadian club was listed in the 1955 *Rockhound Buyers Guide* but the number of clubs had grown to 43 in the 1962 edition, only seven years later. Of the 43 Canadian clubs 37 are in British Columbia.

Few United States citizens realize the size of this beautiful land, but British Columbia has 359,000 square land miles and many thousands of water miles. This is more than twice the size of California and 100,000 more square miles than Texas. Unfortunately, there are very few paved roads in proportion to the land and these roads are practically closed to travel at times because of the weather. Little collecting can be done between November and April. The rugged character of the country and the heavy timber and verdure make prospecting difficult; one should really be a camper

to hunt in this country, as the luxurious motor inn with TV in every room is absent and few accommodations of any kind are available. While the traveler off the beaten path will have to pack almost all of his food, he need not worry about water as he does at many desert locations in the States . . . water is everywhere. And where there is water, such as streams and lake shores, there is agate.

It seems from reports that almost any stream or lake shore will produce gem material of some kind for the collector and just about every type of agate and jasper ever reported in the United States has been found in this province . . . also jade at several spots. There is colored banded agate similar to the Fairburn agate of South Dakota and there are thundereggs similar to those of Oregon. There must be petrified wood but the Canadian rockhounds do not seem interested in it, for they never report any finds. Most of them are principally interested in one thing and that is jade . . . the agate finds are incidental and the wood is scarcely noted. The jade that the Canadian rockhound goes after is the float material found in the rivers, material that has been tumbled down the streams through countless centuries from remote areas where it has not yet been found in place. Jade is never found away from the river banks unless in old stream

172

beds. Perhaps the best collecting area is the Fraser River which is a big rushing stream with many large gravel bars, most of them accessible from Highway 1, sometimes by foot and sometimes by accessory dirt roads. Jade, agates, and jasper occur on practically every bar according to reliable reports the author has received. Collectors should be equipped with wading boots, for most collecting in British Columbia requires them.

No passports are needed to enter or return from Canada. Your auto registration usually is sufficient and we know of no one who has failed to pass customs upon returning because of any rocks he has collected. The best thing to do is to reply, if questioned, that the rocks are just rocks for your hobby collection, of no monetary value. It might be wise to eliminate the word jade from your vocabulary; some too enthusiastic customs employee might think you were hauling back a fortune. The same advice applies to our Canadian readers returning to Canada with United States rocks.

Regulations do change, but the rules at this writing, which have been in effect for many years, are that automobiles may be taken into Canada without a fee. Obtain a free permit good for six months at the port of entry. If a stay is to be less than 48 hours you must surrender your state license registration and get it back when you leave the country. If the driver is not the legal owner of the car he must satisfy customs that he has authority to take the car into Canada. Naturalized citizens of the United States must carry their naturalization certificates and alien residents of the United States must have alien registration cards. It is wise for all United States citizens to carry some proof of citizenship in case of arbitration with some customs officials. People may carry copies of a birth certificate, but the author believes that the simplest proof of citizenship is a certification from one's local voting registrar that one is

registered to vote. This is supplied free by registrars everywhere, it does not mention one's party affiliation, and it is conclusive proof that one is a citizen.

Probably the most explored district lies between Chilliwack and Lillooet, a distance of about 140 miles. Chilliwack is about 90 miles east of Vancouver on Canadian Highway 1. Going directly from the United States, take Highway 99 in Washington state to Blaine and then enter Canada at Clayton and take a road to the right to reach Highway 1, leaving Highway 99 at this point. Turn east on Highway 1 and go about 30 miles to Chilliwack.

Examine bars in the Fraser River between Chilliwack and Lytton and then turn left on Highway 12 for 36 miles to Lillooet where the paved road ends. Most of the larger towns in Canada have tourist offices and they are usually well informed about the rocks of their area and collecting conditions. They are very helpful and should be consulted.

If you do go as far north on Highway 1 as Lytton, the turnoff point to Lillooet, it is suggested that you continue another 60 miles to Cache Creek and turn right and go east 56 miles to Kamloops, still on Highway 1. Good agate locations are reportedly being found in this area all the time, good banded agates being found only a half mile from the city limits. The banded agates from this area are probably the largest and some of the best in Canada. There is a thriving rock club in Kamloops, the Thompson Valley Rock Club, which meets in the Library Museum building on the first Tuesday evening of each month. A visit to a meeting could result in some new friendships and wonderful information about the area.

If one is interested in thundereggs the trip should be extended on Highway 2, which begins at Cache Creek, the turnoff to Kamloops. Clinton is 27 miles north on Highway 2. The country to the west of Clinton is rugged, with high mountains and a favorite game hunting area that is reported to have beautiful thundereggs at several locations, usually on private property. However, information about the locations is vague and inquiry about them should be made of local rockhounds one may meet along the way.

Alberta

In the Province of Alberta, east of British Columbia, there is a very famous petrified wood locality in the vicinity of Drumheller. Going east from Calgary on Highway 1 for 18 miles one comes to Highway 9 turning left and north at Strathmore. Drumheller is 70 miles northeast on Highway 9. The Dinosaur Beds Provincial Park is 8 miles north of the town. No collecting is allowed there but in the surrounding country one can easily find dinosaur bones which are different from the Utah and Colorado bones in that they are frequently hollow and crystal lined. The Drumheller wood is in small limb sections and is very similar to the famous Eden Valley wood of Wyoming. The vast plains provinces of Saskatchewan and Manitoba are evidently not agate country, for nothing can be found in the literature about existing locations.

Ontario

Ontario is noted for having the most beautiful agate in Canada, similar to the Mexican agate shown in color in the frontispiece of this book but not so vivid in coloring, and there are numerous locations of amethyst associated with the dumps of private mines. The agate is found on Michipicoten Island in Lake Superior near the shore at Michipicoten Harbor, reached by Highway 17 north of Sault Ste. Marie, Michigan. Good banded agate is also reported about 15 miles north of Sault Ste. Marie at Goulais Bay on Lake Superior. In western Ontario along Highway 17 from Port Arthur northeast to Nipigon, along the north shore of Lake Superior, there is a belt

about 25 miles wide containing a great many silver, zinc, and lead mines in which good amethyst crystals are an unwanted by-product and may be found in the dumps. The mines will have to be located by private inquiry. Highway 17, running all around Lake Superior, is an extension of Highway 61 in Minnesota. There are two belts of mines, one beginning at Big Trout Bay and running north to Pie Island. The other begins at Port Arthur on Thunder Bay and extends north to Nipigon. Clear, smoky, and amethyst crystals may be gathered at most of the mines and many of the crystals can be faceted into beautiful gems.

Quebec

The Province of Quebec offers very little in the way of quartz gems except jasper of various colors and patterns that is reported to be widely distributed in small amounts. No important locality can be pinpointed at this time. New Brunswick, likewise, has little to offer the collector. Chalcedony geodes, some with amethyst crystals, occur between North Head and Dark Harbor on Grand Manan Island in Charlotte County. Nova Scotia has a few agates on the beaches of the Bay of Fundy and agate is rather widely distributed throughout the province, but in scarce amounts. There appears to be nothing in the literature about quartz deposits in Newfoundland, Prince Edward Island, Labrador, or the trackless vast Northwest Territories. It appears that the rockhound wanting to do some serious and rewarding gemstone collecting has but one real choice in Canada and that is British Columbia—practically untouched and unexplored, rockwise.

MEXICO

There is only one very good reason for going into Mexico for quartz gem materials and that is that the weather is always right for it. There is no snow and

Fig. 116. Beautiful banded fortification agate from Mexico. On display at the Smithsonian Institution. *(Photo courtesy of the Smithsonian Institution.)*

it is usually very hot. The roads go right through the agate fields but the locations are all on private ranches and one is limited to stream beds, usually dry. The author has never heard of a Mexican national who was really interested in rocks but nearly every man, woman, and child knows of the North Americans' great interest and is ready to take advantage of it at any opportunity. If you go to Mexico you will find the friendliest people in the world, but they are sharp in a trade and they know the value of the rocks they sell a lot better than the average rockhound. Whatever you do, never refer to yourself as an American. The Mexicans are Americans too and they strongly resent a United States citizen calling himself anything else than a

North American, which they are too, or *Norte Americano.*

The Mexican agates are the best naturally colored agates in the world. A good selection of them is illustrated in color on the jacket of this book and as the frontispiece. These agates are from the extensive collection of James Mueller, a gemstone dealer in Phoenix, Arizona, who has one of the finest collections of Mexican agates, both cut and uncut, in the United States. A slice of a colorful Mexican banded agate makes about the best bola tie mount one can obtain, usually just the right size and certainly colorful.

Before proceeding further with information on agates it would be well to advise readers of the details of making an extended trip into Mexico. The country is not well supplied with roads as is the United States, but the main roads are fine and better than Canada's. Mexico does not have the deteriorating weather of Canada. Gasoline stations are well spaced along the road but they are out of gas a great part of the time. The oil industry is nationalized but, at this writing, the Mexicans have never succeeded in establishing a system of distribution that keeps all stations supplied at all times. The author has had some very sad and alarming experiences because of this deficiency. Therefore, always keep your tank filled and always carry a spare container of at least ten gallons of fuel. If you do get into a town where no gasoline is available, go to the local tourist bureau and they will help you. The government wants to do everything possible to help, as the tourist business is now one of Mexico's leading "industries." If the town is a sizeable one with an airport, go there, for all airports have gasoline.

One does not need a passport to visit Mexico, but some proof of citizenship should be carried, such as a birth certificate or a certification from your local voters' registrar that you are a registered voter. Each citizen over 15 years of age must carry a tourist card if he is going to go more than 90 miles below the United States border. These cards can be secured from Mexican Consuls in the important cities of the United States or from immigration authorities at border towns. The cards require a $3.00 fee for a six months' visit and $5.00 for a longer stay. Upon returning to the United States you must show a certificate of vaccination within the last three years, so it is best to visit your doctor in the States and be vaccinated before you leave the country. Most large cities will vaccinate you free in their Public Health Clinics. If you are just crossing the border to visit some of the interesting border towns and cities, it is only neces-

sary to give your name and the state where you were born to get back in.

If you are taking a car into Mexico for more than 90 miles south, you must furnish proof of ownership, registration certificate, and driver's license. In case of an accident your car will be impounded unless you furnish proof of financial responsibility or evidence that your car is insured with a company that will pay claims in Mexico. The best procedure is to get a policy from a Mexican insurance company as soon as you enter Mexico, for this protects you immediately and with no question. These policies can be secured for any time you want, a week or a month or more, and the fees are very reasonable, much lower than in American companies. At all border towns you will see the signboards of Mexican insurance companies. Naturalized United States citizens must carry their naturalization certificates and alien residents of the United States must carry valid passports and alien registration cards.

If you do collect any mineral or gem specimens in Mexico, or buy some, it is not difficult to get them back into the United States, but definite advice cannot be given as regulations appear to change almost from day to day. The author has talked to many collectors and dealers who have traveled into Mexico and in all cases he has received different accounts. A truck loaded with rocks is always suspect at any border town. That denotes a commercial venture and is always in dispute. The traveler with a private car or camper-type car is seldom suspect and should just declare that he has *minerales* of no commercial value. There does not seem to be any rule book; each customs officer appears to act as an independent agent and a little graft on big lots of rocks is quite common according to our informants, although we discount some of their wild tales. The author happens to live only 20 miles from the Mexican border and has never had any difficulty of any kind in going back and forth, nor has he ever heard of anyone else having trouble transporting rocks.

The state in Mexico bordering Southern California is Baja California or Lower California. Many reports have been written about gem materials coming out of this almost inaccessible country, but the only gem the author has ever been impressed with is sphene, an entrancingly beautiful gem when faceted and very much desired by collectors. The quartz gems are very mediocre and hardly worth going after, unless for the fun.

Informants tell us that any small amount of rock is usually not taxed at the United States border but, when it appears that the lot is clearly a commercial proposition, 5 per cent of the purchase price is charged and you had better be prepared with a receipt of purchase. Road maps and regulations for tourists can be secured in advance of your trip by applying to the American Chamber of Commerce, San Juan de Letran 24, Mexico City. Ask at the same time about the latest regulations on rocks you may wish to bring back from Mexico, and then you will have this document in case of dispute upon your return.

A word of advice should be given at this point. The average American considers himself a rather superior person and, unfortunately, he conveys this attitude when he leaves his country. Mexico is a strange country containing a proud people, speaking another language, and with an entirely different sense of values. There is a wider class distinction among Mexicans than there is in the United States and the American tourist is usually considered with a quiet contempt . . . women in shorts and slacks are held in utter contempt. Always be courteous and you will be treated with the greatest courtesy you have ever experienced.

It is assumed that any visitor to Mexico who goes to the trouble of getting a tourist's card will visit Mexico City. Few Americans realize that this great and beautiful city is larger than any city in North or South America with the exception of New York . . . a city of about 6 million population. Mexico City was a well organized city of 60,000 homes before Manhattan Island saw its first white man. It has a wonderful cool year-round climate because of its high elevation— 7349 feet.

There are three fine highways to Mexico City from the United States. A highway from Laredo, Texas, crosses over the most spectacular mountain pass in the world on a marvelously engineered highway. The crossing must be made in the midday hours because of the treacherous clouds at other times. This is just the section between Tamazunchale (pron. Thomas and Cholly) and Zimapan, a distance of about 100 miles. There is nothing along this highway for the collector of quartz materials. Some of the finest opals in the world used to come from mines at Zimapan, but none have been recovered there for many years and none are for sale in the area.

Highway 15 is now complete from Nogales, Arizona, south of Tucson, through Guadalajara, Mexico's second city, to Mexico City, but there is nothing along this highway of interest to the quartz collector. The "rockhound highway" is Highway 45, the Christopher Columbus Highway, from El Paso, Texas, to Mexico City, probably the most traveled highway in Mexico. This is part of the Pan-American Highway. The finest quartz gem materials in the world are found along this highway . . . the beautiful naturally-colored banded agates seen in the frontispiece of this book and the Mexican fire opals, the only true "fire" opals, of Querétaro (pronounced ker-ET-ero). Unfortunately, we must offer the information that it is a matter of great difficulty indeed to collect any agates and almost impossible to collect any opal. The traveler will find plenty

Fɪɢ. 117. An excellent example of a scenic agate which leaves nothing to anyone's imagination. Called the Hooded Owl Agate, it is owned by T. B. Williams of Lordsburg, New Mexico, and it may be seen by anyone stopping at his Triangle Rock Shop in that town. The agate was dug up by an Indian boy about 75 miles west of Sueco in the state of Chihuahua, Mexico. It was broken into an oval shape when being dug and Mr. Williams ground and polished it that way, which gave a perfect shape to the owl. No other lapidary treatment was used and the owl is naturally colored in a beautiful carnelian red with a purplish red background. This agate may be seen in color on the cover of the June 1961 issue of the *Lapidary Journal*.

of both for sale but he would be far better off financially if he did his buying from established dealers in the States. There are many good dealers in El Paso and elsewhere in the United States with good stocks of Mexican materials. Their addresses may be secured from their advertisements in the gem magazines.

It was about 1945, when Highway 15 was becoming available, that a few American rockhounds traveling the new highway began to explore the roadside territory for agates. They found, to their great surprise, plenty of small agates, averaging about 2 inches, that were the most colorful agates ever found, being noted particularly for their purples and blues and pinks. Found along with these agates were larger agates that proved to be the finest iris agates that have ever been discovered. The word was not around very long before American dealers had cleared off the surface material by periodic raids with trucks and by having small boys gather all the agates they could find for a few cents a pound. It happens that the best agate locations are on two of the largest and richest cattle ranches in all Mexico, and their owners are so tremendously wealthy that they have so far been open to no inducements to permit bulldozing or digging for the thousands of tons of agates that are probably available. The ranch hands, however, work with the individual roadside operators one comes across and agates do still find their way into the traveler's sack. It is not unusual for one to see huge piles of agate in the yards of some villagers, but they are the culls of agate picked up many years ago and are absolutely worthless.

Villa Ahumada is about 83 miles south of El Paso. Between there and Ojo Laguna, a distance of about 70 miles, is the most important agate producing area in Mexico, particularly on the Gallego and Sueco ranches. A very fine type of agate, called Mexican lace agate, comes from a section west of Villa Ahumada, and the ranch owner permits blasting and digging at this writing. There is another variety of agate from this same location called flame agate because of the flame-like red inclusions in clear chalcedony, a very beautiful gem when cut and polished. While the best agate is found along this particular stretch of Highway 15, there has also been a great deal of agate gathered near the same road for the next 300 miles—so there is a lot of fun and exploring for the rock-

hound traveling this highway and interested in agate. If one is interested in fine mineral crystal specimens other than quartz, then Durango, about halfway to Mexico City, is one of the most interesting collecting spots in the world. Collectors are allowed, in several instances, to visit in the mines.

The quartz gem collector in Mexico will have one thing on his mind above all others and that is to secure some Mexican fire opals, the most beautiful of all the opals and queen of all the quartz gems. But the only opals one will get will be by purchase, for the mines are all privately owned and the dumps yield nothing (what they do contain is usually bottled in water and sold to the unwary as "specimens").

Some advice on buying opal should be offered at this point. The Mexican dollar is the peso, worth eight cents in American money at this writing. The workers in the mines are paid only five pesos, or forty cents, a day. One can then understand the cupidity of the miner who wants to sell a piece of opal in matrix for perhaps eighty cents, a small sum to almost any American tourist but a couple of days' wages to the miner. The glass jugs one will see filled with opal specimens in matrix are very interesting and make some beautiful cabochons, but do not pay more than an American dollar for the biggest jug you may see. If you want a really fine opal you must be prepared to pay from $50.00 to $100.00 for a single fine specimen and none of the street vendors or the miners have such material. There is wide competition among the German and Japanese dealers for the small quantity of fine opal that is ever available and it is a discouraging process for the traveler to find a source of opal that he can trust, plus the fact that relatively few Americans are capable of even judging a good Mexican fire opal. They should be examined in museums and good jewelry stores before making the trip, so that a buyer will know what he is looking for. A lot depends on a person's good fortune at the time. A friend of the author picked up a fire opal for only 75 cents that yielded one of the best Mexican opals he has ever seen. But it was many years ago and the purchase was made at a curio shop in a hotel at the Grand Canyon in Arizona. Such a circumstance may never happen again—but you never know. Probably the best available bargains are still for sale in American dealers' shops, for many of the dealers are hardly more aware of the value of some of their opal merchandise than their customers.

Queretero, a fast-growing city of 66,000, is the center of the opal mining district. Many of the mines are in the hands of the Ontiveros family and contact by telephone or visit with any of them will get you information on opal and perhaps a chance to visit one of the mines, or at least to buy some opal. The visitor will see many urchins along the streets offering jars of matrix specimens for sale. When the word gets along the grapevine that an American is in town looking for opal, vendors usually appear.

If one has the time, a visit should be made on a Sunday to the small village on Tequisquiapan (tekees-keepan). About seven o'clock in the morning the Indians come down out of the hills to sell the opals in the Plaza that they have dug during the previous week from the mountains in back of the village. To get to this small village, take the main highway (45) south of Queretaro for 31 miles to San Juan del Rio and turn off another 10 miles to Tequisquiapan.

This brief account covers only a small part of the great country of Mexico, which is filled with quartz minerals, but there is practically no documentation on specific localities. It is suggested that the rockhound traveler do some personal exploring along the highways and byways he travels, for he just might find a wonderful spot for surface agate and jasper as others have done before him.

Chapter 10

How to Cut and Polish Agates

PRACTICALLY every reader who ever goes on a rock trip and gathers some of his very own gem materials will want to process some of his finds into finished gemstones. Along the way somewhere he will meet other rockhounds with finished products they are only too proud and anxious to show him, or he will visit rock shops where he will see how ugly rocks can be transformed into gems of great beauty or stone objects of usefulness and decorative value.

Gem cutting is no longer difficult. Up until the early thirties there was practically no commercial equipment available and the amateur lapidary had to depend entirely on his own ingenuity to build his own equipment, which still demanded much drudgery and time before passable gems could be produced.

This situation changed very rapidly, and by the forties there were many manufacturers of diamond saw blades, saw carriages, cabochon making machines, and faceting machines. Today, in the sixties, there are a great many dependable manufacturers of good equipment, some of whose wares are shown in this chapter. Machines are now available that turn out beautifully polished tumbled stones that are little credit to the operator, for he does nothing at all in the process but sit and wait, buy the grits, and pay for the power. There is absolutely no skill required.

Time was when the amateur lapidary would take a likely looking slab of petrified wood or agate and laboriously grind the stone on a lap wheel for hours on end. He would achieve with pride a mirror-like finish on his slab and proudly exhibit it in the early gem shows. Now ten men can toss ten slabs into ten self-operating slab polishing machines and come up with ten identical and perfectly polished slabs that are a credit to no one, for no personal skill was involved. The "art" of tumbling stones has become extremely popular and yields a lot of fun, but it requires no lapidary skill to produce tumbled gems with any of the great variety of tumbling equipment available in today's market.

The man or woman who feels an artistic urge toward stone cutting is limited to cabochon cutting, faceting, carving, and the making of novelties. However, the author does not wish to be misunderstood. There is plenty of fun and satisfaction to be had by the many thousands who tumble stones and who slab them in the newer slab polishers. They produce items of great beauty and gemological interest, but they are not lapidaries any more than a woman with a package of prepared cake mix and a hot oven is a skilled baker.

The field where the greatest number of gem cutters work and where they have the most fun is cabochon cutting.

Fig. 118. Master facet unit with a 45° angle dop for faceting the table on a cut crystal gemstone. Manufactured by M. D. R. Mfg. Co., Los Angeles.

Here one can make any shape he desires and expertly select the color, pattern, or design contained in the stone itself. Self expression can be indulged in, as seen in the many cabochon illustrations in this book.

The art of faceting is not so much an art as a skill. It is very rewarding to produce the entrancing form of a cut gem, the ultimate in beauty, but it requires only skill and vast patience. Originality and artistic ability are rarely used because all faceted gems are cut to a norm.

This section does not pretend to offer full advice on gem cutting as that re-

quires a complete book, but the author does wish to explain to the reader the fundamentals of gem cutting. He may be reading for the first time of the possibility of his entering, for his personal fun and pleasure, the world's oldest artistic craft. A very complete book is available on gem cutting. It is a companion book to this one, called *Gemcraft.* This author is co-author of the book, with Hugh Leiper, now editor of the *Lapidary Journal.* There are also many other books available on the lapidary art and of course there are the magazines giving new techniques and current information, listed in Chap. 12.

There is one big problem in the cutting of all gem materials into whatever form and that is the problem of conquering hardness. There is no great problem in sawing a piece of wood with a steel saw, for the steel teeth are much harder than the wood and they cut through it easily. But no metal saw with teeth could be made that would saw a rock, because almost any rock except talc or gypsum is harder than the hardest steel. Rocks used to be sawed by running a steel disk through a mud made of carborundum grits and other hard materials. The disk would pick up the abrasive and it would help to "saw" through the rock. Then the diamond saw was invented and now steel disks have small diamonds inserted into their periphery;

they can saw through the hardest rocks because the diamond is the hardest material in the world.

Agates and all the other quartz materials discussed in this book have a hardness of 7 on the Mohs scale. The only stones harder are the topaz (8), corundum (ruby and sapphire, 9), and the diamond (10). This does not mean that the diamond is only three degrees harder than an agate; it may be untold thousands of times harder . . . no one knows exactly. It is sufficient to say that the quartz materials at 7 are among the hardest things on earth, and that is why they are so durable as gems; they are unlikely to break or chip when struck by other objects and, because of their durability, their polish lasts indefinitely.

FIG. 119. Triple barrel tumbler manufactured by Don Bobo's Lapidary Products, Seattle, Washington, and selling for $87.95. Equipped with removable insert liners, it permits the tumbling or polishing of three 12-pound loads of gem pebbles, such as agate or jasper, at one time. (*Photo by Kaminske Studio, Seattle.*)

183

An agate cabochon must be preshaped to the desired form. Perhaps it is a beach agate that has already been ground small by time's and nature's grinding mills—the tumbling streams and the sea. It will require no sawing and the stone can be preshaped by hand grinding. But if one wants to grind a cabochon from a large rock he must first obtain a section of it. To do this he clamps it into the carriage of a diamond saw, just as a butcher places a bologna in a slicing machine. The rock is set at the point where the operator wishes to slice and the power is turned on. Very slowly the diamond blade chews through the rock until a slice drops off. The slice is then cleaned of the oil through which the blade has been running to avoid the terrible heat that would crack the rock. After an examination of the slice for the best possible section for color, freedom from fractures, pattern, etc., the ca-bochon blank is marked, usually with a template, in the desired shape. Independent shapes, rather than those of the standard templates, are best, for they reflect the individuality of the gem cutter. They may not fit the standard jewelry mountings that are available, but if one must conform in every lapidary operation he will never become an artist. Mountings can always be made to fit *any* stone shape.

The marking on the slab is made with an aluminum or copper pencil, for ordinary lead pencil markings would wash off in the processing. The surplus material around the marking on the slab can be snubbed off with pliers or cut away in a small diamond saw called a trim saw. The material is then shaped by hand as much as possible, the methods being illustrated in the books about gem cutting. After the approximate shape has been achieved, the stone is attached to

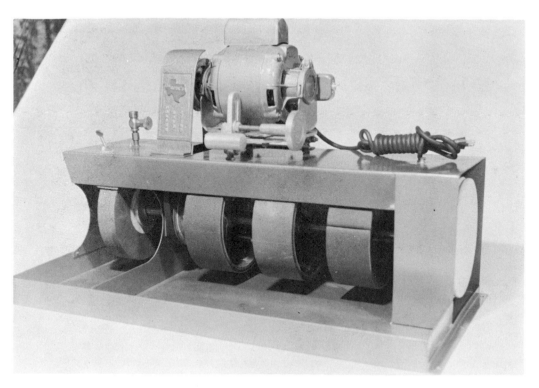

Fig. 120. Compact cabochon maker manufactured by Rock's, San Antonio, Texas, and selling for $189.50. It contains grinding and polishing units only (no saw), but is a very complete outfit. (*Photo by Jack Kinkel, San Antonio.*)

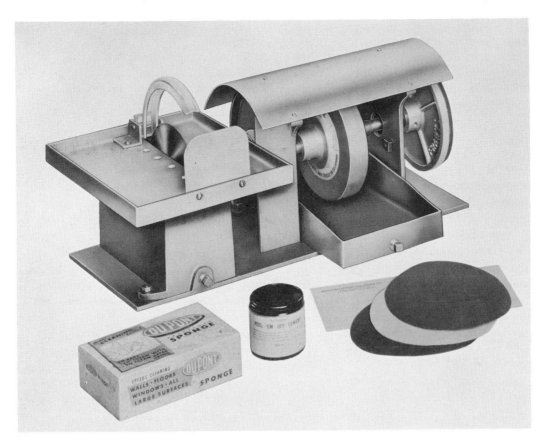

Fig. 121. Junior Pup lapidary outfit for use in a small space such as an apartment. Manufactured by Frantom Lapidary Equipment Company, Gardena, California. Priced at $75.00. Contains saw and blade, grinder, sander, and polisher. *(Photo by Folger, Los Angeles.)*

a stick for easier manipulation. This is called a dop stick and the stone is attached with hot wax. The stone is then manipulated on carborundum grinding wheels until the final shape is achieved.

A gem has now been made by conquering its hardness and bringing it into submission into the shape desired by the operator. But it is dull in appearance and covered with scratches and perhaps some pits. These must be eliminated by further conquering the stone's hardness and achieving a final polish.

The next step is the use of sanding wheels, which are wheels covered with cloth coated with carborundum grits in various grades. The stone is manipulated on these fast moving wheels until all scratches have been removed. It is then washed to be sure all carborundum grits have been cleaned away and the operator moves to a polishing felt or leather wheel to which is applied a thin paste of cerium oxide or tin oxide. The stone is manipulated until there is a perfect mirror-like polish that is absolutely free of scratches or blemishes and until the light from a light bulb can be seen clearly in the surface of the gem no matter which way it is turned, and with no cloudy effect at any spot. If this cannot be achieved, then the stone was not properly sanded and the process should begin all over again. The stone is finally removed from the dop by heating the wax and prying it loose, and using a little acetone on a rag to clean the stone of all polishing agents. In the

185

Fig. 122. Frantom De Luxe model lapidary outfit manufactured by Frantom Lapidary Equipment Company, Gardena, California. Priced at $238.00, complete with motor, saw and blade, grinding wheels, polishing disks and buffs, in addition to all accessories. *(Photo by Folger, Los Angeles.)*

author's opinion this is one of the great thrills of achievement: seeing the new beautiful gem in one's palm.

Faceting is done in much the same way, except that the materials involved are expensive, rare, valuable, and fragile when compared to agates. The faceter begins with a small piece of material and not a slab. The whole operation is one of putting faces or sides on a crystal gem that will reflect light and achieve a sparkle. Reference is made to the gem cutting books for the meticulous methods and procedures of faceting.

Making novelties requires all the procedures of the lapidary: the use of the big and little saws, the lap wheels, and the grinders and polishers. Making beads and hollowing ash trays require drills. Carving gems, the ultimate in the lapidary art, requires the use of many techniques and definitely calls for artistic

Fɪɢ. 123. Combination lapping and polishing machine for making slabs, bookends, and novelties requiring flat surfaces. Manufactured by Vi-Bro-Lap, Yakima, Washington, it sells for $195.00 in a 20″ size.

ability. These details are too long and varied to be given here.

The thing that the author wishes to emphasize in this work is that any man or woman can become a competent artist in the world's oldest art form; and if he does he will probably work most of the time with the quartz materials discussed here. One does not have to be rich to cut rocks, for good machinery is available in a wide price range. One does not have to possess a huge garage or basement to house a lot of machinery, for much of it is designed for the apartment dweller who has little space and who is not allowed to make noise.

If a reader decides he is interested in gem cutting, the author suggests the following procedure. Obtain sample copies at very little expense of *all* the magazines catering to the rock hobby and then buy at least two of the books on gem cutting mentioned in Chapter 12. Sit down with a number of post cards

FIG. 124. Faceting outfit manufactured by Lee Lapidaries, Cleveland, Ohio, and selling for $89.95. This does not include the facet head, which is $39.95, and the lapping wheels.

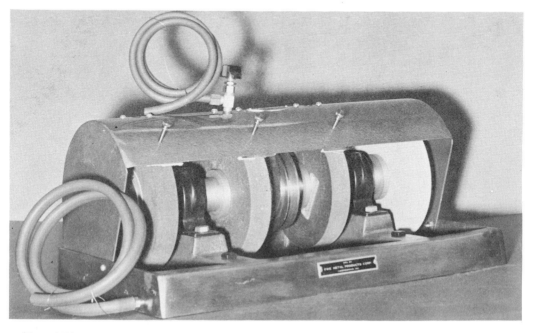

FIG. 125. Low cost grinder and polisher manufactured by Fike Metal Products Corporation, Blue Springs, Missouri, costing approximately $69.00 without the motor.

FIG. 126. Slabbing saw manufactured by Fike Metal Products Corporation, Blue Springs, Missouri, selling for approximately $109.50, less the diamond blade and motor. The illustration shows how a rock is secured in a vise for slabbing.

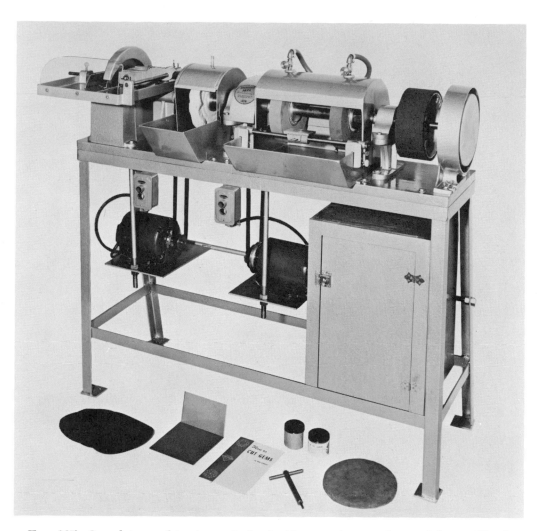

FIG. 127. Complete combination unit for lapidary work, manufactured by Highland Park Manufacturing Company, South Pasadena, California. This unit has everything including a saw with a separate motor, accessories and a storage space for unused polishing felts, etc. It retails complete with motors for approximately $320.00. *(Photo by Allen Hawkins, Pasadena.)*

and address them to the advertisers in the magazines who offer free literature or free catalogs. Some dealers offer elaborate catalogs for a few cents. Buy several of these. Study the catalogs until you have some idea of what you want to pay and what you want to buy for your particular space and desires, and then make your purchases from your local dealer, if you find one, and save shipping costs. If there is a dealer near you, visit his shop several times and study his wares and get advice on your own needs.

A final suggestion is offered: do not skip the fun of cabochon making by jumping right into some other phase like faceting. The making of cabochons will teach you faster than anything else the skills of conquering hardness, shaping materials, and achieving a polish. You will never be a genuine lapidary until you have made many good cabochons.

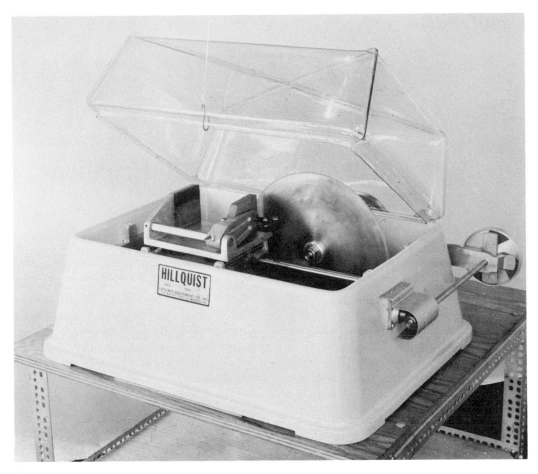

Fɪɢ. 128. The Hillquist combination slabbing and trim saw, manufactured by Lapidary Equipment Company, Seattle, Washington. It sells for about $236.00 without blade or motor.

Chapter 11

Illustrations of Agate Creations

THE QUESTION which has probably occurred at least once to every reader is: "what can be done with all these rocks after gathering or buying them?" The answer is that a thousand things can be done with them just as thousands of things have been done with them since our ancient ancestors used rocks for their first art forms and their first weapons. We no longer use them for weapons, although in a few parts of the world people still use the spear and the bow and arrow.

The things made by man that have survived from the ancient world were made of stone. Such great wonders as the Pyramids of Egypt are no longer attempted but many great buildings in America and elsewhere have been made of stone and a great deal of stone is still being used, although it cannot be used so much in today's tall buildings because of its great weight.

Working with stone today is a matter of making jewelry settings, useful novelties, furnishings, and carvings. The art of intarsia is being increasingly revived by rockhounds who have developed real lapidary skill in doing it. This is the art of making pictures out of inset pieces of stone, similar to mosaics which are made of glass or tile. Unfortunately we have no illustrations of contemporary intarsias but the magazines catering to the hobby frequently carry them.

It was planned at this point to include three chapters on Agates Combined in Jewelry, Novelty Uses for Agate, and Illustrations from Noted Collections, but lack of space has compelled only a brief discussion of these items here. An attempt has been made to cover much of the field of the lapidary art in the following illustrations.

Many will look at these pictures and raise an eyebrow as they say "art?" Yes, it is all art, beauty being in the eye of the beholder. In 1947 the author went to an exhibition of modern art as expressed in jewelry in San Francisco. It was a horrible experience for him to see a thousand safety pins strung on a copper wire awarded a prize. As this is written there are pictures in the current magazines of a piece of statuary made from a mass of several thousand old keys glued together in an oblong mass.

The lapidary art has not gone this far, as a visit to any of the big gem shows will indicate. Few controversial art examples get into the shows although the author has seen some rather frightening table tops that have been made of agate slabs. Many table tops have too many agates of various kinds and too many colors and patterns so that they are not artistic because they are too "busy." But the important thing is that the lapidary is trying self-expression and his creation becomes a source of great satisfaction

Fɪɢ. 129. Butterfly in quartz gems and silver by Madeline Grissom of the Los Angeles Lapidary Society. The pictured butterfly has an all-silver frame for the stones. The body is 5″ long from tip of feelers to tail end. The body, head, and feelers are as authentic as they could be, made of silver. The height is 7″ and the length is 9″. The top and lower wings are separate units. Black and white shadow agate from Mexico is in the middle with lavender Quinn River agate from Nevada at the top, then going down to the bottom with light lavender Laguna agate from Mexico. Twelve cabochons compose each of the two top wings. In the bottom wing the top cabochon is Idaho plume agate, yellow and brown in color, then two small cabochons and a clear agate of the same material. The large cabochon is red and green plume agate from Oregon. In the corner, close to the body, is an interesting sagenite agate in blue and black from Owl Hole, California. Another piece of Owl Hole sagenite agate is white, beige, and light blue. There are 7 cabochons in each of these two wings. A spike holds the butterfly suspended in the driftwood.

FIG. 130. Varieties of cryptocrystalline quartz in tumbled gems. This batch, tumbled by Walter Shirey of the Los Angeles Lapidary Society, contains varieties of jasper, agate, and tigereye. The gems are used in making many types of jewelry and novelties. *(Photo by O. D. Smith.)*

to him and is perhaps appreciated by many others.

Unfortunately there are no illustrations of jewelry here except rings. The modern silvercrafter sometimes strives for a combination of his skill with that of the lapidary, in producing display pieces useful only for ornamentation. A fine example of what these artists are striving for is shown in the accompanying illustration of the butterfly. It should be pointed out, however, that the main use of cabochons and faceted stones is still in conventional jewelry for everyday use, such as rings for both sexes, brooches, pins, pendants, bracelets, tie clasps, earrings, cuff links, and the newer bola ties that have become so popular with men for casual wear.

Tumbled stones have become immensely popular during the last few years, for the unusual shapes of the stones and the various colors encourage the artistic instinct and drive of thousands of amateurs who make entrancing things with them and much unusual jewelry. Illustrations are shown herewith of tumbled agates and jasper and a batch of crystal gems tumbled from amethyst, citrine, and rose quartz for use in bracelets. Buttons made from stone are becoming very popular.

Many lapidaries do nothing with the larger slabs they polish except to display them in hobby rooms or elsewhere for their own frequent admiration and as discussion pieces for their visiting friends. Some people insert their pieces into

FIG. 131. Tumbled gems of crystal quartz varieties such as amethyst, citrine, rutilated quartz, rose quartz, and smoky quartz. Used in making many types of jewelry and novelties. These gems were tumbled by Walter Shirey of the Los Angeles Lapidary Society. *(Photo by O. D. Smith.)*

FIG. 132. Buttons made of agate. Button backs are glued to the back of the buttons so they can be sewed. The center stone is black onyx with pure gold embossed into the stone by a supersonic machine. The design is the rear of the Great Seal of the United States as it appears on the back of a dollar bill. Buttons to the left are of tigereye. All stones are enlarged to show detail. From the author's collection. *(Photo by O. D. Smith.)*

196

FIG. 133. Two slabs of Brazilian agate from the author's collection. The upper slab is 8″ long and has rich olive-green coloring with a clear crystal center. The lower slab is 6″ long with alternating blue and white bands and a carnelian edge. Not heat-treated. These slabs are fine for fountain-pen stands. (*Photo by O. D. Smith.*)

their fireplaces or into table tops and many use them as bases for fountain pen desk sets. Lamps have been made from thin transparent slabs.

Probably the most useful objects made of agate are ash trays and bookends. Most bookends never fulfill their function (to hold up books) because they are not heavy enough; the weight of the books makes the ends fall over. But stone bookends are heavy and serve their purpose well. One of the most interesting uses of agate is in making agate handled silverware as illustrated herewith. This requires the skill of both the lapidary and the silversmith and it is productive of some beautiful and practical pieces.

Thousands of amateurs in recent years have turned to carving gemstones, almost always in the quartz family group. A lot of very competent work has been achieved in this field and it can be seen

197

FIG. 134. Two fine slabs of Brazilian agate that are not heat-treated. Upper slab is yellowish brown with a crystal center, 9″ long. Lower slab is gray and blue with a crystal center, 6½″ long. From the author's collection. *(Photo by O. D. Smith.)*

in the many gem shows every year. Methods and current work are regularly shown in such magazines as the *Lapidary Journal* and *Gems and Minerals.* These pieces fit in well with almost any scheme of decoration and they will be the treasured heirlooms of tomorrow and the years to follow.

Faceted stones are, of course, the ultimate in lapidary work and they make the finest gem settings, usually deserv-

ing of the best of the silversmith's and the goldsmith's art. The crystal varieties of quartz are particularly favored by the amateur lapidary, especially in the rich purple of the amethyst and the brilliant yellow of the citrine, sold too often as topaz.

Yes, thousands of useful things can be made from the agates, petrified wood, jasper, and crystal rocks that you gather on unforgettable journeys. The bookends

FIG. 135. Interesting ash trays made in Idar-Oberstein, **West Germany, from** dyed Brazilian agate. Bright red with white bandings. From the author's collection. *(Photo by O. D. Smith.)*

you make from a petrified log you picked up in Arizona or Washington, pieces of jewelry you make from your finds, or have someone else make for you, even the unpolished specimens you gather, will combine for a happier and fuller life. The people who become interested in agates and other gem materials are very happy people in their hobby for it is a wholesome activity that gets them outdoors, allows them to travel with a purpose, permits them to develop art forms and skills, and enlarges their horizons through study—an activity in which the whole family can indulge. It is becoming increasingly popular everywhere.

FIG. 136. Bookends made from two quarters of a large Brazilian agate 11″ wide. The center was unattractive, containing no crystal and no bandings. The maker, Charles T. Kennedy of Redlands, California, conceived the idea of sandblasting the profiles of Washington and Lincoln into the white interior of the agate, thereby producing a unique set of bookends. From the author's collection. *(Photo by O. D. Smith.)*

FIG. 137. Pair of bookends 15″ wide and weighing 20 pounds, made from Arizona petrified wood. The wood has several shades of rich red coloring mixed with milky chalcedony. This wood is exactly like the wood from the Petrified Forest in Arizona, although this piece did not come from there. From the author's collection. *(Photo by O. D. Smith.)*

Fig. 138. A goose holding a water lily. Carved in chalcedony with carnelian wings. From the author's collection. (*Photo by O. D. Smith.*)

Fig. 139. Goat carved in chalcedony with carnelian markings and a hen carved in carnelian. From the author's collection. (*Photo by O. D. Smith.*)

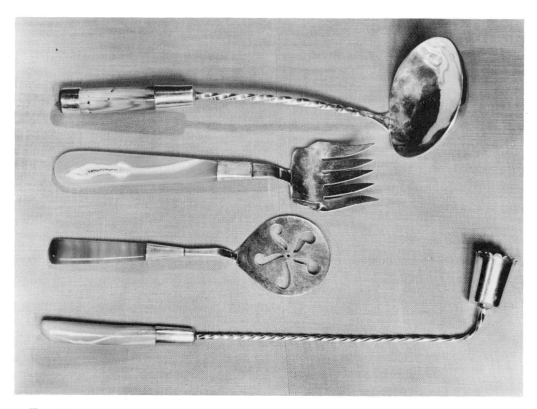

Fig. 140. Agate-handled table silverware originated by, and made by, the late James W. Anderson of Baltimore, founder of the Gem Cutters Guild of Baltimore, one of America's leading amateur lapidary societies. Beautiful silverware has since been produced by many lapidaries and silversmiths in the United States and is on view at many of the amateur shows, but Mr. Anderson's pieces always had that hand-crafted look. He once said to the author, "When I finish a piece I always look at it, and if it looks too good I hit it a whack with a hammer so people will be sure it didn't come from some store." The piece shown at the top is a 13" sterling silver punch ladle with a handle of petrified wood from Washington, showing the worm holes. The next item below is a large meat fork with an Idaho agate handle showing a geode type cavity in the center of the stone. The next item below is a tomato server with a handle of Montana carnelian agate. The bottom piece is a candle snuffer with a handle of New Mexico agate. This is from the author's collection and the three top pieces are from the collection of Mr. Anderson's daughter, Mrs. Charles Critchfield, Los Alamos, New Mexico. *(Photo by O. D. Smith.)*

FIG. 141. More items from the hand-crafted agate table silverware made by the late James W. Anderson of Baltimore. Item at the left is a sterling silver cheese scoop with a mouse on the handle, headed for the cheese. The gemstone handle is New Mexico green ricolite. The next item is a large pickle fork with a handle of banded Brazilian agate. The next item is a small hors d'oeuvre fork with a Montana moss agate handle. The next piece is a pickle fork with a Montana agate handle from the author's collection. The item on the extreme right is a small ladle set with brown jasper from an unknown location. All pieces except number four from the left are from the collection of Mr. Anderson's daughter, Mrs. Charles Critchfield, Los Alamos, New Mexico. (Photo by O. D. Smith.)

FIG. 142. A superb carved chalcedony bowl from the author's collection.
(Photo by O. D. Smith.)

FIG. 143. Goddess of Mercy carved in rose quartz. From the author's collection. *(Photo by O. D. Smith.)*

FIG. 144. Carved carnelian dog, amethyst fish, and smoky quartz crab. All from the author's collection. *(Photo by O. D. Smith.)*

FIG. 145. Some of the better agates from the author's collection. The cabochon at the top left is an unusual but interesting shape in carnelian. Below it is another carnelian agate with a convex top. The chalcedony cabochon at the center top has a dog attached to it carved from carnelian. Below it is an intaglio with a dragon carved in the rich carnelian. At the top right is a figure of Jesus carved in real agate onyx by Ewald Leyendecker, famous gem engraver of New York. The agate at bottom left is a fine example of a tree agate from India. *(Photo by O. D. Smith.)*

FIG. 146. Interesting paperweights made from half spheres of plastic into which are embedded minute opal chips. The bottoms of the spheres are enameled in black and the curved surface of the plastic greatly magnifies the opal pieces to make an entrancingly beautiful desk accessory. An excellent way in which to use opal refuse that cannot be cut. From the author's collection. *(Photo by O. D. Smith.)*

FIG. 147. A 12″ sphere of Brazilian agate, cut in Idar-Oberstein, West Germany. The sphere rests on a base of Utah carnelian agate cut by the author. Note the sagenitic needles in the eye of the agate. From the author's collection. *(Photo by O. D. Smith.)*

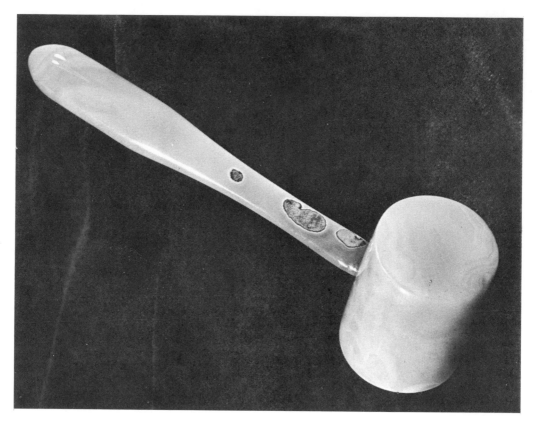

FIG. 148. A gavel made of chalcedony from the bean fields near Nipomo, California. Material gathered, polished, and presented to the author upon completion of his term as president of the Los Angeles Lapidary Society in 1942 by Jane Hagar of Manhattan Beach, California. From the author's collection. *(Photo by O. D. Smith.)*

FIG. 149. Interesting paperweight cut with a tuna fish can from New Mexico green ricolite, with an inset of the blue core of an Oregon thunderegg. Cut by the late James W. Anderson of Baltimore, Md., founder of the Gem Cutters Guild of Baltimore. Its width is 2¾" across. From the author's collection. *(Photo by O. D. Smith.)*

Fig. 150. Faceted quartz gems and ring settings from the author's collection. The large brilliant at the bottom center is an amethyst setting weighing 24 carats. The large ring to the right of it is set with a 52½ carat citrine. The stone to the left of the rings is amethyst. The large oval brilliant at the top left is quartz and the round brilliant to its right is smoky quartz, both of them being over 100 carats. The two stones to the left and center of the middle group of three are citrine and the one on the right is a synthetic titania cut by the author. It is 22½ carats and was one of the first titanias ever cut in America. All of the quartz is from Brazil with the exception of the amethyst stones, which were cut by the author from Arizona material. (*Photo by O. D. Smith.*)

Fig. 151. An excellent display of petrified wood slabs of C. E. Cramer at a show of the Los Angeles Lapidary Society. The wood is from California and Nevada locations and the small "logs" are from Eden Valley, Wyoming. All of the pieces in the Old Wood Pile display are of petrified wood, including the axe, saw horse, and saw. *(Photo courtesy of the Los Angeles Lapidary Society.)*

FIG. 152. Display of nodules and petrified wood by Louis Goss at a show of the Los Angeles Lapidary Society in Hollywood in 1945. *(Photo courtesy of the Los Angeles Lapidary Society.)*

FIG. 153. An interesting display of the lapidary work of Roy L. Cass at a show of the Los Angeles Lapidary Society. (*Photo courtesy of the Los Angeles Lapidary Society.*)

Fig. 154. One of the exhibits in the first amateur lapidary show ever held, that of the Los Angeles Lapidary Society in March, 1941. Present shows are usually held with row after row of uniform cases. This makes a compact and well-organized show but it lacks the openness and freer display ideas of the earlier shows. Note the number of desk pen sets in this exhibit of geodes, nodules, and petrified wood. From the collections of Dr. H. Marsden Heard and H. N. Freeman. (*Photo courtesy of the Los Angeles Lapidary Society.*)

213

Fig. 155. A few of the famous gemstone bowls carved from various materials by one of America's most accomplished craftsmen, George Ashley of Pala, California. The bowl to the left was carved from amethystine agate from the Creede district of Colorado. Progressing to the right, the bowl at the top is made of paisley agate from Imperial County, California. The bowl below it was carved from Mexican agate. The next bowl to the right was carved from plume agate from Carey, Oregon, and the bowl on the far right was carved from angel wing agate from Carey, Oregon. The bowls are on permanent exhibit at the Smithsonian Institution in Washington, D.C., with other gemstone bowls carved by Ashley. *(Photo courtesy of the Smithsonian Institution.)*

Chapter 12

Bibliography of Agate and Earth Science Books

AN OFTEN repeated maxim is the phrase "knowledge is power," but in following any kind of a hobby a person will find that knowledge is not only power but *fun*. For the more information one posesses about his hobby and the things related to it, the more fun and pleasure he has with it.

In Chapter 3 we have given a list of travel books in relation to rock collecting. They are repeated here in a complete list of most of the books available at this writing on various phases of the earth science, of which agate collecting is a small part. Certainly one's interest in agates cannot help but be enhanced and more thoroughly enjoyed if the collector also has some knowledge of geology, gemology, mineralogy, and gemcraft. The great majority of people enjoy their automobiles with no knowledge whatever of the workings of the internal combustion engine, and it is just as possible to enjoy agates without any great knowledge of earth science. However, it is easily understandable that the collector will enjoy his gem collection much more if he is possessed of a knowledge, even in a small degree, of gemology and gem cutting; even more with a knowledge of mineralogy and geology. Often the study of these related subjects opens new vistas and horizons of interest in the mineral kingdom. The reader is urged to consult his local library for any of the books mentioned here or to visit a local gem and mineral dealer and examine the books he may have for sale. By writing to the magazines serving the gem cutting hobby (addresses given in this chapter) a current book list can be obtained free for the asking. A visit to a local book store usually avails little, as few booksellers carry these specialized texts. However, almost any bookseller will order for you any book in the list if you give him the name of the publisher.

The titles given here and the prices are the books that are available as of the winter of 1963, with the prices current at that time. Books do go out of print and prices do change, so that the list will no doubt need correction from time to time. The title of the book is followed by the author's name, the publisher's name and the price. Complete addresses of the publishers will be found at the end of the chapter. All books can be purchased direct from the publishers. There appears to be no good reason for listing here any of the more than one hundred books that discuss quartz gems that have gone out of print, as they are not available except in libraries, where the file cards should be consulted under "agate" and "quartz."

BOOKS ABOUT AGATE COLLECTING AND GEM MINERAL LOCATIONS

Gemstones and Minerals, How and Where to Find Them, by John Sinkankas, D. Van Nostrand Co., Inc.

The Agates of North America (paper back), *Lapidary Journal*

Midwest Gem Trails, by June Culp Zeitner, Gemac Corp.

Northwest Gem Trails, by Dr. Henry C. Dake, Gemac Corp.

California Gem Trails, by Darold J. Henry, Gordon's

Gem Trails of Texas, by Bessie W. Simpson, Gem Trails Publishing Co.

Arizona Gem Fields, by Alton Duke, Alton Duke

The Rock Collector's Nevada and Idaho, by Darold J. Henry, Gordon's

Colorado Gem Trails and Mineral Guide, by Richard M. Pearl, Sage Books

Petrified Forest Trails, by J. Ellis Ransom, Gemac Corp.

Arizona Gem Trails (and the Colorado Desert in California), by J. Ellis Ransom, Gemac Corp.

Mineralogical Journeys in Arizona, by Arthur L. Flagg, Bitner's

Lake Superior Agate, by Theodore C. Vanasse, The Spring Valley Sun

Gemstones of North America, by John Sinkankas, D. Van Nostrand Co., Inc.

Crystal and Mineral Collecting, by William B. Sanborn, Lane Book Co.

New Mexico Gem Trails, by Bessie W. Simpson, Gem Trails Publishing Co.

Successful Mineral Collecting and Prospecting, by Richard M. Pearl, McGraw-Hill Book Co., Inc.; New American Library (paper back)

The Gem Hunter's Guide, Science and Mechanics Magazine

We Walk on Jewels (Treasure Hunting in Maine for Gems and Minerals), by Jean Blakemore, Seth Lowe Press

The Rock-Hunter's Range Guide, by J. Ellis Ransom, Harper & Row

Popular Prospecting, by Dr. Henry C. Dake, Gemac Corp.

The Agate Book, by Dr. Henry C. Dake, Gemac Corp.

BOOKS ABOUT GEM CUTTING

Gemcraft—How to Cut and Polish Gemstones, by Lelande Quick & Hugh Leiper, Chilton Co. (a companion book to this one)

Gem Cutting—A Lapidary's Manual, by John Sinkankas, D. Van Nostrand Co., Inc.

Art of Gem Cutting (paper back), by Henry C. Dake, Gemac Corp.

Books of Gem Cuts (loose leaf, on faceting), M.D.R. Mfg. Co., Inc., in two volumes

Working With Agate, by Melvin L. Kathan, Melvin L. Kathan (booklet)

How and Why of Picking Agates, by Robert R. & Hazel C. Minton, Minton's (booklet)

The Agate Book (paper back), by Henry C. Dake, Gemac Corp.

Jewelry, Gem Cutting and Metalcraft, by William T. Baxter, McGraw-Hill Book Co., Inc.

Facet Cutters Handbook, by Edward J. Soukup, Gemac Corp.

Tumbling Techniques, by G. L. Daniel, Gordon's (booklet)

Gem Tumbling and Baroque Jewelry Making (paper back), by Arthur and Lila Victor, the Victors

How to Cut Gems, by Dan and Marie O'Brien, O'Brien Lapidary Equipment Co. (paper back)

The Diamond Saw and Its Operation, by Wilfred C. Eyles, *Lapidary Journal* (booklet)

Faceting, by Louis Eaton Shaw, Craftsman Photo Lithographers

The Art of the Lapidary, by Francis J. Sperisen, Bruce Publishing Co.

BOOKS ABOUT GEMOLOGY
(The Science of Gems)

Handbook of Gems and Gemology, by Charles J. Parsons and Edward J. Soukup, Gemac Corp.

Practical Gemology, by Robert Webster, N.A.G. Press, Ltd.

Gemologists' Compendium, by Robert Webster, N.A.G. Press, Ltd.

Gemstones, by G. F. Herbert Smith, Pitman Publishing Corp.

Inclusions as a Means of Gemstone Identification, by E. J. Gubelin, Gemological Institute of America

Popular Gemology, by Richard M. Pearl, Sage Books

Dictionary of Gems and Gemology, by Robert M. Shipley, Gemological Institute of America

The Diamond Dictionary, Gemological Institute of America

Gems and Gem Materials, by Edward H. Kraus and Chester B. Slawson, McGraw-Hill Book Co., Inc.

Gem Testing, by B. W. Anderson, Emerson Books, Inc.

Gem Materials Data Book, by Charles J. Parsons and Edward J. Soukup, Gemac Corp.

A Key to Precious Stones, by L. J. Spencer, Emerson Books, Inc.

Roman Book of Precious Stones, by Sydney H. Ball, Gemological Institute of America

The Story of Jade, by Herbert P. Whitlock and Martin L. Ehrmann, Sheridan House

Diamond Technology, by Paul Grodzinski, N.A.G. Press, Ltd.

Gems: Their Sources, Descriptions and Identification, Volumes 1 and 2, by Robert Webster, F.G.A., Butterworth, Inc.

BOOKS ABOUT JEWELRY MAKING

The Design and Creation of Jewelry, by Robert von Neumann, Chilton Co. (a companion book to this one)

Enameling on Metal, by Oppi Untracht, Chilton Co. (a companion book to this one)

Jewelry Making for the Beginning Craftsman, by Greta Pack, D. Van Nostrand Co., Inc.

Handmade Jewelry, by Louis Weiner, D. Van Nostrand Co., Inc.

Jewelry and Enameling, by Greta Pack, D. Van Nostrand Co., Inc.

Jewelry Making, by Murray Bovin, Murray Bovin (publisher)

Enameling Principles and Practice, by Kenneth F. Bates, World Publishing Co.

Cabochon Jewelry Making, by Arthur and Lucille Sanger, Charles A. Bennett Co.

Chains and Beads, by Greta Pack, D. Van Nostrand Co., Inc.

The Jewelry Repair Manual, by R. Allen Hardy and John J. Bowman, D. Van Nostrand Co., Inc.

Jewelry Engravers Manual, by John J. Bowman, D. Van Nostrand Co., Inc.

Navajo and Pueblo Silversmiths, by John Adair, University of Oklahoma Press

Hand Made Jewelry, by Louis Weiner, D. Van Nostrand Co., Inc.

BOOKS ABOUT MINERALS AND ROCKS

Getting Acquainted with Minerals, by George L. English and David E. Jensen, McGraw-Hill Book Co., Inc.

Quartz Family Minerals, by Dake, Fleener and Wilson, McGraw-Hill Book Co., Inc.

Rocks and Minerals, by Richard M. Pearl (paper back), Barnes & Noble, Inc.

Chambers' Mineralogical Dictionary, Chemical Publishing Co.

My Hobby Is Collecting Rocks and Minerals, by David E. Jensen, Hart Book Co.

Ultra-Violet Guide to Minerals, by Sterling Gleason, D. Van Nostrand Co., Inc.

Identification and Qualitative Analysis of Minerals, by O. C. Smith, D. Van Nostrand Co., Inc.

The Rock Book, by Carroll and Mildred Fenton, Doubleday & Co., Inc.

Rocks and Minerals, by Herman C. Zim, Paul R. Schaffer, and Raymond Perlman, Simon & Schuster

The First Book of Stones, by M. B. Cormack (for children), Franklin Watts, Inc.

Rocks and Their Stories, by Carroll and Mildred Fenton, Doubleday & Co., Inc.

A Field Guide to Rocks and Minerals, by Frederick L. Pough, Houghton Mifflin Co.

Wonders of Rocks and Minerals, by Richard M. Pearl, Dodd-Mead & Co. (for children)

Field Book of Common Rocks and Minerals, by Frederic B. Loomis, G. P. Putnam's Sons

How to Know the Minerals and Rocks, by Richard M. Pearl, McGraw-Hill Book Co., Inc.

The Story of Rocks and Minerals, by David M. Seaman, Harvey House (for teen-agers)

Dana's System of Mineralogy, by C. Palache, H. Berman, C. Frondel, John Wiley & Sons, Inc. Vol. 1 (1944), Vol. 2 (1951), Vol. 3 (1962). [Vols. 4 and 5 in preparation.]

Dana's Textbook of Mineralogy, by Ford, John Wiley & Sons, Inc.

BOOKS ON MISCELLANEOUS SUBJECTS

Popular Prospecting, by Henry C. Dake, Gemac Corp.

The Fossil Book, by Carroll and Mildred Fenton, Doubleday

The Uranium and Fluorescent Minerals, by Dr. Henry C. Dake, Gemac Corp.

The Opal Book, by Frank Leechman, distributed in America by Gemac Corp.

Handbook for Prospectors, by M. M. von Bernewitz, McGraw-Hill

Rocks, Rivers and the Changing Earth, by Herman and Nina Schneider, William R. Scott, Inc.

Treasures of the Earth, by Fred Reinfeld, Doubleday & Co., Inc.

Field Geology, by Frederic H. Lahee, McGraw-Hill Book Co., Inc.

1001 Questions Answered About Earth Science by Richard M. Pearl, Dodd, Mead & Co.

Chinese Jade Throughout the Ages, by Stanley Charles Knott, Charles E. Tuttle Co.

PUBLICATIONS ABOUT GEMS AND MINERALS

The Lapidary Journal, P. O. Box 2369, San Diego 12, California.

A monthly magazine about gem cutting, silvercraft, gemology and collecting. $4.50 a year in the United States and its possessions and all American countries from Canada to Patagonia; $5.00 a year elsewhere. Subscription includes the huge *Rockhound Buyers Guide* as the regular April issue. Sample current issue 50 cents postpaid. (*Guide* issue $1.00)

Gems and Minerals, P. O. Box 687, Mentone, California.

A monthly magazine about gem cutting, silvercraft, gemology, and collecting. $3.00 a year in the United States and its possessions, $3.50 elsewhere. Sample issue 35 cents.

The Mineralogist, P. O. Box 808, Mentone, California.

A bi-monthly magazine about minerals and mineral collecting. $2.00 a year in the United States and its possessions, $2.50 a year elsewhere. Sample current issue 35 cents postpaid.

Earth Science, P. O. Box 1357, Chicago, Illinois.

A bi-monthly magazine about mineral and fossil collecting and geology. $2.50 a year in the United States and Canada, $3.00 elsewhere. Sample current issue 45 cents.

Rocks and Minerals, P. O. Box 29, Peekskill, New York.

A bi-monthly magazine about rock and mineral collecting. $3.00 a year everywhere. Sample current issue 60 cents postpaid.

LIST OF PUBLISHERS
(Arranged Alphabetically)

Barnes & Noble, Inc., 105 Fifth Ave., New York 3, N. Y.

Charles A. Bennett Co., 237 N. E. Monroe St., Peoria, Ill.

Bitner's, P. O. Box 1012, Scottsdale, Ariz.

Murray Bovin, 68-36 108th St., Forest Hills, L. I., N. Y.

Bruce Publishing Co., 400 N. Broadway, Milwaukee 1, Wis.

Butterworth, Inc., 7235 Wisconsin Ave., Washington 14, D. C.

Chemical Publishing Co., Inc., 212 Fifth Ave., New York 10, N. Y.

Chilton Books, 525 Locust St., Philadelphia 6, Pa.

Craftsmen Photo Lithographers, Hanover, N. J.

Dodd, Mead & Co., 432 Park Ave. So., New York 16, N. Y.

Doubleday & Co., Inc., Garden City, N. Y.

Emerson Books, Inc., 251 W. 19th St., New York 11, N. Y.

Gem Trails Publishing Co., P. O. Box 537, Granbury, Tex.

Gemac Corp., P. O. Box 808, Mentone, Calif.

Gemological Institute of America, 11940 San Vicente Blvd., Los Angeles 49, Calif.

Gordon's, P. O. Box 4073, Long Beach, Calif.

Harper & Row, 49 E. 33 St., New York 16, N. Y.

Hart Publishing Co., 74 Fifth Ave., New York 11, N. Y.

Harvey House, Inc., Publishers, Irvington-on-Hudson, N. Y.

Houghton Mifflin Co., 2 Park St., Boston 7, Mass.

Melvin L. Kathan, 316 N. E. 44th Ave., Portland 13, Ore.

Lane Book Co., Menlo Park, Calif.

Lapidary Journal, P. O. Box 2369, San Diego, Calif.

Seth Lowe Press, Rockland, Me.

McGraw-Hill Book Co., Inc., 330 W. 42nd St., New York 36, N. Y.

M.D.R. Mfg. Co., Inc., 4853 W. Jefferson Blvd., Los Angeles 16, Calif.

Minton's, Route 2, Box 97-A, Portland 10, Ore.

N.A.G. Press, Ltd., 226 Latymer Court, Hammersmith, London W. 6, England.

New American Library, 501 Madison Ave., New York 22, N. Y.

O'Brien Lapidary Equipment Co., 1108 N. Wilcox Ave., Hollywood 38, Calif.

Pitman Publishing Corp., 2 W. 45th St., New York 36, N. Y.

G. P. Putnam's Sons, 200 Madison Ave., New York 16, N. Y.

Sage Books, 2679 S. York St., Denver 10, Colo.

Science and Mechanics Magazine, 450 E. Ohio St., Chicago 11, Ill.

William R. Scott, Inc., 8 W. 13th St., New York 11, N. Y.

Sheridan House, 257 Park Ave. S., New York 10, N. Y.

Simon and Schuster, Inc., 630 Fifth Ave., New York 20, N. Y.

The Spring Valley Sun, Spring Valley, Wis.

Charles E. Tuttle Co., Inc., 28 S. Main St., Rutland, Vt.

University of Oklahoma Press, Norman, Okla.

D. Van Nostrand Co., Inc., 120 Alexander St., Princeton, N. J.

The Victors, 1415 W. 3rd Ave., Spokane 43, Wash.

Franklin Watts, Inc., 575 Lexington Ave., New York 22, N. Y.

John Wiley & Sons, Inc., 440 Park Ave. S., New York 16, N. Y.

World Publishing Co., 2231 W. 110th St., Cleveland 2, Ohio.

INDEX

Index

Page numbers set in **boldface** refer to illustrations in the text

229

LELANDE QUICK

long a recognized authority on the amateur lapidary movement in the United States, was one of the founders of the Los Angeles Lapidary Society and was its first president.

He assisted in the organization of a number of other clubs all over the country and organized the Michigan Lapidary Society and the Lapidary and Gem Society of New York. With a committee from the Los Angeles society, he organized many other amateur gem-cutting groups in the Los Angeles area, including the Hollywood Lapidary and Mineral Society.

In 1947, he began publication of the *Lapidary Journal* in Hollywood. During his thirteen years as editor and publisher, Mr. Quick traveled widely and lectured on gem-cutting at many universities from coast to coast. He retired in 1960 to devote his time to writing books and magazine articles about gems.